FUNCTIONAL PROGRAMMING AND INPUT/OUTPUT

Functional Programming and Input/Output

Andrew D. Gordon

University of Cambridge

CAMBRIDGE
UNIVERSITY PRESS

CAMBRIDGE UNIVERSITY PRESS
Cambridge, New York, Melbourne, Madrid, Cape Town, Singapore, São Paulo

Cambridge University Press
The Edinburgh Building, Cambridge CB2 8RU, UK

Published in the United States of America by Cambridge University Press, New York

www.cambridge.org
Information on this title: www.cambridge.org/9780521471039

© Cambridge University Press 1994

First published 1994
This digitally printed version 2008

A catalogue record for this publication is available from the British Library

ISBN 978-0-521-47103-9 hardback
ISBN 978-0-521-07007-2 paperback

Contents

List of Tables

Summary

A common attraction to functional programming is the ease with which proofs can be given of program properties. A common disappointment with functional programming is the difficulty of expressing input/output (I/O) while at the same time being able to verify programs. In this dissertation we show how a theory of functional programming can be smoothly extended to admit both an operational semantics for functional I/O and verification of programs engaged in I/O.

The first half develops the operational theory of a semantic metalanguage used in the second half. The metalanguage $\mathcal{M}$ is a simply-typed λ-calculus with product, sum, function, lifted and recursive types. We study two definitions of operational equivalence: Morris-style contextual equivalence, and a typed form of Abramsky's applicative bisimulation. We prove operational extensionality for $\mathcal{M}$—that these two definitions give rise to the same operational equivalence. We prove equational laws that are analogous to the axiomatic domain theory of LCF and derive a co-induction principle.

The second half defines a small functional language, $\mathcal{H}$, and shows how the semantics of $\mathcal{H}$ can be extended to accommodate I/O. $\mathcal{H}$ is essentially a fragment of Haskell. We give both operational and denotational semantics for $\mathcal{H}$. The denotational semantics uses $\mathcal{M}$ in a case study of Moggi's proposal to use monads to parameterise semantic descriptions. We define operational and denotational equivalences on $\mathcal{H}$ and show that denotational implies operational equivalence. We develop a theory of $\mathcal{H}$ based on equational laws and a co-induction principle.

We study simplified forms of four widely-implemented I/O mechanisms: side-effecting, Landin-stream, synchronised-stream and continuation-passing I/O. We give reasons why side-effecting I/O is unsuitable for lazy languages. We extend the semantics of $\mathcal{H}$ to include the other three mechanisms and prove that the three are equivalent to each other in expressive power.

We investigate monadic I/O, a high-level model for functional I/O based on Wadler's suggestion that monads can express interaction with state in a functional language. We describe a simple monadic programming model, and give its semantics as a particular form of state transformer. Using the semantics we verify a simple programming example.

Prayer

Let the light of truth, and the help of grace, be vital principles of action in us;
that we may, in the time of life, attain the ends for which we live;
and that our religion, which begins in knowledge,
may proceed in action, settle in temper, and end in happiness.

Preface

This dissertation is the result of my own work and includes nothing which is the outcome of work done in collaboration. This dissertation is not substantially the same as any that I have submitted or am currently submitting for a degree, diploma or any other qualification at any other university.

I acknowledge here many people who have helped me complete this work; whether named here or not, I thank all the people who have been good to me over my time in Cambridge.

I am extremely grateful to my supervisor, Larry Paulson, who has read, commented and discussed many drafts of my work. Perhaps the most important thing I've learnt from Larry is to keep computer science relevant to practical computational concerns. I am grateful also to Alan Mycroft who acted as joint supervisor for fruitful discussions about many drafts and ideas.

I have had many useful conversations with my friend Roy Crole. His help over the years with understanding many mathematical ideas has been invaluable. I am particularly grateful to him for explaining Moggi's approach to denotational semantics to me in simple terms, and for commenting on an early draft of this dissertation in detail. Robin Milner's ideas have been an enormous influence on this dissertation. I am grateful to have been in his undergraduate concurrency class at Edinburgh, and to have had many helpful conversations with him during his sabbatical in Cambridge. Jon Fairbairn enlivened my early years in Cambridge with his idiosyncratic views; he graciously passed on to me debates about I/O in the Haskell committee. During his absence from the Lab he is greatly missed. I thank Andy Pitts for reading and discussing this work on many occasions, and for his encouragement. Mike Gordon provided funding for me to try out my semantic ideas on a dataflow language for hardware description, a good way to work out how semantics can serve practical needs. Ken Moody offered me students to teach, many encouraging conversations, and the odd bottle of wine. I thank Roger Needham, head of department, for many things, not least that he suggest I apply for an internship at DEC SRC in Palo Alto. I learnt a great deal from my host, Jim Horning, and others at DEC, for which I am very grateful.

I thank Ian Poole of the Medical Research Council at the Western General Hospital in Edinburgh for the time he spent explaining their system to me, asking searching questions about functional I/O, and suggesting the example that motivates Chapter 8.

This work was supported partially by an SERC studentship. This dissertation was prepared on a Firefly computer donated by DEC. Martyn Johnson keeps the Fireflies going, one of his many services to the Lab. The experimental side of this work owes much to Dave Matthews and Mark Jones. Dave Matthews made available his port of Poly/ML to the Firefly, and Mark Jones his Gofer interpreter for Haskell.

Juanito Camilleri, Joe Dixon, Lee Fedder and Mads Rosendahl started with me; they are good friends. Thanks to the following who read and discussed drafts of this work: Nick Benton, Gavin Bierman, Paul Curzon, Eike Ritter and Stuart Wray. My officemates in 205 and TM1 have been good company; Mike Burrows was a good friend in my first year and during my time at DEC. Mike Gordon's Hardware Verification Group is a stimulating and friendly environment. I've enjoyed conversation with Tom Melham in all sorts of places. I thank the following for helpful conversations about functional I/O and semantics: Peter Breuer, John Cupitt, Andrew Dwelly, Nicholas Graham, John Hughes, Eugenio Moggi, Luke Ong, Nigel Perry, Gordon Plotkin, Raman Sundaresh, Allen Stoughton, Simon Thompson, David N. Turner, John Williams and Ed Wimmers.

I do not know how I could have sustained this work without the support of people in two good veggie-shared-houses: Bryant's Bend in Palo Alto and Glob House in Cambridge. Evensong at King's signifies beyond what I can say. My opening prayer, used often at King's, is by Benjamin Whichcote, provost 1644–1660. Stephen Cherry, the present chaplain, has given me much. My friends in the Student Christian Movement, at Holy Trinity, St. Columba's and the Romsey Labour Club have been good to know. Thanks especially to Shelagh, Phil, Sue, Cathy and Julie. Yvonne is an Irish blessing.

Thanks to my brother Dave for haggis and thuds, amongst other gifts. My first and greatest debt is to my Mum and Dad, who never fail to love and support me.

Andrew D. Gordon
14 August 1992

Preface to the Book Edition

This book is a slight revision of the submitted dissertation. I have simplified the language $\mathcal{M}$ introduced in Chapter 3, incorporated some changes made to Chapter 7 when it was published in FPCA'93 [45] and simplified Chapter 8 somewhat. I have not, however, attempted to take account in the main text of the publications that have appeared or come to my attention since submission. These include the following.

Semantics of Functional Languages Recent textbooks [48, 152] cover domain-theoretic semantics of recursively-typed languages such as $\mathcal{M}$. Pitts gives a simple proof of adequacy [115] in the context of recursively-defined domains, a result derived from his theory of relational properties of domains [113]. A domain theoretic semantics for a fragment of $\mathcal{M}$ appears in a paper with Crole [26]. Mason and Talcott [81] and Felleisen et al. [39] have written series of papers on entirely operational theories of functional programming. Their work goes beyond this dissertation in considering side-effects. It does not however take advantage of applicative bisimulation and co-induction in the way Chapter 6 does. Applicative bisimulation is studied by Pitts and Stark [111] in the presence of dynamically allocated names and by Sands [128] as a measure of performance. Jeffrey [65] and Launchbury [78] have recently developed theories of call-by-need evaluation.

Graphical User Interfaces Several recent implementations, including Concurrent Clean [4], Fudgets [20] and Budgets [125], express graphical user interfaces in a functional style. Noble [103] is an extensive survey.

Monadic I/O Peyton Jones and Wadler's work [110] has been further developed by Launchbury and Peyton Jones [79]. The MRC project using monadic I/O is still in progress. Programs and specifications are based on the monadic model suggested in Chapter 8, although formal proofs of program properties are impractical at present.

This is a good opportunity to thank my examiners, Simon Jones and Andrew Pitts. Finally, I want to thank Lindy for all her support and encouragement. Her company is good.

Andrew D. Gordon

4 May 1994

Chapter 1

Introduction

One of the main arguments in favour of functional programming is that it is easier to prove properties of functional programs than of imperative programs. Proofs of functional programs are claimed to be easier to construct than proofs of imperative programs. On the other hand, input/output (I/O) has long been viewed as problematic for functional languages. I/O mechanisms for functional languages have either been impractically inexpressive or not been integrated into the language semantics. The working programmer can argue that there is no published evidence—such as realistic examples—of how properties can be proved of functional programs that perform realistic I/O. Hence a major theoretical advantage of functional programming—that programs are easy to understand and verify—does not carry over to practical programs engaged in I/O.

This dissertation is a study of how to give semantics to I/O mechanisms for functional languages, and how to use such semantics to prove properties of programs engaged in I/O. It is meant as a step towards convincing the working programmer that functional programming can be practical, though much remains to be done.

The purpose of this chapter is to introduce the problem of functional I/O, survey previous work, and outline the contribution of this dissertation. §1.1 defines terminology used here concerning functional programming. §1.2 discusses previous work on I/O in functional languages, and identifies four widely-implemented mechanisms. Any semantics of functional I/O has to build on a semantics of functional languages; §1.3 reviews semantic methods suitable for functional languages. §1.4 states the hypothesis of this dissertation. §1.5 outlines each chapter. §1.6 states the original results of this dissertation and §1.7 offers advice to the reader. Finally, §1.8 introduces some of the mathematical material needed here.

1.1 Functional programming

Many functional (or applicative) languages have been put forward since the pioneering work on LISP [83], ISWIM [77] and POP-2 [17] in the 1960s. For the purpose of this dissertation, we distinguish two classes of functional languages, depending on the semantics of function application. Recall the terms call-by-value and call-by-name from ALGOL

60. When a function is applied to an actual parameter under **call-by-value** semantics the function's formal parameter is bound to the value obtained by evaluating the actual parameter. Under **call-by-name** semantics, the formal parameter is bound to the un-evaluated actual parameter, and each time the value of the formal is required, the actual parameter is evaluated. An **eager** language is one in which function application has call-by-value semantics; a **lazy** language is one in which function application has call-by-name semantics. By this definition, LISP, Scheme and ML are eager, whereas Miranda, Lazy ML and Haskell are lazy. For the sake of efficiency, application in lazy languages is usually implemented using call-by-need, as in graph reduction [109, 143] for instance. **Call-by-need** is the same as call-by-name, except that after the first evaluation of the actual parameter its value is retained and used whenever the formal parameter is subsequently used.

The primary focus of this dissertation is I/O for lazy languages such as Miranda or Haskell, although we discuss eager languages briefly. We make no claim to have considered all the varieties of functional language; for instance, the work here is not immediately applicable to dataflow languages like Lucid [6, 147] or Silage [44] in which every expression stands for an infinite stream.

Much has been written in praise of functional programming. The curious reader is referred to the paper by Hughes [61] or any of the many textbooks on functional programming [1, 13, 40, 52, 106]. My own motivation when beginning this research was the thought that unlike imperative programs, lazy functional programs are easy to manipulate when proving program properties, but it was not clear how to reason about programs engaged in I/O.

1.2   A brief history of functional I/O

Many mechanisms have been implemented and proposed for functional I/O. We identify four classes of I/O mechanism which together cover most of the proposed schemes.

Side-effecting I/O

Like functional programming, functional I/O begins with McCarthy [83]. LISP 1.5 had a **side-effecting** I/O mechanism. The core of LISP 1.5 can be explained as applications of functions to arguments, but the LISP Programming System needed other operations such as "commands to effect an action such as the operation of input-output" which were called "pseudo-functions" [83]. The pseudo-function `print` wrote its S-expression argument to the printer. The pseudo-function `read` took no arguments, but returned an S-expression from the input device. This side-effecting style of I/O persists in LISP and is also used in other eager languages such as Scheme or ML. Many language theorists have viewed side-effecting I/O with suspicion because unlike pure LISP, the evaluation of programs using side-effects cannot simply be explained as the applications of functions to arguments. To paraphrase Stoy [134], there is more to the meaning of an expression than just its value; the side-effects and order of evaluation of subexpressions become significant. The same suspicions are aroused by LISP or ML programs that use the assignment statement.

Although suspicious to some, side-effecting I/O is by far the most widely-used I/O mechanism in eager languages. In an eager language it is fairly easy to predict the order in which expressions are evaluated so programs using side-effecting I/O can be fairly simple to write and debug, if not to reason about formally. To the best of the author's knowledge, Williams and Wimmers' paper [151] is the only work to consider how to prove properties of programs using side-effecting I/O in an eager language. They develop an algebra for FL [9], a descendant of Backus' FP [8]. I/O is achieved in FL by operations on **histories**, objects that encode the status of all I/O devices and which are implicitly passed to and from every function. One can view this as a form of side-effecting I/O.

On the other hand, it is not usually easy to predict the order in which a program in a lazy language will call such side-effecting "pseudo-functions." Evaluation order is determined by data dependencies which can be hard to predict in advance. Side-effects mixed with lazy evaluation make programs hard to understand. Another reason why side-effecting I/O is hard to use with a lazy language is that call-by-need can cease to be a correct implementation of call-by-name, as we show in Chapter 7.

Landin-stream I/O

A stream is a potentially endless list of values, generated as need arises. Streams were used by Landin in his λ-calculus semantics of ALGOL 60 to represent the values of loop variables [76]; he remarked that streams could have been used to represent I/O in ALGOL 60. Streams were being used about the same time by Strachey in his (imperative) GPM language to represent I/O [137]. Streams can be represented as elements of certain recursively defined domains. In an influential paper [71], Kahn applied domain theory to concurrency using collections of stream-processing functions to model the semantics of certain kinds of process network. With MacQueen [72] he showed that these process networks could be implemented in POP-2 extended with certain side-effecting operations on streams.

About the same time, the pioneers of lazy languages [41, 54] argued that the list cons operation, like any other function, should not evaluate its arguments. In an eager language like LISP, every list is finite. On the other hand, if the cons operation does not evaluate its arguments, infinite lists can be represented whose elements are computed on demand. Notionally infinite lists are an important tool for the programmer in a lazy language [61].

The idea emerged that the input and output streams used in giving semantics to I/O could be implemented within a lazy language itself. In what we call **Landin-stream** I/O, interaction with a teletype is specified by a functional program that maps a lazy list of input characters to a lazy list of output characters. The reduction mechanism needs to be extended so that demand for values in the input stream is met by obtaining fresh input from the keyboard. Jones and Sinclair [67] credit Henderson [53] as being the first to propose the use of a stream-processing function to implement teletype I/O. By the mid-1980s this was a standard technique [5, 142, 154] covered in introductory textbooks [13, 109].

Synchronised-stream I/O

Synchronised-stream I/O is a generalisation of Landin-stream I/O where the program is a function mapping a stream of acknowledgements to a stream of requests. In Landin-stream I/O, inputs and outputs need not be synchronised: inputs occur when demand arises for the value in the input stream; outputs occur when the value of the next item in the output stream has been determined. In synchronised-stream I/O, input and output is synchronised: the functional program must produce an output request before examining the corresponding input acknowledgement. The power of synchronised-streams is that the type of requests can encode any kind of imperative command. Synchronised-streams were first reported as the underlying implementation technique for Karlsson's Nebula operating system [74]. The same essential idea was independently discovered by Stoye [136] in his operating system for SKIM-II and also by O'Donnell [104]. Synchronised-streams were chosen as the basic I/O mechanism in Haskell [59].

Continuation-passing I/O

Karlsson derived **continuation-passing** I/O operations from the underlying synchronised-stream mechanism of Nebula [74]. In the context of teletype I/O, continuation-passing I/O is based on a type CPS (short for "continuation-passing style") with three operations INPUT::(Char -> CPS) -> CPS, OUTPUT::Char -> CPS -> CPS and DONE::CPS. The type CPS can be implemented as an algebraic type within the functional language. There is no change to the language's evaluation mechanism, but a top-level program of type CPS can be interpreted or **executed** as follows. To execute INPUT(k), input a character v from the keyboard and then execute k v. To execute OUTPUT v q, output character v to the printer, and then execute program q. To execute DONE, simply terminate. The style is called continuation-passing because the argument k to the INPUT operation is reminiscent of continuations in denotational semantics [127, 134]. Holmström used a continuation-passing style in PFL [57], an eager dialect of ML extended with concurrency primitives. Perry [107] and McLoughlin and Hayes [86] implemented continuation-passing I/O mechanisms in lazy dialects of Hope. Rebelsky's recent proposal of **I/O trees** is essentially a form of continuation-passing I/O [123]. Unlike side-effecting and either kind of stream-based I/O, the continuation-passing style is suitable for either lazy or eager languages.

The Haskell I/O system [59] is based on synchronised-stream I/O (based on a type called **Dialogue**) but there is a standard set of continuation-passing operations. These operations are programmed in terms of the underlying synchronised-stream mechanism (in the same spirit as Nebula). Hudak and Sundaresh discuss translations between the two mechanisms that were discovered by the Haskell committee [60]. One fruit of the formal semantics for functional I/O developed in Chapter 7 is a proof of correctness of translations between Landin-stream, synchronised-stream and continuation-passing I/O.

Combinators for I/O

Programmers using eager languages find that programs using side-effecting I/O are fairly easy to understand, if not to reason about formally. The order of evaluation, and hence of side-effects, is fairly easy to control. On the other hand, programs using stream-based I/O can be hard to develop for two reasons: explicit "plumbing" of streams around a program is easy to get wrong; the order in which input and output is interleaved can be hard to predict because of lazy evaluation. Wray [154] and Dwelly [32] report problems of this sort.

Several authors have derived combinators to abstract operations that are commonly needed with stream-based programming. Karlsson [74] programmed continuation-passing operations using a synchronised-stream mechanism. Wray [154] suggested combinators for sequential composition and iteration. In his seminal work on the semantics and pragmatics of Landin-stream I/O in lazy languages, Thompson suggested a range of combinators with which to construct Landin-stream programs. The combinators construct programs of type interact a b; a program of this type is intended to represent an interactive computation with state of type a that when executed will return a value of type b. Thompson's combinators include operations such as sequential composition and iteration. He developed a trace theory to verify their correctness—the first work on semantics of I/O for lazy languages.

In developing the Kent Applicative Operating System (KAOS) [28, 144], a 14,000 line Miranda program, John Cupitt refined Thompson's combinators. He worked with a type interact a, which represented interactive computations that return values of type a. He used two basic combinators, return and comp.

```
return :: a -> interact a
comp   :: (a -> interact b) -> interact a -> interact b
```

A program return v is the trivial computation that immediately returns the value v; a program comp f p is a sequential composition: first execute p to return a value v, and then execute program f v. Stream-based programs, such as KAOS, written using these and other combinators have neither of the disadvantages mentioned earlier. There is no explicit plumbing of streams. The order of input and output is controlled by sequential composition.

Moggi [100, 101] has shown that structures of the form (interact, return, comp) occur often in the denotational semantics of programming languages. The semantics of such a structure can be given as a computational model, in the sense of Moggi, a categorical structure based on a strong monad. Wadler [149, 150] showed that such structures are a versatile tool for functional programming, particularly when writing programs to interact with state.

Influenced by the work of Cupitt, Moggi and Wadler, Chapter 8 of this dissertation advocates what we call **monadic I/O**, in which combinators like Cupitt's are used to structure programs. Monadic I/O is a high-level construct that can be implemented using any of the four low-level I/O mechanisms. Monadic programs are easier to understand than programs written in the three low-level styles suitable for lazy languages; there are no explicit streams or continuations to tangle a program.

Summary of previous work on functional I/O

We have discussed four classes of I/O mechanism. These will be covered in greater length in Chapter 7 in the context of teletype I/O. The semantic tools developed earlier in the dissertation will allow us to give semantics to each of the four I/O mechanisms.

To summarise, we considered side-effecting, Landin-stream, synchronised-stream and continuation-passing mechanisms of I/O. Side-effecting I/O is not suitable for lazy languages because of the difficulty of predicting the order in which side-effects occur. The semantics of both eager and lazy languages are complicated by the presence of side-effects, making program properties harder to prove. Although the input stream needs to be implemented specially, the semantics of a lazy language need not be affected by the presence of stream-based I/O; input and output streams are simply lazy lists. (I/O mechanisms in certain eager languages [18, 72, 98] have been based on streams, but the type of streams is kept distinct from lists and used only for I/O.) Continuation-passing I/O has been used with both lazy and eager languages. Evaluation of expressions remains unchanged, but some kind of interpreter needs to be added to the implementation to execute continuation-passing programs. Various sets of combinators have been proposed for programming at a higher level than the basic I/O mechanism.

The four classes cover the most widely-implemented mechanisms for functional I/O. To the best of the author's knowledge, the only mechanism suitable for teletype I/O not covered here is the extension of Landin-stream I/O with hiatons [147] as implemented in Lazy ML [7]. The problem is for a program to be able to poll the keyboard. Landin-stream I/O has blocking input in the sense that once demand arises for the next input value, computation is halted until a key is typed. The solution is that a special value, a **hiaton**, appears in the input stream whenever demand has arisen for a character, but none is available from the keyboard. Hiatons have not been widely implemented. Another solution to the polling problem is to add a command to poll the keyboard to synchronised-stream [136] or continuation-passing I/O [43], but we do not pursue this idea here.

There are good literature surveys on functional I/O by Hudak and Sundaresh [60], Jones [67] and Perry [108]. Historically, many ideas about functional I/O have arisen from adding nondeterminism or concurrency to functional languages. We do not study such mechanisms in this dissertation. We refer the interested reader to papers containing surveys on the following topics: functional programming and operating systems [67], nondeterminism and stream-based semantics [15], real-time functional programming [22, 50] and concurrent extensions of ML [11]. Kelly's book [75] cites many works on parallel systems based on functional languages.

Although there has been a great deal of work on functional I/O, there has been very little work on semantics. The primary goal of this dissertation is to explain the semantics of functional I/O, and hence make properties provable of functional programs engaged in I/O. To the best of the author's knowledge, Thompson's paper [141] on the semantics of Landin-streams in Miranda, is the only prior work on the semantics of I/O in lazy languages. In the context of eager languages , there is Williams and Wimmers' [151] work on semantics for what is essentially side-effecting I/O, and several papers giving operational semantics for concurrent constructs [11, 19, 57, 126], but with no development of a theory for program proofs. Dybjer and Sander [34] report work on the related problem of expressing concurrency using streams. They verify a communications protocol expressed as a concurrent network of stream-based functions.

1.3 Semantics of functional languages

To obtain a theory of functional I/O, we must begin with a theory of functional programming itself. In the context of this dissertation, such a theory has two purposes: to specify precisely the computational behaviour of functional programs so that implementations could be verified; and to enable program properties to be stated and proved.

Abramsky [2] points out that although the untyped λ-calculus has often been viewed as the prototypical functional language, actual implementations of lazy languages do not conform to the standard theory [10]. Abramsky considers two functional programs, (\x -> Ω) and Ω, where Ω is a looping or divergent program. He points out that according to the standard theory, the two are equal, but in the implementation of lazy languages such as Miranda or Lazy ML, evaluation of the first converges whereas evaluation of the second diverges. Motivated by this example, Abramsky develops his lazy λ-calculus as a step towards a theory of lazy functional programming. Following Plotkin's study of PCF [117], Abramsky equips the lazy λ-calculus with a structural operational semantics [55, 119] and a domain-theoretic denotational semantics. He then proves an adequacy theorem to relate the two semantics.

As far as this dissertation is concerned, Abramsky's key manoeuvre is to view his lazy λ-calculus as a process calculus. Led by Milner, a great many operationally-based methods have been developed for the CCS theory of concurrency [93, 94]. Bisimilarity, found by taking the greatest fixpoint of a certain functional [31], is a cornerstone of this theory. Since it is a greatest fixpoint it admits **co-inductive** proofs [97, 114]. Abramsky builds a bridge between CCS and the λ-calculus by proposing **applicative bisimulation** as the notion of operational equivalence in the lazy λ-calculus. Applicative bisimulation is a reworking of CCS bisimulation for the λ-calculus.

We follow Abramsky and construct a theory of functional programming based on structural operational semantics and applicative bisimulation. Verification of an implementation could be based on the operational semantics, but this is beyond the scope of the dissertation. Proofs of program properties are based on a theory of applicative bisimulation that parallels that of CCS. It is important that applicative bisimulation is a congruence relation, that is, a substitutive equivalence relation. Abramsky's original proof that application bisimulation is a congruence depended on domain-theoretic results. Stoughton and Howe made two suggestions for how congruence could be proved directly from the operational semantics. Stoughton suggested a variant of Milner's context lemma [12, 91]. Howe, with an ingenious construction, proved congruence for a broad range of lazy computation systems [58]. In Chapter 4 we will investigate both the context lemma and Howe's method. In related work, Milner [95] and Sangiorgi [129] link the lazy λ-calculus with the theory of π-calculus, a development of CCS with mobile processes [96]. Smith [133] builds on Howe's work to construct semantic domains from operational semantics.

A semantics of functional programs [21, 54] has often been based on domain-theoretic denotational semantics [102, 118, 130, 134]. Stoy's classic paper [135] shows how domain-theoretic methods such as Scott induction can be applied to prove properties of functional programs. Instead of domain theory we use operational semantics to specify the I/O behaviour of functional programs. Were we to appeal to domain-theoretic principles in proofs of functional programs, we would need to relate the operational and domain-theoretic semantics. Lester [80], Simpson [132] and Burn [16] have proved such a relation (usually known as **adequacy**) in the context of a lazy functional language; other related work is more theoretical [25, 90, 117, 120, 139]. We leave the relation between the operational and domain-theoretic semantics of the functional languages studied here as future work. For the purpose of proving program properties we have not felt the lack of a domain-theoretic semantics as a loss; examples arising here that might have required Scott induction in a domain-theoretic setting have been proved using co-induction.

In summary, as a step towards a theory of functional I/O, we develop a theory of functional programming in which the functional language is viewed as a kind of process calculus. The theory is based on structural operational semantics and applicative bisimulation.

1.4   Hypothesis

This dissertation aims to show the following.

- An operational theory of functional programming is suitable for precisely specifying a functional language and proving properties of functional programs.

- Such an operational theory can be extended to specify and prove properties of the most widely-implemented mechanisms for I/O in lazy functional languages.

- A semantics for a simple form of monadic I/O may be expressed within the functional language. Hence programs using monadic I/O may be verified using standard techniques.

1.5   Synopsis

The first half of the dissertation defines a semantic metalanguage, $\mathcal{M}$, which is used in the second half for the investigation of functional I/O.

Chapter 2: A calculus of recursive types. In this chapter we prove a technical result needed in Chapter 3. Mendler has proved confluence and strong normalisation for the Girard-Reynolds polymorphic λ-calculus extended with positive recursive types. This chapter proves strong normalisation for an extension, called $\mu\nu\lambda 2$, of Mendler's calculus.

Chapter 3: A metalanguage for semantics. The metalanguage $\mathcal{M}$ is a simply-typed λ-calculus with product, sum, function, lifted and recursive types. This chapter defines its syntax, type assignment relation and its lazy and deterministic operational semantics. The main result of this chapter is a convergence theorem—that, apart from terms of lifted types, evaluation of every term converges.

Chapter 4: Operational precongruence. We investigate two operationally defined preorders on the terms of $\mathcal{M}$: contextual order (after Morris and Plotkin) and applicative similarity (after Milner and Abramsky). We define a notion of operational adequacy to mean that a preorder respects evaluation in a certain way. We show that each preorder is an operationally adequate precongruence. The proofs use a variant of Milner's context lemma [91] for contextual order, and a typed reworking of a method due to Howe [58] for applicative similarity. Given that applicative similarity is a precongruence, it is routine to establish **operational extensionality** [14]: that applicative similarity coincides with contextual order.

Chapter 5: Theory of the metalanguage. We adopt applicative bisimilarity, the equivalence corresponding to contextual order and applicative similarity as equivalence on terms of $\mathcal{M}$. We prove equational laws that are analogues of the axiomatic domain theory of LCF [46, 105]. We derive a principle of co-induction from the definition of applicative bisimilarity. We investigate properties of empty, one-point, iterated sum, iterated product, boolean and natural number types.

The second half investigates a range of ways in which functional languages can be extended to express I/O:

Chapter 6: An operational theory of functional programming. We define a functional language, $\mathcal{H}$, which is essentially a subset of Haskell. $\mathcal{H}$ has lazy algebraic types and both call-by-name and call-by-value function applications. We give a deterministic operational semantics and a denotational semantics using $\mathcal{M}$. The denotational semantics is a case study of Moggi's proposal to use monads to parameterise semantic descriptions. We prove a close correspondence between the operational and denotational semantics. We define operational and denotational equivalences as object-level applicative bisimilarity and equivalence in the metalanguage respectively. We show that a theory of programming, which consists of a set of equational laws together with a co-induction principle, holds for operational equivalence. The equational laws are valid for denotational equivalence, but we leave open whether the co-induction principle holds. We conclude the chapter by considering the semantics and theory of $\mathcal{HX}$, a language obtained from $\mathcal{H}$ by adding a parameterless exception mechanism.

Chapter 7: Four mechanisms for teletype I/O. We take teletype I/O—interaction with a keyboard and printer—as a simple I/O model. In this context, we discuss the formal semantics of four widely-implemented mechanisms for functional I/O: side-effecting, Landin-stream, synchronised-stream and continuation-passing I/O. We explain why side-effecting I/O combines badly with call-by-name semantics of function application. The other three mechanisms are suitable for use with call-by-name semantics. We prove in a precise sense that they are of equal expressive power.

Chapter 8: Monadic I/O. We develop a monadic style of functional I/O to support an application of functional I/O at the Medical Research Council (MRC) in Edinburgh. We describe a simple monadic programming model, and express its semantics within $\mathcal{H}$ as a particular form of state transformer. Using the semantics we verify a simple programming example.

Chapter 9: Conclusion. Conclusions are drawn and further work suggested.

1.6   Results

The main contribution of this dissertation is to develop an operational theory of lazy functional programming, to extend it to accommodate various I/O constructs, and to show how it can be applied to prove properties of functional programs engaged in I/O. Here are specific original results.

- A theory of a non-trivial functional language, $\mathcal{H}$, based on equational reasoning and co-induction, and developed operationally from first principles.

- A case-study of the monadic approach to denotational semantics, based on an operationally-defined metalanguage, $\mathcal{M}$. Proof that the denotational semantics corresponds closely to the operational semantics.

- A formal semantics for side-effecting, Landin-stream, synchronised-stream and continuation-passing I/O.

- A proof that Landin-stream, synchronised-stream and continuation-passing I/O are equally expressive in the context of teletype I/O.

- A case-study of the monadic approach to I/O, motivated by an application of functional programming to medical electronics.

- An investigation of the relationship between the context lemma and Howe's method of proving precongruence for operationally-defined preorders.

1.7   How to read the dissertation

A bird's eye view can be had by reading this chapter, reading the unnumbered introductory sections of Chapters 2 to 8, and then the whole of the last chapter. The introductory sections are intended to motivate and sketch the results of each chapter without mentioning any mathematical details.

As mentioned above, the first half develops a semantic metalanguage, $\mathcal{M}$, for use in the second half to give denotational semantics for a functional object language, $\mathcal{H}$. $\mathcal{H}$ is the basis for the study of functional I/O in the second half. The argument in the dissertation is linear in that almost every chapter depends on all its predecessors to some degree, but none on its successors. That said, a great deal of the second half can be understood without knowing the development of $\mathcal{M}$ in detail. After obtaining a bird's eye view, the reader primarily interested in functional I/O might skim §3.1 to §3.3 to get an impression of the definition of $\mathcal{M}$, browse Chapter 5 on the theory of $\mathcal{M}$, and begin reading more thoroughly at Chapter 6.

The extension of Mendler's calculus developed in Chapter 2 is only used explicitly in §3.4. The reader wishing to understand $\mathcal{M}$ in detail is advised to begin at Chapter 3 and skip §3.4 on first reading, and then to study Chapter 2 before reading §3.4.

1.8 Mathematical preliminaries

Syntax, alpha-conversion and the variable convention

We deal with three formal languages in this dissertation: $\mu\nu\lambda 2$ introduced in Chapter 2, $\mathcal{M}$ introduced in Chapter 3, and $\mathcal{H}$ introduced in Chapter 6. Chapter 6 also introduces a variant of $\mathcal{H}$, called $\mathcal{HX}$. Here we state general syntactic conventions that apply to all these languages (except that term variables are treated specially in $\mu\nu\lambda 2$).

We assume two countably infinite sets of **type variables** and **term variables**, ranged over by the metavariables X, Y, Z and f, g, u, v, w, x, y, z, respectively. We almost always refer to term variables simply as variables. We will point out binding occurrences of variables when defining each formal language. If t is a phrase of syntax, we write $ftv(t)$ and $fv(t)$ for the sets of type and term variables respectively that occur free in t. The iterated notation $fv(t_1, \ldots, t_n)$ is short for $fv(t_1) \cup \cdots \cup fv(t_n)$; we use a similarly iterated form of ftv. If t and t' are phrases of syntax, we write $t[t'/X]$ and $t[t'/x]$ for the outcomes of substituting t' for each free occurrence of X or x, respectively, in t, with change of bound variables in t to avoid variable capture. We refer the reader to Hindley and Seldin's textbook for a clear treatment of substitution and alpha-conversion [56]. We make free use of the properties of substitution and alpha-conversion developed in Section 1B of their book.

We follow the standard practice of identifying phrases of syntax up to alpha-conversion, that is, treating a syntactic phrase as if it were its alpha-equivalence class. We use the symbol $\equiv$ for alpha-conversion. We adopt Barendregt's variable convention [10] and assume that all the bound variables in a term are distinct from each other and from any free variables. This is legitimate when phrases of syntax are identified up to alpha-conversion.

We will make it clear whenever we are not treating a phrase of syntax as its alpha-equivalence class. When we are not, we can write $bv(t)$ for the set of bound term variables in t. A **context**, $\mathcal{C}$ or $\mathcal{D}$, is a term possibly containing one or more holes, written as $[]$. We write $\mathcal{C}[t]$, which we call an **instantiation**, for the term obtained by filling in each hole in $\mathcal{C}$ with the term t. Contexts are not identified up to alpha-conversion; we write $\mathcal{C} = \mathcal{D}$ to mean that contexts $\mathcal{C}$ and $\mathcal{D}$ are literally the same. The only significant use of contexts is in Chapter 4; contexts are covered in greater detail in §4.1.

Types and polymorphic definitions

Each of the formal languages $\mu\nu\lambda 2$, $\mathcal{M}$ and $\mathcal{H}$ is a typed λ-calculus in which terms are tagged with type information. Such type information can often be inferred from the narrative text, and then we omit it. Occasionally we omit type information from the defining equation of an $\mathcal{M}$ or $\mathcal{H}$ term, and specify a type scheme. For instance, we might make the definition $\mathsf{id} \stackrel{\text{def}}{=} (\lambda x.\, x)$ and comment that term id has type scheme $(\sigma \to \sigma)$. The idea of type schemes or polymorphic types [92] is widely used in functional languages like ML or Haskell. Rather than burden the reader with a formal mechanism of polymorphic types, we trust that the equation $\mathsf{id} \stackrel{\text{def}}{=} (\lambda x.\, x)$ (and others like it) can be understood as the definition of a whole family of terms, $\mathsf{id}^\sigma \equiv (\lambda x{:}\sigma.\, x)$ for each type σ.

Relations

If S and T are sets, we treat a binary relation between S and T as a subset of the product $S \times T$. If $\mathcal{R} \subseteq S \times T$ we write $s\mathcal{R}t$ and $(s, t) \in \mathcal{R}$ interchangeably. Relational composition is written as juxtaposition; that is, if $\mathcal{R}_1 \subseteq S_1 \times S_2$ and $\mathcal{R}_2 \subseteq S_2 \times S_3$, then $\mathcal{R}_1\mathcal{R}_2 \subseteq S_1 \times S_3$ is the composition of $\mathcal{R}_1$ and $\mathcal{R}_2$. If $\mathcal{R} \subseteq S \times S$, then $\mathcal{R}^+$ and $\mathcal{R}^*$ are its transitive closure and reflexive transitive closure respectively. We write Id for the identity relation. If $\mathcal{R}$ is a relation, $\mathcal{R}^{-1}$ is its inverse.

Bisimulation and co-induction

We make extensive use of preorders and equivalence relations defined to be the greatest fixpoints of certain functionals. The prototypical use of this technique in computer science is bisimilarity in CCS [94], suggested by Park and developed by Milner.

We will introduce such relations by first defining the functional, denoted parenthetically by $[\cdot]$ or $\langle \cdot \rangle$. Then we define notions of simulation and similarity as introduced in the following theorem, which states general properties of the relations defined in this way:

Proposition 1.1 *Suppose the following:*

- *Metavariable t ranges over a set of terms, Term.*
- *Metavariable S ranges over subsets of Term $\times$ Term.*
- *Functional $[\cdot]$ is a monotone function over subsets of Term $\times$ Term (that is, if $S_1 \subseteq S_2$ then $[S_1] \subseteq [S_2]$).*
- *A **simulation** is a relation S such that $S \subseteq [S]$.*
- ***Similarity**, $\lesssim$, is defined to be the union of all simulations.*

We have:

(1) *Similarity is the greatest fixpoint of $[\cdot]$.*
    *(A **fixpoint** of $[\cdot]$ is a relation S such that $S = [S]$.)*

(2) *Similarity is the greatest simulation.*

(3) *$t \lesssim t'$ iff there is a simulation S such that tSt'.*

(4) *If the identity relation on Term is a simulation, then $\lesssim$ is reflexive.*

(5) *If S_1S_2 is a simulation whenever both S_1 and S_2 are, then $\lesssim$ is transitive.*

(6) *If S^{-1} is simulation whenever S is, then $\lesssim$ is symmetric.*

Proof. Part (1) is a special case of the Knaster-Tarski theorem in fixpoint theory; see Davey and Priestley [31, pages 93–94].

(2) That similarity is a simulation follows from (1). It is the largest since by definition it contains any other.

(3) For the forwards direction, take the simulation S to be $\lesssim$ itself. For the backwards direction, we have $S \subseteq \lesssim$, so $(t, t') \in S$ implies $(t, t') \in \lesssim$.

(4) For any t, pair (t, t) is in a simulation (the identity relation), so by part (3), we have

$t \lesssim t$.

(5) For arbitrary t_1, t_2 and t_3, suppose that $t_1 \lesssim t_2$ and $t_2 \lesssim t_3$. Since similarity is a simulation, so is the composition $\lesssim\lesssim$. We have $t_1 \lesssim\lesssim t_3$ by definition of relational composition, so pair (t_1, t_3) is contained in a simulation. Hence by (3) we have $t_1 \lesssim t_3$, as required.

(6) Suppose that $t \lesssim t'$. Since $\lesssim$ is a simulation, we have $t' \lesssim t$ as required. ∎

Property (3) of this proposition is an important proof technique: to prove $t \lesssim t'$, it suffices to find some S containing pair (t, t') and prove that $S \subseteq [S]$. This technique has been called Park's rule or greatest fixpoint induction or **co-induction** [97, 114].

If the relation $\lesssim$ defined by a functional $[\cdot]$ is a preorder (a reflexive and transitive relation), we call $\lesssim$ a **similarity** and any S such that $S \subseteq [S]$ we call a **simulation** (as we did above). On the other hand, if relation $\lesssim$ is an equivalence, we call $\lesssim$ a **bisimilarity** and any S such that $S \subseteq [S]$ we call a **bisimulation**.

Chapter 2

A calculus of recursive types

This chapter prepares the way for Chapter 3, where we will define a simply-typed metalanguage for programming language semantics, $\mathcal{M}$. We wish to prove in Chapter 3 that for every term in a certain class of $\mathcal{M}$ types, evaluation cannot diverge. This result is used in Chapter 5 where we will develop a theory of $\mathcal{M}$. We obtain this result by translating such terms of $\mathcal{M}$ into a polymorphic λ-calculus that possesses a strong normalisation property: that no infinite reduction sequence starts from any term.

The types of $\mathcal{M}$ we wish to encode are sums, products, functions and a certain class of recursive types, called **positive recursive types**. A recursive type $\mu X.\sigma$ is **positive** just when each occurrence of the bound type variable X within type σ is to the left of an even number of function arrows. For instance, the types $(\mu X.1+X)$, of natural numbers, or $(\mu X.1+(\tau \times X))$, of finite lists of type τ, are positive recursive types. As an example of a non-positive type, consider $(\mu X.X \to X)$ which can encode any term of the untyped λ-calculus. Evidently there are terms of this type whose evaluation diverges.

We seek a calculus with a strong normalisation result whose type structure is expressive enough to encode the types of $\mathcal{M}$, and hence to be the basis of a normalisation proof for $\mathcal{M}$. One candidate is the polymorphic λ-calculus, $\lambda 2$, of Girard and Reynolds, which has a rich type structure able to encode a wide range of types. Functions are primitive in $\lambda 2$ and there are standard encodings of sums and products. As for recursive types, Girard [42] outlines a scheme for encoding the class of recursive types which are sums of products, and equipping each with primitive recursive functions. Wraith [153] describes a general scheme for encoding any positive recursive type and primitive recursion within $\lambda 2$. A second candidate is Mendler's extension of $\lambda 2$ [89, 88][1] which adds new type constructors for positive recursive types, together with constants and reduction rules to construct terms of recursive types, and compute primitive recursive functions. Mendler proves that his extension of $\lambda 2$ is Church-Rosser and strongly normalising.

We use Mendler's calculus because it allows a direct representation of recursive types. In this chapter we augment Mendler's calculus with two new families of constants that are needed to simulate certain operators in $\mathcal{M}$. The purpose of the chapter is to prove that even with the additional constants, and their reduction rules, all the terms of the calculus

---

[1] Paul Francis Mendler is also known as Nax Paul Mendler.

are strongly normalisable.

§2.1 defines the type structure of $\mu\nu\lambda2$, the calculus developed in this chapter, to be the same as in Mendler's calculus. §2.2 defines the term structure of $\mu\nu\lambda2$ to be the same as in Mendler's calculus, but for the addition of two new families of constants. §2.3 defines the reduction relation for terms of $\mu\nu\lambda2$, and states Mendler's theorem, that any term of $\mu\nu\lambda2$ is strongly normalisable, provided none of the new constants occurs in it. §2.4 defines combinators in Mendler's calculus that correspond to the new constants. §2.5 shows in two examples that the combinators can simulate the new constants. §2.6 proves that the new constants can always be simulated by combinators contained within Mendler's original calculus.

2.1   Types of $\mu\nu\lambda2$

Calculus $\mu\nu\lambda2$ is a generalisation of $\lambda2$, the Girard-Reynolds polymorphic λ-calculus. We assume a countably infinite set of type variables, ranged over by metavariables X, Y, Z. The set of **types**, with metavariables σ and τ, is given by the grammar:

$$
\begin{aligned}
\sigma ::=\ & X && \text{(type variable)} \\
\mid\ & (\sigma \rightarrow \tau) && \text{(function type)} \\
\mid\ & (\forall X.\,\sigma) && \text{(polymorphic type, } X \text{ bound in } \sigma) \\
\mid\ & \rho && \text{(recursive type)} \\
\rho ::=\ & \mu \mid \nu \\
\mu ::=\ & (\mu X.\,\sigma) && \text{(initial type, } X \text{ bound in } \sigma) \\
\nu ::=\ & (\nu X.\,\sigma) && \text{(terminal type, } X \text{ bound in } \sigma)
\end{aligned}
$$

Conventional notions of free type variables and substitution apply, as stated in §1.8. Types are identified up to alpha-conversion.

We say that a type variable X **occurs positively** in a type τ iff each occurrence of X in τ is to the left of an even number of $\rightarrow$'s. Dually, a type variable X **occurs negatively** in a type τ iff each occurrence of X in τ is to the left of an odd number of $\rightarrow$'s.

Recursive types take one of the forms $(\mu X.\,\sigma)$ or $(\nu X.\,\sigma)$. Beware that the symbol μ (or ν) is used both as a metavariable for initial types (or terminal types) and as part of the syntax as the type constructor itself. For an $\mathcal{M}$ type τ to be **well-formed** we require two properties of any recursive type, $(\mu X.\,\sigma)$ or $(\nu X.\,\sigma)$, that occurs in τ. First, we require that each such recursive type is **positive**, which is to say that the bound variable X occurs positively in σ. Second, we require that each recursive type is closed, or equivalently that $ftv(\sigma) \subseteq \{X\}$. For instance, type $(\mu X.\,X \rightarrow X)$ is closed but not positive; type $(\mu X.\,\mu Y.\,X)$ is closed and positive, but is not well-formed because it contains a type $(\mu Y.\,X)$ which is positive but not closed. If we make the standard definitions of sums and products,

$$
\begin{aligned}
\sigma + \tau &\stackrel{\text{def}}{=} (\forall Z.\,(\sigma \rightarrow Z) \rightarrow (\tau \rightarrow Z) \rightarrow Z) \quad Z \notin ftv(\sigma,\tau) \\
\sigma \times \tau &\stackrel{\text{def}}{=} (\forall Z.\,(\sigma \rightarrow \tau \rightarrow Z) \rightarrow Z) \qquad\quad Z \notin ftv(\sigma,\tau)
\end{aligned}
$$

Mendler points out that X occurs positively in such types iff X occurs positively in types σ and τ. Let type 1 be $(\nu X.\,X)$, a one-point type (which we investigate in the context of $\mathcal{M}$ in §5.2). If τ is a well-formed closed type, we can define well-formed types $(\mu X.\,1 + X)$,

$(\mu X.\, 1 + (\tau \times X))$ and $(\nu X.\, \tau \times X)$ of natural numbers, finite τ-lists and notionally infinite τ-streams respectively.

We insist that recursive types be **closed and positive** for the following reasons. Recursive types that are not positive are problematic because they can type terms that are not normalisable. For instance, the type $(\mu X.\, X \to X)$ can type a version of the Ω combinator from the untyped λ-calculus. Positive recursive types that are not closed complicate some of the syntactic constructions used in this chapter. We rule them out as a convenience just for this reason. Mendler requires recursive types to be positive, but not necessarily closed. We will assume implicitly that any type we deal with is well-formed. Note that the set of well-formed types is closed under substitution.

Parentheses will often be omitted when the intended grouping is implied by associativity and scope rules. These rules are that the function arrow, "$\to$," associates to the right, and the scope of bound variables continues as far to the right as possible. For example, the type $\sigma_1 \to \sigma_2 \to \sigma_3$ is short for $(\sigma_1 \to (\sigma_2 \to \sigma_3))$.

2.2 Terms of $\mu\nu\lambda 2$

As mentioned in §1.8, type variables are treated specially in $\mu\nu\lambda 2$. We assume given a countably infinite set of **names**, ranged over by metavariables f, g, x, y, z. (This set of names is the same as the set of term variables used in $\mathcal{M}$ and $\mathcal{H}$.) In $\mu\nu\lambda 2$, a **term variable** (called simply a variable in the following) is of the form x^σ, where x is a name, and σ is a type. The **raw terms** of $\mu\nu\lambda 2$, with metavariables L, M and N, are produced by the grammar:

$$
\begin{array}{llll}
M & ::= & x^\sigma & \text{(typed variable)}\\
  & \mid & (\lambda x^\sigma.\, M) & \text{(abstraction, variable } x^\sigma \text{ bound in } M)\\
  & \mid & (M\, N) & \text{(application)}\\
  & \mid & (\Lambda X.\, M) & \text{(type abstraction, } X \text{ bound in } M,\\
  & & & \quad X \text{ not free in any type occurring in } fv(M))\\
  & \mid & (M\, \sigma) & \text{(type application)}\\
  & \mid & k & \text{(constant)}
\end{array}
$$

where constants k are drawn from the set of constants, Con, given below:

$$Con \stackrel{\text{def}}{=} \{\mathsf{Intro}^\mu, \mathsf{Elim}^\mu, \mathsf{R}^\mu, \mathsf{Intro}^\nu, \mathsf{Elim}^\nu, \mathsf{S}^\nu\}$$

Let $ftv(M)$ and $fv(M)$ be the sets of all type and term variables that occur free in M:

M	$ftv(M)$	$fv(M)$
x^σ	$ftv(\sigma)$	$\{x^\sigma\}$
$(\lambda x^\sigma.\, M)$	$ftv(\sigma) \cup ftv(M)$	$fv(M) - \{x^\sigma\}$
$(M\, N)$	$ftv(M) \cup ftv(N)$	$fv(M) \cup fv(N)$
$(\Lambda X.\, M)$	$ftv(M) - \{X\}$	$fv(M)$
$(M\, \sigma)$	$ftv(M) \cup ftv(\sigma)$	$fv(M)$
k	$\varnothing$	$\varnothing$

Type and term substitution is written as $M[\sigma/X]$ and $M[N/x]$. Alpha-conversion is up to renaming of the names of bound term variables, but not their type labels; $(\lambda x^\sigma.\, M) \equiv$

$(\lambda y^\sigma . (M[y^\sigma / x^\sigma]))$ if $y^\sigma \notin fv(M)$. We identify terms up to alpha-conversion. The restriction on variables in type abstractions comes from the $\lambda 2$; without it, $fv(\Lambda X. x^X)$ is not well defined up to alpha-conversion of terms [42]. We adopt a **name convention** for $\mu\nu\lambda 2$, that all the names of all the bound variables in a term are distinct from each other and from the names of any free variables; we can always achieve this by alpha-conversion.

The only difference between the calculus $\mu\nu\lambda 2$ given here and Mendler's calculus is the presence of the constants Elim^μ and Intro^ν. To obtain his calculus, Mendler added the initial and terminal types to $\lambda 2$, the Girard-Reynolds calculus, together with the constants Intro^μ, R^μ, Elim^ν and S^ν. (We use a notation slightly different from Mendler's: Elim instead of In, Intro instead of out, $\forall X. \tau$ instead of $\Delta X. \tau$, and different metavariables.) We need the extra constants so as to model corresponding Intro and Elim operators in $\mathcal{M}$.

The type assignment relation of $\mu\nu\lambda 2$, a predicate of the form $M{:}\sigma$, where M is a raw term and σ is a type, is defined inductively by the rules

$$\mathsf{Intro}^\mu{:}\sigma[\mu/X] \to \mu$$
$$\mathsf{Elim}^\mu{:}\mu \to \sigma[\mu/X]$$
$$\mathsf{R}^\mu{:}(\forall Y. (\forall X. (X \to \mu) \to (X \to Y) \to \sigma \to Y) \to \mu \to Y)$$
$$\mathsf{Intro}^\nu{:}\sigma[\nu/X] \to \nu$$
$$\mathsf{Elim}^\nu{:}\nu \to \sigma[\nu/X]$$
$$\mathsf{S}^\nu{:}(\forall Y. (\forall X. (\nu \to X) \to (Y \to X) \to Y \to \sigma) \to Y \to \nu)$$
$$x^\sigma{:}\sigma$$

$$\frac{M{:}\tau}{(\lambda x^\sigma. M){:}(\sigma \to \tau)} \qquad \frac{M{:}\sigma}{(\Lambda X. M){:}(\forall X. \sigma)} \qquad \frac{M{:}(\sigma \to \tau) \quad N{:}\sigma}{(M\,N){:}\tau} \qquad \frac{M{:}(\forall X. \tau)}{(M\,\sigma){:}\tau[\sigma/X]}$$

where $\mu \equiv \mu X. \sigma$ and $\nu \equiv \nu X. \sigma$. If $M{:}\sigma$ can be inferred we say that M is a **term**, and that it has type σ. Henceforth the metavariables L, M and N will range over just the terms, rather than all the raw terms.

For the sake of legibility type superscripts will often be omitted. Parentheses will often be omitted when the intended grouping is implied by associativity and scope rules. These rules are that type and term applications associate to the left, and the scope of bound variables continues as far to the right as possible. For example, the term $L\,M\,N$ is short for $((L\,M)\,N)$; and the term $\lambda x. (\lambda y. x\,y)\,y$ is short for $(\lambda x. ((\lambda y. (x\,y))\,y))$.

2.3   Reduction in $\mu\nu\lambda 2$

Let us say that a binary relation $\mathcal{R}$ on terms of $\mu\nu\lambda 2$ is **compatible** just when it is closed under the following rules:

$$\frac{M\mathcal{R}N}{(\lambda x^\sigma. M)\mathcal{R}(\lambda x^\sigma. N)} \qquad \frac{M\mathcal{R}N}{(M\,L)\mathcal{R}(N\,L)} \qquad \frac{M\mathcal{R}N}{(L\,M)\mathcal{R}(L\,N)}$$

$$\frac{M\mathcal{R}N}{(\Lambda X. M)\mathcal{R}(\Lambda X. N)} \qquad \frac{M\mathcal{R}N}{(M\,\sigma)\mathcal{R}(N\,\sigma)}$$

Let Id$^\sigma$ stand for the identity function $(\lambda x^\sigma. x^\sigma)$. The reduction relation on terms, $\rightarrow$, is the least compatible relation closed under the following eight axiom schemes:

- $(\lambda x^\sigma. M) N \rightarrow M[N/x^\sigma]$
- $\lambda x^\sigma. (M x^\sigma) \rightarrow M$ if $x^\sigma \notin fv(M)$
- $(\Lambda X. M) \sigma \rightarrow M[\sigma/X]$
- $\Lambda X. (M X) \rightarrow M$ if $X \notin ftv(M)$
- Elim$^\mu$ (Intro$^\mu$ M) $\rightarrow M$
- R$^\mu$ σ M (Intro$^\mu$ N) $\rightarrow M \mu$ Id$^\mu$ (R$^\mu$ σ M) N
- Elim$^\nu$ (Intro$^\nu$ M) $\rightarrow M$
- Elim$^\nu$ (S$^\nu$ σ M N) $\rightarrow M \nu$ Id$^\nu$ (S$^\nu$ σ M) N

In this dissertation we take advantage of the following theorem.

Theorem 2.1 (Mendler) *If no constant* Elim$^\mu$ *or* Intro$^\nu$ *occurs in a term M, then M is strongly normalisable, which is to say that there is no infinite sequence of reductions starting from M.*

Proof. The proof is contained in an article by Mendler [88]. His calculus does not contain the new families of constants Elim$^\mu$ or Intro$^\nu$. The reduction rules applicable to terms of $\mu\nu\lambda2$ that do not contain the new constants are exactly the same as the rules in Mendler's article. If $M \rightarrow M'$ is a reduction, and M does not contain one of the new constants, then neither does M'. Therefore any sequence of reductions starting from a term not containing the new constants can be exactly simulated by a sequence of reductions in Mendler's calculus. Therefore his result tells us that any term M in $\mu\nu\lambda2$ is strongly normalisable, provided that none of the new constants occurs in M. ∎

In a private communication (June 1991) Mendler said that he omitted the Elim$^\mu$ and Intro$^\nu$ constants from his calculus to simplify the confluence proof (which we make no use of in this dissertation), and was not concerned at the loss of expressiveness because they can be mimicked using the recursion constants R$^\mu$ or S$^\nu$, respectively. This present work appears to be the first to work through a construction of combinators to mimic the constants omitted by Mendler.

The rest of this chapter is devoted to a proof that any term of $\mu\nu\lambda2$ is strongly normalisable.

2.4 Combinators to simulate Elim$^\mu$ and Intro$^\nu$

We prove that every term of $\mu\nu\lambda2$ is strongly normalisable by simulating the new constants Elim$^\mu$ and Intro$^\nu$ with combinators *elim*$^\mu$ and *intro*$^\nu$, definable in Mendler's original calculus from constants R$^\mu$ and S$^\mu$ respectively. Before defining these combinators in Definition 2.3 we define two auxiliary functions, *Spec* and *Gen*:

Definition 2.2 *We define the partial functions (not terms of the calculus), Spec and Gen, that map quadruples of the form (ρ, X, σ, M) to a term, where ρ is a recursive type, X is a type variable, σ is a type and M is a term. First choose some name f. Then define* the two functions simultaneously by structural induction on σ (the third argument):

$$Spec(\mu, X, X, M) \overset{\text{def}}{=} (f^{X \to \mu} M)$$
$$Spec(\rho, X, Y, M) \overset{\text{def}}{=} M \qquad \text{if } X \neq Y$$
$$Spec(\rho, X, \rho', M) \overset{\text{def}}{=} M$$
$$Spec(\rho, X, (\forall Y. \tau), M) \overset{\text{def}}{=} \Lambda Y.\, Spec\,(\rho, X, \tau, M\,Y) \quad \text{where } Y \notin ftv(X, M)$$
$$Spec(\rho, X, (\tau_1 \to \tau_2), M) \overset{\text{def}}{=} \lambda x^{\hat{\tau}_1}.\, Spec\,(\rho, X, \tau_2, M\,(Gen(\rho, X, \tau_1, x^{\hat{\tau}_1})))$$
$$\text{where } \hat{\tau}_1 \equiv \tau_1[\rho/X]$$
$$\text{and name } x \neq f \text{ does not occur in } fv(M)$$

$$Gen(\nu, X, X, M) \overset{\text{def}}{=} (f^{\nu \to X} M)$$
$$Gen(\rho, X, Y, M) \overset{\text{def}}{=} M \qquad \text{if } X \neq Y$$
$$Gen(\rho, X, \rho', M) \overset{\text{def}}{=} M$$
$$Gen(\rho, X, (\forall Y. \tau), M) \overset{\text{def}}{=} \Lambda Y.\, Gen\,(\rho, X, \tau, M\,Y) \quad \text{where } Y \notin ftv(X, M)$$
$$Gen(\rho, X, (\tau_1 \to \tau_2), M) \overset{\text{def}}{=} \lambda x^{\tau_1}.\, Gen\,(\rho, X, \tau_2, M\,(Spec(\rho, X, \tau_1, x^{\tau_1})))$$
$$\text{where name } x \neq f \text{ does not occur in } fv(M)$$

The functions are partial only so far as $Spec(\nu, X, \tau, M)$ and $Gen(\mu, X, \tau, M)$ are undefined when τ is the type variable X; this is unproblematic because we only apply $Spec$ to a terminal type $(\nu X.\sigma)$ or Gen to an initial type $(\mu X.\sigma)$ when X occurs negatively in τ.

Definition 2.3 For each initial type $\mu \equiv (\mu X.\sigma)$, let $\hat{\sigma}$ be the type $\sigma[\mu/X]$, and define the combinator family, $elim^\mu$, as follows:

$$elim^\mu \overset{\text{def}}{=} \mathsf{R}^\mu \, \hat{\sigma} \, (\Lambda X. \lambda f^{X \to \mu}. \lambda g^{X \to \hat{\sigma}}. \lambda x^\sigma.\, Spec\,(\mu, X, \sigma, x^\sigma))$$

Dually, for each terminal type $\nu \equiv (\nu X.\sigma)$, let $\hat{\sigma}$ be $\sigma[\nu/X]$, and define the combinator family, $intro^\nu$, as follows:

$$intro^\nu \overset{\text{def}}{=} \mathsf{S}^\nu \, \hat{\sigma} \, (\Lambda X. \lambda f^{\nu \to X}. \lambda g^{\hat{\sigma} \to X}. \lambda x^{\hat{\sigma}}.\, Gen\,(\nu, X, \sigma, x^{\hat{\sigma}}))$$

The name f is the same as the one chosen in the definition of $Spec$ and Gen.

In §2.6 we will prove that these combinators possess the following properties:

- $elim^\mu(\mathsf{Intro}^\mu(M)) \to^+ M$
- $\mathsf{Elim}^\nu(intro^\nu(M)) \to^+ M$

for any suitably typed term M. Given these properties it is not hard to show that every term in $\mu\nu\lambda2$ is strongly normalising. First we show two examples.

2.5   Two examples

First, recall the type $1 \equiv (\nu X. X)$. We can calculate the combinator $intro^1$ as follows:

$$intro^1 \equiv \mathsf{S}^1 1 \, (\Lambda X. \lambda f^{1 \to X}. \lambda g^{1 \to X}. \lambda x^1.\, Gen\,(1, X, X, x^1))$$
$$\equiv \mathsf{S}^1 1 \, (\Lambda X. \lambda f^{1 \to X}. \lambda g^{1 \to X}. \lambda x^1.\, f^{1 \to X} x^1)$$

Now we can check that $\mathsf{Elim}^1(intro^1(M)) \to^+ M$ for any term M of type 1.

$$
\begin{aligned}
\mathsf{Elim}^1(intro^1(M)) &\equiv \mathsf{Elim}^1(\mathsf{S}^1 \, 1 \, (\Lambda X. \, \lambda f^{1\to X}. \, \lambda g^{1\to X}. \, \lambda x^1. \, f^{1\to X} x^1) \, M) \\
&\to (\Lambda X. \lambda f^{1\to X}. \lambda g^{1\to X}. \lambda x^1. f^{1\to X} x^1) \, 1 \, \mathsf{Id}^1 \, intro^1 \, M \\
&\to (\lambda f^{1\to 1}. \lambda g^{1\to 1}. \lambda x^1. f^{1\to 1} x^1) \, \mathsf{Id}^1 \, intro^1 \, M \\
&\to (\lambda g^{1\to 1}. \lambda x^1. \mathsf{Id}^1 \, x^1) \, intro^1 \, M \\
&\to (\lambda x^1. \mathsf{Id}^1 \, x^1) \, M \\
&\to \mathsf{Id}^1 \, M \\
&\to M
\end{aligned}
$$

Second, let σ be the type $(X \to 1) \to 1$ and initial type μ be $(\mu X. \sigma)$. We begin by calculating $Spec(\mu, X, \sigma, x^\sigma)$, which has type $(\mu \to 1) \to 1$.

$$
\begin{aligned}
Spec(\mu, X, \sigma, x^\sigma) &\equiv \lambda y^{\mu \to 1}. \; Spec \, (\mu, X, 1, x^\sigma \, (Gen(\mu, X, (X \to 1), y^{\mu \to 1}))) \\
&\equiv \lambda y^{\mu \to 1}. \; Spec \, (\mu, X, 1, x^\sigma \\
&\qquad (\lambda z^X. \; Gen \, (\mu, X, 1, y^{\mu \to 1} \, (Spec(\mu, X, X, z^X)))))) \\
&\equiv \lambda y^{\mu \to 1}. \; Spec \, (\mu, X, 1, x^\sigma \\
&\qquad (\lambda z^X. \; Gen \, (\mu, X, 1, y^{\mu \to 1} \, (f^{X \to \mu} z^X)))) \\
&\equiv \lambda y^{\mu \to 1}. \; Spec \, (\mu, X, 1, x^\sigma \, (\lambda z^X. y^{\mu \to 1} \, (f^{X \to \mu} z^X))) \\
&\equiv \lambda y^{\mu \to 1}. x^\sigma \, (\lambda z^X. y^{\mu \to 1} \, (f^{X \to \mu} z^X))
\end{aligned}
$$

The combinator $elim^\mu$ is defined as follows, where $\hat\sigma$ is $(\mu \to 1) \to 1$.

$$
elim^\mu \equiv \mathsf{R}^\mu \, \hat\sigma \, (\Lambda X. \lambda f^{X \to \mu}. \lambda g^{X \to \hat\sigma}. \lambda x^\sigma. \; Spec \, (\mu, X, \sigma, x^\sigma))
$$

We can check that $elim^\mu(\mathsf{Intro}^\mu(M)) \to^+ M$ for any term M of type $\hat\sigma$.

$$
\begin{aligned}
elim^\mu(\mathsf{Intro}^\mu(M)) &\equiv \mathsf{R}^\mu \, \hat\sigma \, (\Lambda X. \lambda f^{X \to \mu}. \lambda g^{X \to \hat\sigma}. \lambda x^\sigma. \; Spec \, (\mu, X, \sigma, x^\sigma)) \\
&\qquad (\mathsf{Intro}^\mu(M)) \\
&\to (\Lambda X. \lambda f^{X \to \mu}. \lambda g^{X \to \hat\sigma}. \lambda x^\sigma. \; Spec \, (\mu, X, \sigma, x^\sigma)) \\
&\qquad \mu \, \mathsf{Id}^\mu \, elim^\mu \, M \\
&\to (\lambda f^{\mu \to \mu}. \lambda g^{\mu \to \hat\sigma}. \lambda x^\sigma. \\
&\qquad \lambda y^{\mu \to 1}. x^\sigma \, (\lambda z^\mu. y^{\mu \to 1} \, (f^{\mu \to \mu} z^\mu))) \\
&\qquad \mathsf{Id}^\mu \, elim^\mu \, M \\
&\to (\lambda g^{\mu \to \hat\sigma}. \lambda x^\sigma. \lambda y^{\mu \to 1}. x^\sigma \, (\lambda z^\mu. y^{\mu \to 1} \, (\mathsf{Id}^\mu \, z^\mu))) \\
&\qquad elim^\mu \, M \\
&\to (\lambda x^\sigma. \lambda y^{\mu \to 1}. x^\sigma \, (\lambda z^\mu. y^{\mu \to 1} \, (\mathsf{Id}^\mu \, z^\mu))) \, M \\
&\to (\lambda y^{\mu \to 1}. M \, (\lambda z^\mu. y^{\mu \to 1} \, (\mathsf{Id}^\mu \, z^\mu))) \\
&\to (\lambda y^{\mu \to 1}. M \, (\lambda z^\mu. y^{\mu \to 1} \, z^\mu)) \\
&\to (\lambda y^{\mu \to 1}. M \, y^{\mu \to 1}) \\
&\to M
\end{aligned}
$$

Notice that the reductions make use of the beta and eta rules, and depend on the variable named f being replaced by the identity function.

2.6 Strong normalisation for $\mu\nu\lambda2$

We prove a series of propositions that culminates in a strong normalisation result for $\mu\nu\lambda2$. The first proposition states all the properties that we rely on in the functions *Spec* and

Gen; parts (1a) and (1d) are of particular interest.

Proposition 2.4   Let μ be any initial type $\mu X.\sigma_0$ and let s be the substitution $\cdot[\mu/X][\mathsf{Id}^\mu/f^{\mu\to\mu}]$. Then for any type τ and term M,

(1) If $M{:}\tau$ and X occurs positively in τ, let $N \equiv Spec(\mu, X, \tau, M)$, and then
  (a) N has type $\tau[\mu/X]$,
  (b) $fv(N) \subseteq fv(M)$ and name f does not occur in $fv(N)$,
  (c) $ftv(N) \subseteq ftv(\tau) \cup ftv(M) \cup \{X\}$, and
  (d) $Ns \to^* Ms$.

(2) If $M{:}\tau[\mu/X]$ and X occurs negatively in τ, let $N \equiv Gen(\mu, X, \tau, M)$, and then
  (a) N has type τ, and
  (b) $fv(N) \subseteq fv(M)$ and name f does not occur in $fv(N)$,
  (c) $ftv(N) \subseteq ftv(\tau) \cup ftv(M) \cup \{X\}$, and
  (d) $Ns \to^* Ms$.

Proof. We prove all parts simultaneously by induction on the size of the type τ, and proceed by analysis of its structure. For the sake of brevity, we omit all the details of parts (b) and (c). They are no harder to prove than the other parts.

Case $\tau \equiv X$.
  (1a) Here $N \equiv (f^{X\to\mu} M)$ which has type μ, which equals $\tau[\mu/X]$.
  (1d) $Ns \equiv (\mathsf{Id}\,(Ms)) \to Ms$.
  (2) $Gen(\mu, X, X, M)$ is undefined, but this case cannot arise because X occurs positively in X.

Case $\tau \equiv Y \neq X$.
  (1a) $N \equiv M{:}Y$ and $Y \equiv \tau[\mu/X]$.
  (1d) $Ns \equiv Ms \to^* Ms$.
  (2a) $N \equiv M{:}Y$ and $Y \equiv \tau$.
  (2d) $Ns \equiv Ms \to^* Ms$.

Case $\tau \equiv \rho$.   This case is trivial because of the restriction in $\mu\nu\lambda2$ that all recursive types be closed. If we had not made this restriction, the definitions of *Spec* and *Gen* would be rather more complicated.
  (1a) Here $N \equiv M$, which has type ρ. All recursive types are closed, so $\rho \equiv \tau[\mu/X]$.
  (1d) $Ns \equiv Ms \to^* Ms$.
  (2a) $N \equiv M$, which has type $\tau[\mu/X] \equiv \tau$, since all recursive types are closed.
  (2d) $Ns \equiv Ms \to^* Ms$.

Case $\tau \equiv (\forall Y.\sigma)$.   We may assume $Y \notin ftv(X, M)$ since types are identified up to alpha-conversion.
  (1a) Here $N \equiv \Lambda Y.\ Spec\,(\mu, X, \sigma, MY)$. By IH, we have that $Spec(\mu, X, \sigma, MY)$ is of type $\sigma[\mu/X]$. Therefore N is of type $\forall Y.\,(\sigma[\mu/X]) \equiv \tau[\mu/X]$.

$$
\begin{aligned}
(1\mathrm{d})Ns &\equiv \Lambda Y.\,(Spec(\mu, X, \sigma, MY)s) \\
&\to^* \Lambda Y.\,((MY)s) \qquad\qquad \text{(IH)} \\
&\equiv \Lambda Y.\,(Ms)Y \\
&\to Ms
\end{aligned}
$$

(2a) $N \equiv \Lambda Y.\ Gen\ (\mu, X, \sigma, MY)$. By IH, $Gen(\mu, X, \sigma, MY)$ is of type σ. Therefore N is of type $(\forall Y.\ \sigma) \equiv \tau$.

$$
\begin{aligned}
(2d)Ns &\equiv \Lambda Y.\ (Gen(\mu, X, \sigma, MY)s) \\
&\to^* \Lambda Y.\ ((MY)s) &&\text{(IH)} \\
&\equiv \Lambda Y.\ (Ms)Y \\
&\to Ms
\end{aligned}
$$

Case $\tau \equiv (\tau_1 \to \tau_2)$.

(1a) $N \equiv \lambda x.\ Spec\ (\mu, X, \tau_2, M\ (Gen(\mu, X, \tau_1, x)))$, where x has type $\tau_1[\mu/X]$. Since X occurs negatively in τ_1, by IH we have $Gen(\mu, X, \tau_1, x){:}\tau_1$. Then $M\ (Gen(\mu, X, \tau_1, x))$ has type τ_2. Since X occurs positively in τ_2, by IH we have $Spec(\mu, X, \tau_2, M\ (Gen(\mu, X, \tau_1, x)))$ has type $\tau_2[\mu/X]$. Therefore N has type $\tau_1[\mu/X] \to \tau_2[\mu/X]$ which equals $\tau[\mu/X]$.

$$
\begin{aligned}
(1d)Ns &\equiv \lambda x.\ (Spec(\mu, X, \tau_2, M\ (Gen(\mu, X, \tau_1, x)))s) \\
&\to^* \lambda x.\ ((M\ (Gen(\mu, X, \tau_1, x)))s) &&\text{(IH)} \\
&\equiv \lambda x.\ (Ms)\ (Gen(\mu, X, \tau_1, x)s) \\
&\to^* \lambda x.\ (Ms)\ (xs) &&\text{(IH)} \\
&\equiv \lambda x.\ (Ms)\ x \\
&\to Ms
\end{aligned}
$$

(2a) Dually, $N \equiv \lambda x.\ Gen\ (\mu, X, \tau_2, M\ (Spec(\mu, X, \tau_1, x)))$, where x has type τ_1. Since X occurs positively in τ_1, by IH we have $Spec(\mu, X, \tau_1, x)$ has type $\tau_1[\mu/X]$. Then $M\ (Spec(\mu, X, \tau_1, x))$ has type $\tau_2[\mu/X]$. Since X occurs negatively in τ_2, by IH we have $Gen(\mu, X, \tau_2, M\ (Spec(\mu, X, \tau_1, x)))$ has type τ_2. Finally, N has type $\tau_1 \to \tau_2$ which equals τ.

$$
\begin{aligned}
(2d)Ns &\equiv \lambda x.\ (Gen(\mu, X, \tau_2, M\ (Spec(\mu, X, \tau_1, x)))s) \\
&\to^* \lambda x.\ ((M\ (Spec(\mu, X, \tau_1, x)))s) &&\text{(IH)} \\
&\equiv \lambda x.\ (Ms)\ (Spec(\mu, X, \tau_1, x)s) \\
&\to^* \lambda x.\ (Ms)\ (xs) &&\text{(IH)} \\
&\equiv \lambda x.\ (Ms)\ x \\
&\to Ms \qquad\blacksquare
\end{aligned}
$$

The following is analogous to Proposition 2.4, but for terminal types.

Proposition 2.5 *Let ν be any terminal type $\nu X.\ \sigma_0$ and let s be the substitution* $\cdot[\nu/X][\mathsf{Id}^\nu/f^{\nu\to\nu}]$. *Then for any type τ and term M,*

(1) If $M{:}\tau$ and X occurs negatively in τ, let $N \equiv Spec(\nu, X, \tau, M)$, and then
   (a) N has type $\tau[\nu/X]$, and
   (b) $fv(N) \subseteq fv(M)$ and name f does not occur in $fv(N)$,
   (c) $ftv(N) \subseteq ftv(\tau) \cup ftv(M) \cup \{X\}$, and
   (d) $Ns \to^* Ms$.

(2) If $M{:}\tau[\nu/X]$ and X occurs positively in τ, let $N \equiv Gen(\nu, X, \tau, M)$, and then
   (a) N has type τ, and
   (b) $fv(N) \subseteq fv(M)$ and name f does not occur in $fv(N)$,
   (c) $ftv(N) \subseteq ftv(\tau) \cup ftv(M) \cup \{X\}$, and
   (d) $Ns \to^* Ms$.

Proof. Omitted, but dual to the previous proof.   ■

Now we prove properties of the combinators $elim^\mu$ and $intro^\nu$:

Proposition 2.6 *For any recursive types $\mu \equiv \mu X. \sigma$ and $\nu \equiv \nu X. \sigma$,*

(1) *There are no type or term variables free in $elim^\mu$ or $intro^\nu$, that is, they are combinators.*

(2) *The type assignments $elim^\mu:(\mu \to \sigma[\mu/X])$ and $intro^\nu:(\sigma[\nu/X] \to \nu)$ are derivable, that is, the combinators are well-typed.*

(3) *For any term M,*

(a) *if $M:\sigma[\mu/X]$ then $elim^\mu(\mathsf{Intro}^\mu(M)) \to^+ M$.*

(b) *if $M:\sigma[\nu/X]$ then $\mathsf{Elim}^\nu(intro^\nu(M)) \to^+ M$.*

Proof. (1) Consider the term $elim^\mu$.   Let $\hat{\sigma}$ be the type $\sigma[\mu/X]$.   Since $fn(Spec(\mu, X, \sigma, x^\sigma)) \subseteq \{x, f\}$, we can calculate $fn(elim^\mu) = fn(Spec(\mu, X, \sigma, x^\sigma)) - \{f, x, g\} = \varnothing$. Therefore $fv(elim^\mu) = \varnothing$. Similarly, $ftv(Spec(\mu, X, \sigma, x^\sigma)) \subseteq ftv(\sigma) \cup \{X\} = \{X\}$, since $ftv(\sigma) \subseteq \{X\}$. We have:

$$ftv(elim^\mu) = (ftv(\mu, \hat{\sigma}, X \to \mu, X \to \hat{\sigma}, \sigma) \cup ftv(Spec(\mu, X, \sigma, x^\sigma)) - \{X\} = \varnothing$$

Similarly we can check that the term $intro^\nu$ has no free type or term variables.

(2) Combinator $elim^\mu$ will be well-typed if $Spec(\mu, X, \sigma, x^\sigma)$ is of type $\sigma[\mu/X]$, and Proposition 2.4(1a) says so. Similarly, for $intro^\nu$ to be well-typed, the term $Gen(\nu, X, \sigma, x^{\sigma[\nu/X]})$ needs to have type σ, and according to Proposition 2.4(2a) it does.

(3) Again let $\hat{\sigma}$ be $\sigma[\mu/X]$. By appeal to Proposition 2.4(1d) let us calculate:

$$
\begin{aligned}
&elim^\mu(\mathsf{Intro}^\mu(M)) \\
&\equiv\ \mathsf{R}^\mu\,\hat{\sigma}\,(\Lambda X. \lambda f^{X \to \mu}. \lambda g^{X \to \hat{\sigma}}. \lambda x^\sigma.\ Spec\,(\mu, X, \sigma, x^\sigma))(\mathsf{Intro}^\mu(M)) \\
&\to\ (\Lambda X. \lambda f^{X \to \mu}. \lambda g^{X \to \hat{\sigma}}. \lambda x^{\hat{\sigma}}.\ (Spec(\mu, X, \sigma, x^\sigma)) \\
&\qquad \mu\ \mathsf{Id}^\mu\ elim^\mu M \\
&\to\ (\lambda f^{\mu \to \mu}. \lambda g^{\mu \to \hat{\sigma}}. \lambda x^{\hat{\sigma}}.\ (Spec(\mu, X, \sigma, x^\sigma)[\mu/X])) \\
&\qquad \mathsf{Id}^\mu\ elim^\mu\ M \\
&\to\ (\lambda g^{\mu \to \hat{\sigma}}. \lambda x^{\hat{\sigma}}.\ (Spec(\mu, X, \sigma, x^\sigma)[\mu/X][\mathsf{Id}^\mu/f^{\mu \to \mu}])) \\
&\qquad elim^\mu M \\
&\to\ (\lambda x^{\hat{\sigma}}.\ (Spec(\mu, X, \sigma, x^\sigma)[\mu/X][\mathsf{Id}^\mu/f^{\mu \to \mu}][elim^\mu/g^{\mu \to \hat{\sigma}}]))M \\
&\equiv\ (\lambda x^{\hat{\sigma}}.\ (Spec(\mu, X, \sigma, x^\sigma)[\mu/X][\mathsf{Id}^\mu/f^{\mu \to \mu}]))M \\
&\to^*\ (\lambda x^{\hat{\sigma}}.\ (x^\sigma[\mu/X][\mathsf{Id}^\mu/f^{\mu \to \mu}]))M \\
&\equiv\ \mathsf{Id}^{\hat{\sigma}} M \\
&\to\ M
\end{aligned}
$$

By a similar calculation we can compute the other part of the proposition.   ■

Now that we know how to simulate the new constants that appear in our extended calculus in terms of the original calculus, we can simulate each term N of the extended calculus by a term M with each of the new constants replaced by one of the combinators we have just defined.

Definition 2.7 *Define the* **simulation relation**, $M > N$, *on terms of* $\mu\nu\lambda2$, *as the least compatible relation closed under the following axiom schemes:*

- $elim^\mu > \mathsf{Elim}^\mu$
- $intro^\nu > \mathsf{Intro}^\nu$
- $k > k$ *for any* $k \in Con - \{\mathsf{Elim}^\mu, \mathsf{Intro}^\nu\}$.

Later we will rely on the fact that simulation is preserved by substitution:

Lemma 2.8 *For any terms M and N such that $M > N$,*

(1) *If $M > N$ then $fv(M) = fv(N)$ and $ftv(M) = ftv(N)$.*

(2) *$M[\sigma/X] > N[\sigma/X]$ for any σ and X; and*

(3) *$M[L/x] > N[L'/x]$ for any L, L' and x with $L > L'$.*

Proof. Part (1) is an easy induction on the depth of inference of $M > N$. Part (2) is also by induction on the depth of inference of $M > N$. We show several cases:

Case $M \equiv elim^\mu > \mathsf{Elim}^\mu \equiv N$. Since neither side contains any free type variable, $M[\sigma/X] \equiv M > N \equiv N[\sigma/X]$. Similarly, since neither side contains a free term variable, $M[L/x] > N[L'/x]$.

Case $M \equiv intro^\nu > \mathsf{Elim}^\mu \equiv N$. The result follows by the same argument as the previous case, that neither side contains a free type or term variable.

Case $M \equiv k > k \equiv N$. Same again.

Case $M \equiv y^\tau > y^\tau \equiv N$. We have $M[\sigma/X] \equiv N[\sigma/X]$, so $M[\sigma/X] > N[\sigma/X]$. For (2), either $x = y$ or not. If so, $M[L/x] \equiv L > L' \equiv N[L'/x]$. If not, $M[L/x] \equiv y^\tau > y^\tau \equiv N[L'/x]$.

Case $M \equiv (\lambda y^\tau. M_1) > (\lambda y^\tau. N_1) \equiv N$. We may pick the bound variable y such that $y \neq x$. By induction hypothesis we have $M_1[\sigma/X] > N_1[\sigma/X]$ and $M_1[L/x] > N_1[L'/x]$. Then we can derive that $M[\sigma/X] \equiv (\lambda y^{\tau[\sigma/X]}. M_1[\sigma/X]) > (\lambda x^{\tau[\sigma/X]}. M_2[\sigma/X]) \equiv N[\sigma/X]$ and $M[L/x] \equiv (\lambda y^\tau. M_1[L/x]) > (\lambda x^\tau. M_2[L'/x]) \equiv N[L'/x]$ as required.

Case $M \equiv (M_1\, M_2) > (N_1\, N_2) \equiv N$. By induction hypothesis, $M_i[\sigma/X] > N_i[\sigma/X]$ and $M_i[L/x] > N_i[L/x]$ for $i = 1, 2$. Then we have

$$M[\sigma/X] \equiv (M_1[\sigma/X]\, M_2[\sigma/X]) > (N_1[\sigma/X]\, N_2[\sigma/X]) \equiv N[\sigma/X]$$

and $M[L/x] \equiv (M_1[L/x]\, M_2[L/x]) > (N_1[L'/x]\, N_2[L'/x]) \equiv N[L'/x]$ as required.

The case for Λ-abstractions is similar. Part (3) follows by a similar argument. ∎

Now we come to the key property of the simulation relation: that if $M > N$, then any reduction of N can be mimicked by a non-empty sequence of reductions starting from M:

Proposition 2.9 *If $M > N$ and $N \to N'$ then there exists M' such that $M \to^+ M'$ and $M' > N'$.*

Proof. The proof is by induction on the depth of inference of $N \to N'$, proceeding by an analysis of how the inference was derived. We show here only the two cases where combinators do the work of constants, and one of the inductive cases:

Case $N \equiv \mathsf{Elim}^{\mu}(\mathsf{Intro}^{\mu} N_1) \to N_1 \equiv N'$.

    Since $M > N$ we have $M \equiv elim^{\mu}(\mathsf{Intro}^{\mu} M_1)$ with $M_1 > N_1$.

    Set $M' \equiv M_1$ and by Proposition 2.6(3a) we have $M \to^+ M'$, and we know $M' > N'$.

Case $N \equiv \mathsf{Elim}^{\nu}(\mathsf{Intro}^{\nu} N_1) \to N_1 \equiv N'$.

    Since $M > N$ we have $M \equiv \mathsf{Elim}^{\nu}(intro^{\nu} N_1)$ with $M_1 > N_1$.

    Set $M' \equiv M_1$ and by Proposition 2.6(3b) we have $M \to^+ M'$, and we know $M' > N'$.

Case $N \equiv (\lambda x. N_1) \to (\lambda x. N_1') \equiv N'$.

    where $N_1 \to N_1'$. Since $M > N$ we have $M \equiv (\lambda x. M_1)$ with $M_1 > N_1$.

    By induction hypothesis, there is M_1' such that $M_1 \to^+ M_1'$ and $M_1' > N_1'$.

    Set $M' \equiv (\lambda x. M_1')$ and we have $M \to^+ M'$ and $M' > N'$.

The other cases of the proof follow the same pattern.   ■

A simple consequence of Proposition 2.9 is strong normalisation:

Theorem 2.10 *Each term N of $\mu\nu\lambda 2$ is strongly normalisable.*

Proof. Suppose to the contrary, that there is a well-typed term N that admits an infinite chain of reductions. Construct a term M such that $M > N$ by replacing each constant of form Elim^{μ} or Intro^{ν} that occurs in N by the corresponding combinator $elim^{\mu}$ and $intro^{\nu}$ respectively. From Proposition 2.9 it follows that since there is an infinite chain of reductions starting from N, there is also one starting at M. But M is a term of Mendler's published calculus, which is known to be strongly normalising, Theorem 2.1, so we have reached a contradiction. Therefore each term of $\mu\nu\lambda 2$ is strongly normalisable.   ■

We have extended Mendler's second-order λ-calculus with recursive types, to have two new families of constants, Elim^{μ} and Intro^{ν}. This provides a basis for the normalisation proof of the semantic metalanguage, $\mathcal{M}$, developed in later chapters of this dissertation.

Chapter 3

A metalanguage for semantics

The purpose of this chapter is to define a metalanguage for programming language semantics, called $\mathcal{M}$. In Chapter 6 we define a small functional language, called $\mathcal{H}$. We will
give a denotational semantics for $\mathcal{H}$ in terms of $\mathcal{M}$, and also show how the denotational
semantics can be extended to account for an exception mechanism and side-effecting I/O.
Hence each of the four classes of functional I/O discussed in Chapter 7 can be defined
from the denotational semantics for $\mathcal{H}$, extended as necessary.

We adopt a variant of Plotkin's threefold methodology for denotational semantics [120].
First, he developed a theory of partial functions and so-called bottomless domains. Second,
he proposed a typed λ-calculus as a semantic metalanguage; his calculus had product,
sum, function, lifted and recursive types. His calculus had both domain-theoretic and
operational semantics. He proved adequacy results relating the operational and domain-
theoretic semantics of his metalanguage. Third, to study a particular object language, he
gave a direct operational semantics and an indirect domain-theoretic semantics induced by
mapping the object language into the metalanguage. Proof of the correspondence between
the operational and domain-theoretic semantics of the object language can take advantage
of the adequacy results for the metalanguage. This approach is general in that for each
object language studied, the proof of adequacy factors into two: a general result proved
once and for all for the metalanguage, and a comparatively simpler proof relating the
semantics of the object and metalanguages. Plotkin's work has been developed by Moggi
[99] and Jones [66].

We develop in this dissertation a simply-typed λ-calculus called $\mathcal{M}$ for the denotational
semantics of $\mathcal{H}$ and its variants. The most important difference between the operational
semantics of Plotkin's calculus and $\mathcal{M}$ is that in $\mathcal{M}$ the evaluation of any term of a certain
class of types cannot diverge. In Plotkin's calculus, there is a divergent term at every type.
We partition the types of $\mathcal{M}$ in two: the **possibly-divergent** types are the lifted types;
the **certainly-convergent** types are all the others. One reason for this is to convey
information about operational behaviour in the type system; for instance, any numeral in
$\mathcal{H}$ is mapped to an $\mathcal{M}$ term of type Num, which is a certainly-convergent type representing
the natural numbers. The type of the translation of the numeral conveys that it cannot
diverge.

In this and the following two chapters we investigate $\mathcal{M}$ before applying it to the study of functional programming and I/O in Chapters 6 and 7. In this chapter we define $\mathcal{M}$ and assign it an operationally-based rather than domain-theoretic semantics. $\mathcal{M}$ has a type system similar to Plotkin's calculus: product, sum, function, lifted and recursive types. Using a methodology similar to Plotkin's, we use the metalanguage to decompose a more complex object language, $\mathcal{H}$. In Chapter 4 we investigate two operationally-defined preorders on the terms of $\mathcal{M}$: Morris-style contextual order and a typed form of Abramsky's applicative bisimulation. We will prove them to be equal, and take the equivalence they generate as equivalence on terms of $\mathcal{M}$. In Chapter 5 we develop a theory of $\mathcal{M}$ based on equational laws and a co-induction principle. We study certain derived $\mathcal{M}$ types that are needed for the semantics of $\mathcal{H}$: booleans, natural numbers and iterated sums and products.

§3.1 defines the syntax of $\mathcal{M}$. The type system is defined in §3.2 and the operational semantics in §3.3. §3.4 proves the major result of this chapter, that only terms of lifted type can diverge.

3.1   Syntax of $\mathcal{M}$

We assume countably infinite sets of type variables and term variables, ranged over by letters X, Y, Z and f, g, x, y, z respectively. The syntactic conventions of §1.8 apply to $\mathcal{M}$. The types are given by the following grammar

$$\sigma, \tau ::= X \mid \sigma \times \tau \mid \sigma + \tau \mid \sigma \to \tau \mid \sigma_\perp \mid \mu X.\sigma$$

and the terms by the grammar in Table 3.1.

A type is **possibly-divergent** iff it is a **lifted type**, that is, has the form $\sigma_\perp$. Any other type is **certainly-convergent**. The main result of this chapter is a convergence theorem (Theorem 3.11) which says that evaluation of any closed term of a certainly-convergent type must converge. A corollary is that only terms of a possibly-divergent type may diverge. The product, disjoint sum and function types, $(\sigma \times \tau)$, $(\sigma + \tau)$ and $(\sigma \to \tau)$ respectively, are certainly-convergent types.

Recursive types are certainly-convergent. They take the form $(\mu X.\sigma)$. Just as in Chapter 2 the symbol μ is used both as a metavariable for recursive types and as part of the syntax as the type constructor itself. There are two syntactic restrictions on these types: (1) each free occurrence of the type variable X in σ must be to the left of an even number of $\to$'s; and (2) the only type variable free in σ can be X. Restriction (2) rules out mutually recursive types. These conditions are required so that the convergence theorem can be proved by mapping any certainly-convergent type in $\mathcal{M}$ to a corresponding type in $\mu\nu\lambda 2$. We will assume implicitly that types are well-formed. The set of well-formed types is closed under substitution.

3.2   Type assignment in $\mathcal{M}$

An **environment**, Γ, is a finite mapping from variables to closed types, written as $x_1{:}\sigma_1, \ldots, x_n{:}\sigma_n$, where the variables in the list are pairwise distinct. The domain of

---

Syntax

$$U, V \ ::= \ \langle M, N \rangle \qquad \text{(pair)}$$

$$\mid \ \mathsf{Inl}^\tau(M) \mid \mathsf{Inr}^\sigma(M) \qquad \text{(injection)}$$

$$\mid \ (\lambda x{:}\sigma.\, M) \qquad \text{(abstraction, } x \text{ bound in } M)$$

$$\mid \ \mathsf{Lift}(M) \qquad \text{(Lift-term)}$$

$$\mid \ \mathsf{Intro}^\mu(M) \qquad \text{(Intro-term)}$$

$$L, M, N \ ::= \ x \qquad \text{(variable)}$$

$$\mid \ V \qquad \text{(canonical term)}$$

$$\mid \ \mathsf{Split}(M, x.\, y.\, N) \qquad \text{(Split-term, } x, y \text{ bound in } N)$$

$$\mid \ \mathsf{Case}(M, x_1.\, N_1, x_2.\, N_2) \quad \text{(Case-term, } x_i \text{ bound in } N_i \ (i=1,2))$$

$$\mid \ (M\,N) \qquad \text{(application)}$$

$$\mid \ \mathsf{Seq}(M, x.\, N) \qquad \text{(Seq-term, } x \text{ bound in } N)$$

$$\mid \ \mathsf{Fix}^\sigma(x.\, M) \qquad \text{(Fix-term, } x \text{ bound in } M)$$

$$\mid \ \mathsf{Elim}(M) \qquad \text{(Elim-term)}$$

Table 3.1: Terms of $\mathcal{M}$

$$\overline{\Gamma \vdash x : \Gamma(x)}$$

$$\frac{\Gamma \vdash M : \sigma \qquad \Gamma \vdash N : \tau}{\Gamma \vdash \langle M, N \rangle : (\sigma \times \tau)} \qquad \frac{\Gamma \vdash M : (\sigma \times \tau) \qquad \Gamma, x{:}\sigma, y{:}\tau \vdash N : \tau'}{\Gamma \vdash \mathsf{Split}(M, x.\, y.\, N) : \tau'}$$

$$\frac{\Gamma \vdash M : \sigma}{\Gamma \vdash \mathsf{Inl}^\tau(M) : (\sigma + \tau)} \qquad \frac{\Gamma \vdash M : \tau}{\Gamma \vdash \mathsf{Inr}^\sigma(M) : (\sigma + \tau)}$$

$$\frac{\Gamma \vdash M : (\sigma + \tau) \qquad \Gamma, x_1{:}\sigma \vdash N_1 : \sigma' \qquad \Gamma, x_2{:}\tau \vdash N_2 : \sigma'}{\Gamma \vdash \mathsf{Case}(M, x_1.\, N_1, x_2.\, N_2) : \sigma'}$$

$$\frac{\Gamma, x{:}\sigma \vdash M : \tau}{\Gamma \vdash (\lambda x{:}\sigma.\, M) : (\sigma \to \tau)} \qquad \frac{\Gamma \vdash M : (\sigma \to \tau) \qquad \Gamma \vdash N : \sigma}{\Gamma \vdash (M\,N) : \tau}$$

$$\frac{\Gamma \vdash M : \sigma}{\Gamma \vdash \mathsf{Lift}(M) : \sigma_\perp} \qquad \frac{\Gamma \vdash M : \sigma_\perp \qquad \Gamma, x{:}\sigma \vdash N : \tau_\perp}{\Gamma \vdash \mathsf{Seq}(M, x.\, N) : \tau_\perp} \qquad \frac{\Gamma, x{:}\sigma_\perp \vdash M : \sigma_\perp}{\Gamma \vdash \mathsf{Fix}^\sigma(x.\, M) : \sigma_\perp}$$

$$\frac{\Gamma \vdash M : \sigma[\mu/X] \qquad \mu \equiv (\mu X.\, \sigma)}{\Gamma \vdash \mathsf{Intro}^\mu(M) : \mu} \qquad \frac{\Gamma \vdash M : \mu \qquad \mu \equiv (\mu X.\, \sigma)}{\Gamma \vdash \mathsf{Elim}(M) : \sigma[\mu/X]}$$

Table 3.2: Type assignment rules for $\mathcal{M}$

an environment Γ is denoted by $Dom(\Gamma)$. We write (Γ, Γ') for the concatenation of two environments; this notation is **well-formed** only when $Dom(\Gamma) \cap Dom(\Gamma') = \varnothing$.

Definition 3.1 *The $\mathcal{M}$ type assignment relation, $\Gamma \vdash M : \sigma$, is inductively defined by the rules in Table 3.2. Each rule has the implicit side-condition that any environments appearing in the rule are well-formed.*

We show that the type assignment relation possesses some standard properties.

Proposition 3.2

(1) *If $\Gamma \vdash M : \sigma$ and $\Gamma \vdash M : \tau$ then $\sigma \equiv \tau$.*

(2) *If $\Gamma, x{:}\tau \vdash M : \sigma$ and $\Gamma \vdash N : \tau$ then $\Gamma \vdash M[N/x] : \sigma$.*

(3) *If $\Gamma \vdash M : \sigma$ then $fv(M) \subseteq Dom(\Gamma)$.*

(4) *If $\Gamma \vdash M : \sigma$ and $\Gamma \subseteq \Gamma'$ then $\Gamma' \vdash M : \sigma$.*

Proof. (1) By structural induction on M. The proof is straightforward because terms are labelled with type information where necessary to ensure unique type assignment.

(2) By induction on the depth of inference of the type assignment $\Gamma, x{:}\tau \vdash M : \sigma$.

(3,4) By simple inductions on the depth of inference of $\Gamma \vdash M : \sigma$.   ∎

We define classes of programs and confined terms.

Definition 3.3

(1) *A **program** is a term M such that $\varnothing \vdash M : \tau$ (and hence $ftv(M, \tau) = \varnothing$), for some (necessarily unique) type τ. The type τ is called the **type of** M, which itself is called a τ-**program**.*

(2) *A **confined term** is a pair $(\Gamma \vdash M)$ such that there is a (necessarily unique) type τ with $\Gamma \vdash M : \tau$. The type τ is called the **type of** $(\Gamma \vdash M)$ and Γ is called the **environment of** $(\Gamma \vdash M)$. Occasionally we represent a confined term $(\Gamma \vdash M)$ of type τ with the type assignment sentence $(\Gamma \vdash M : \tau)$ itself.*

3.3 Operational semantics of $\mathcal{M}$

We define a deterministic operational semantics for $\mathcal{M}$ programs. We use an auxiliary notion of an experiment, E, which is a function on programs such that $E(M)$ is obtained by wrapping a selector around program M. Experiments are discussed at greater length in §4.2. They are an alternative to Felleisen's **evaluation contexts** [38].

Definition 3.4 Experiments, E, *are defined by the grammar at the top of Table 3.3. Write $E(M)$ for the term obtained by replacing the occurrence of "$\cdot$" in E by the term M.*

*The **reduction** and **evaluation** relations for $\mathcal{M}$ are the binary relations on $\mathcal{M}$ programs, $\rightarrow$ and $\Downarrow$ respectively, defined inductively by the rules in Table 3.3.*

The canonical programs are the outcomes of evaluation. The operational semantics is lazy in the sense that subterms of canonical programs may be non-canonical. Witness

Reduction Semantics

$$E \ ::= \ \mathsf{Split}(\cdot, x.\, y.\, M) \mid \mathsf{Case}(\cdot, x_1.\, N_1, x_2.\, N_2) \mid (\cdot \, M) \mid \mathsf{Seq}(\cdot, x.\, N) \mid \mathsf{Elim}(\cdot)$$

$$\frac{M \to N}{E(M) \to E(N)}$$

$$\mathsf{Split}(\langle M_1, M_2 \rangle, x_1.\, x_2.\, N) \to N[M_1/x_1][M_2/x_2]$$

$$\mathsf{Case}(\mathsf{Inl}(M), x_1.\, N_1, x_2.\, N_2) \to N_1[M/x_1]$$

$$\mathsf{Case}(\mathsf{Inr}(M), x_1.\, N_1, x_2.\, N_2) \to N_2[M/x_2]$$

$$((\lambda x.\, M)\, N) \to M[N/x]$$

$$\mathsf{Seq}(\mathsf{Lift}(M), x.\, N) \to N[M/x]$$

$$\mathsf{Fix}(x.\, M) \to M[\mathsf{Fix}(x.\, M)/x]$$

$$\mathsf{Elim}(\mathsf{Intro}(M)) \to M$$

Evaluation Semantics

$$\frac{}{V \Downarrow V}$$

$$\frac{L \Downarrow \langle M_1, M_2 \rangle \qquad N[M_1/x_1][M_2/x_2] \Downarrow V}{\mathsf{Split}(L, x_1.\, x_2.\, N) \Downarrow V}$$

$$\frac{L \Downarrow \mathsf{Inl}(M) \qquad N_1[M/x_1] \Downarrow V}{\mathsf{Case}(L, x_1.\, N_1, x_2.\, N_2) \Downarrow V} \qquad \frac{L \Downarrow \mathsf{Inr}(M) \qquad N_2[M/x_2] \Downarrow V}{\mathsf{Case}(L, x_1.\, N_1, x_2.\, N_2) \Downarrow V}$$

$$\frac{L \Downarrow (\lambda x.\, M) \qquad M[N/x] \Downarrow V}{(L\, N) \Downarrow V}$$

$$\frac{L \Downarrow \mathsf{Lift}(M) \qquad N[M/x] \Downarrow V}{\mathsf{Seq}(L, x.\, N) \Downarrow V}$$

$$\frac{M[\mathsf{Fix}(x.\, M)/x] \Downarrow V}{\mathsf{Fix}(x.\, M) \Downarrow V}$$

$$\frac{M \Downarrow \mathsf{Intro}(N) \qquad N \Downarrow V}{\mathsf{Elim}(M) \Downarrow V}$$

Table 3.3: Evaluation rules for $\mathcal{M}$

Inr(Fix($x.\,x$)), which is canonical but has non-canonical Fix($x.\,x$) as a subterm.

Proposition 3.5

(1) If $\varnothing \vdash M : \sigma$ and $M \to N$ then $\varnothing \vdash N : \sigma$.

(2) If $\varnothing \vdash M : \sigma$ and $M \Downarrow V$ then $\varnothing \vdash V : \sigma$.

(3) If $L \to M$ and $L \to N$ then $M \equiv N$.

(4) If $L \Downarrow U$ and $L \Downarrow V$ then $U \equiv V$.

(5) The canonical terms are the normal forms of one-step reduction, where a **normal form** is a program that cannot be reduced, that is, a term M such that for no term N does $M \to N$.

(6) Suppose $M \to N$. Then for any V, $N \Downarrow V$ implies $M \Downarrow V$.

(7) $M \Downarrow V$ just when $M \to^* V$.

Proof. Parts (1) and (2) follow by straightforward inductions on the depth of inference of $M \to N$ and $M \Downarrow V$ respectively. Parts (3) and (4) follow similarly by inductions on the depth of inference of $L \to M$ and $L \Downarrow U$ respectively.

For part (5), we must show that each canonical program has no reductions, and that if a term has no reductions, then it is canonical. First, no canonical program has any reductions, because none of the reduction rules in Table 3.3 is applicable to any canonical program. Second, each program is either canonical, a Fix-term, or of the form $E(M)$ for some experiment E and program M. There are rules in Table 3.3 to reduce a Fix-term and each possible well-typed term $E(M)$, so any program with no reductions must be canonical.

Part (6) is by induction on the depth of inference of the reduction $M \to N$. The forwards direction of (7) is by induction on the depth of inference of evaluation $M \Downarrow V$. We prove the backwards direction of (7) via a method used in Crole's dissertation [25]. Suppose that $M \equiv M_0 \to M_1 \to \cdots \to M_{n-1} \to M_n \equiv V$. We show that $M \Downarrow V$ by filling in the following diagram from right to left, starting with the fact that $M_n \equiv V \Downarrow V$, and establishing for each i that $M_i \Downarrow V$ from $M_{i+1} \Downarrow V$ and part (4) of the proposition.

$$
\begin{array}{ccccccccc}
M & \equiv & M_0 & \to & M_1 & \to & \cdots & \to & M_{n-1} & \to & M_n & \equiv & V \\
 & & \Downarrow & & \Downarrow & & & & \Downarrow & & \Downarrow \\
 & & V & & V & & & & V & & V
\end{array}
$$

Both directions established, part (7) is proved. ∎

We define terminology for termination of evaluation.

Definition 3.6 Suppose that M is a program. Say that M **converges** and write $M\Downarrow$ iff there is a (necessarily unique) canonical program V such that $M \Downarrow V$. Conversely, say that M **diverges** and write $M\Uparrow$ iff M does not converge.

3.4 Convergence

The argument that certainly-convergent types deserve the name proceeds as follows:

Types

$$[X] \overset{\text{def}}{=} X$$

$$[\sigma \times \tau] \overset{\text{def}}{=} (\forall X. ([\sigma] \to [\tau] \to X) \to X) \qquad \text{where } X \notin ftv(\sigma, \tau)$$

$$[\sigma + \tau] \overset{\text{def}}{=} (\forall X. ([\sigma] \to X) \to ([\tau] \to X) \to X) \quad \text{where } X \notin ftv(\sigma, \tau)$$

$$[\sigma \to \tau] \overset{\text{def}}{=} ([\sigma] \to [\tau])$$

$$[\sigma_\perp] \overset{\text{def}}{=} (\forall X. X \to X)$$

$$[\mu X. \sigma] \overset{\text{def}}{=} (\mu X. [\sigma])$$

Terms

$$[\Gamma \vdash x] \overset{\text{def}}{=} x^{[\Gamma(x)]}$$

$$[\Gamma \vdash \langle M, N \rangle : (\sigma \times \tau)] \overset{\text{def}}{=} (\Lambda X. \lambda f^{[\sigma] \to [\tau] \to X}. f [\Gamma \vdash M] [\Gamma \vdash N])$$

$$[\Gamma \vdash \mathsf{Split}(M, x_1. x_2. N) : \tau] \overset{\text{def}}{=} [\Gamma \vdash M][\tau]$$
$$(\lambda x_1^{[\sigma_1]}. \lambda x_2^{[\sigma_2]}. [\Gamma, x_1{:}\sigma_1, x_2{:}\sigma_2 \vdash N])$$
$$\text{where } \Gamma \vdash M : (\sigma_1 \times \sigma_2)$$

$$[\Gamma \vdash \mathsf{Inl}(M) : (\sigma + \tau)] \overset{\text{def}}{=} \Lambda X. \lambda f^{[\sigma] \to X}. \lambda g^{[\tau] \to X}. f [\Gamma \vdash M]$$

$$[\Gamma \vdash \mathsf{Inr}(M) : (\sigma + \tau)] \overset{\text{def}}{=} \Lambda X. \lambda f^{[\sigma] \to X}. \lambda g^{[\tau] \to X}. g [\Gamma \vdash M]$$

$$[\Gamma \vdash \mathsf{Case}(M, x_1. N_1, x_2. N_2) : \tau] \overset{\text{def}}{=} [\Gamma \vdash M][\tau]$$
$$(\lambda x_1^{[\sigma_1]}. [\Gamma, x_1{:}\sigma_1 \vdash N_1])$$
$$(\lambda x_2^{[\sigma_2]}. [\Gamma, x_2{:}\sigma_2 \vdash N_2])$$
$$\text{where } \Gamma \vdash M : (\sigma_1 + \sigma_2)$$

$$[\Gamma \vdash (\lambda x{:}\sigma. M)] \overset{\text{def}}{=} (\lambda x^{[\sigma]}. [\Gamma, x{:}\sigma \vdash M])$$

$$[\Gamma \vdash (M \, N)] \overset{\text{def}}{=} ([\Gamma \vdash M][\Gamma \vdash N])$$

$$[\Gamma \vdash \mathsf{Lift}(M)] \overset{\text{def}}{=} (\Lambda X. \lambda x^X. x^X)$$

$$[\Gamma \vdash \mathsf{Seq}(M, x. N)] \overset{\text{def}}{=} (\Lambda X. \lambda x^X. x^X)$$

$$[\Gamma \vdash \mathsf{Fix}(x. M)] \overset{\text{def}}{=} (\Lambda X. \lambda x^X. x^X)$$

$$[\Gamma \vdash \mathsf{Intro}^\rho(M)] \overset{\text{def}}{=} (\mathsf{Intro}^{[\rho]}[\Gamma \vdash M])$$

$$[\Gamma \vdash \mathsf{Elim}(M)] \overset{\text{def}}{=} (\mathsf{Elim}^{[\rho]}[\Gamma \vdash M]) \qquad \text{where } \Gamma \vdash M : \rho$$

Table 3.4: A translation of $\mathcal{M}$ types and terms into $\mu\nu\lambda2$

---

(1) In Table 3.4 we define a translation of $\mathcal{M}$ types and terms into $\mu\nu\lambda2$. Proposition 3.8 proves that well-typed terms of $\mathcal{M}$ are translated into well-typed terms of $\mu\nu\lambda2$. Lemma 3.9 is a substitution lemma saying that the translation of an $\mathcal{M}$ term into $\mu\nu\lambda2$ is preserved under type and term substitution.

(2) We prove a simulation theorem, Theorem 3.10: if an $\mathcal{M}$ program M of certainly-convergent type reduces to program N, then the translation of M into $\mu\nu\lambda2$ reduces to the translation of N.

(3) The Convergence Theorem for certainly-convergent programs, Theorem 3.11, then follows easily from the simulation theorem and the fact (Theorem 2.10) that no infinite chains of reductions exists in $\mu\nu\lambda2$.

Definition 3.7 *Each $\mathcal{M}$ type σ is translated to a $\mu\nu\lambda2$ type $[\sigma]$ according to the mapping inductively defined by the rules in Table 3.4.*

Each $\mathcal{M}$ confined term $(\Gamma \vdash M)$ is translated to a $\mu\nu\lambda2$ term $[\![\Gamma \vdash M]\!]$ according to the mapping inductively defined by the rules in Table 3.4. Any bound names that appear in the right-hand side of translations but not in the left-hand side are assumed to be new.

The purpose of this construction is to show that each reduction of a certainly-convergent term in $\mathcal{M}$ is simulated by one or more reduction steps in $\mu\nu\lambda2$, so as to prove by contradiction that no certainly-convergent term diverges. The translations of products and sums are the standard ones mentioned in §2.1. For the present purpose there is no need for reductions of possibly-divergent terms to be simulated by their translations; indeed, it would be impossible. Hence we simply map each possibly-divergent type to $(\forall X. X \to X)$ and can map any possibly-divergent term to $(\Lambda X. \lambda x^X. x^X)$.

Proposition 3.8

(1) *For any $\mathcal{M}$ type σ, $ftv([\![\sigma]\!]) = ftv(\sigma)$.*

(2) *For any $\mathcal{M}$ confined term $(\Gamma \vdash M)$ of type τ, $ftv([\![\Gamma \vdash M]\!]) = \varnothing$ and the set of $\mu\nu\lambda2$ names free in $[\![\Gamma \vdash M]\!]$ equals the set of $\mathcal{M}$ variables free in M.*

(3) *If $\mathcal{M}$ confined term $(\Gamma \vdash M)$ has type τ, $\mu\nu\lambda2$ term $[\![\Gamma \vdash M]\!]$ has type $[\![\tau]\!]$.*

Proof. Parts (1) and (2) are by induction on the structure of σ and the depth of inference of $(\Gamma \vdash M : \tau)$ respectively.

(3) By induction on the depth of inference of the type assignment $\Gamma \vdash M : \tau$.   ∎

We need some substitution properties of the translation.

Proposition 3.9

(1) $[\![\tau]\!][[\![\sigma]\!]/X] \equiv [\![\tau[\sigma/X]]\!]$.

(2) *If $(\Gamma, x{:}\tau \vdash M : \sigma)$ and $(\Gamma \vdash N : \tau)$*
    then $[\![\Gamma \vdash M[N/x]]\!] \equiv [\![\Gamma, x{:}\tau \vdash M]\!][[\![\Gamma \vdash N]\!]/x]$.

Proof. (1) By induction on the structure of τ. We show several cases. Suppose $\tau \equiv Y$. If $X = Y$ then both sides equal $[\![\sigma]\!]$. If not, then both sides equal $[\![\tau]\!]$. Suppose $\tau \equiv (\tau_1 \times \tau_2)$. Then $lhs \equiv (\forall Y. ([\![\tau_1]\!][[\![\sigma]\!]/X] \to [\![\tau_2]\!][[\![\sigma]\!]/X] \to Y) \to Y)$ where we may assume that bound variable $Y \notin ftv(\sigma, \tau, X)$. By IH, $lhs \equiv (\forall Y. ([\![\tau_1[\sigma/X]]\!] \to [\![\tau_2[\sigma/X]]\!] \to Y) \to Y) \equiv rhs$. The other cases are similar.

(2) By induction on the depth of inference of $\Gamma, x{:}\tau \vdash M : \sigma$.   ∎

Here is the key theorem of the argument.

Proposition 3.10 *For any two $\mathcal{M}$ programs of the same certainly-convergent type, M and N, if $M \to N$, then $[\![\varnothing \vdash M]\!] \to^+ [\![\varnothing \vdash N]\!]$.*

Proof. The proof is by induction on the depth of inference of $M \to N$. As one might expect as the translations are standard, the reductions of products, sums and functions go through straightforwardly. We show the case of products as an example, and also the inductive case.

Case $M \equiv \mathsf{Split}(\langle M_1, M_2 \rangle, x_1.\, x_2.\, M_3) \to M_3[M_1/x_1][M_2/x_2] \equiv N$. We may assume type assignments $\varnothing \vdash \langle M_1, M_2 \rangle : \sigma_1 \times \sigma_2$, $\varnothing \vdash N : \tau$ and $x_1{:}\sigma_1, x_2{:}\sigma_2 \vdash M_3 : \tau$. We have

$$\llbracket \varnothing \vdash M \rrbracket \equiv \llbracket \varnothing \vdash \langle M_1, M_2 \rangle \rrbracket \llbracket \tau \rrbracket (\lambda x_1^{\llbracket \sigma_1 \rrbracket}.\, \lambda x_2^{\llbracket \sigma_2 \rrbracket}.\, \llbracket x_1{:}\sigma_1, x_2{:}\sigma_2 \vdash M_3 \rrbracket)$$

and

$$\llbracket \varnothing \vdash \langle M_1, M_2 \rangle \rrbracket \equiv (\Lambda X.\, \lambda f^{\llbracket \sigma_1 \rrbracket \to \llbracket \sigma_2 \rrbracket \to X}.\, f \llbracket \varnothing \vdash M_1 \rrbracket \llbracket \varnothing \vdash M_2 \rrbracket).$$

So

$$\llbracket \varnothing \vdash M \rrbracket \to^2 (\lambda x_1^{\llbracket \sigma_1 \rrbracket}.\, \lambda x_2^{\llbracket \sigma_2 \rrbracket}.\, \llbracket x_1{:}\sigma_1, x_2{:}\sigma_2 \vdash M_3 \rrbracket) \llbracket \varnothing \vdash M_1 \rrbracket \llbracket \varnothing \vdash M_2 \rrbracket$$
$$\to^2 \llbracket x_1{:}\sigma_1, x_2{:}\sigma_2 \vdash M_3 \rrbracket [\llbracket \varnothing \vdash M_1 \rrbracket / x_1][\llbracket \varnothing \vdash M_2 \rrbracket / x_2]$$

and hence by the substitution lemma, Proposition 3.9(2), we have

$$\llbracket \varnothing \vdash M \rrbracket \to^+ \llbracket \varnothing \vdash N \rrbracket$$

as required.

Case $M \equiv E(M_1) \to E(N_1) \equiv N$ where $M_1 \to N_1$. First note from the type assignment rules in Table 3.2 that since M is a program of certainly-convergent type, then so too are M_1 and N_1. Therefore the induction hypothesis applies to the reduction $M_1 \to N_1$, and we have $\llbracket \varnothing \vdash M_1 \rrbracket \to^+ \llbracket \varnothing \vdash N_1 \rrbracket$. Then the conclusion, that $\llbracket \varnothing \vdash M \rrbracket \to^+ \llbracket \varnothing \vdash N \rrbracket$, follows by inspection of the translation in Table 3.4 of any possible $E(M_1)$ and $E(N_1)$.

Reductions involving recursive types also go through straightforwardly. Reductions concerning lifted types do not arise, because only terms of certainly-convergent type are considered. ∎

Theorem 3.11 *If σ is a certainly-convergent type and M is a σ-program, then there is a canonical program V for which $M \Downarrow V$.*

Proof. By contradiction: assume that there is an infinite chain of $\mathcal{M}$ terms, beginning $M \to M_1 \to M_2 \to \cdots$. By the previous proposition, there is a chain of $\mu\nu\lambda 2$ terms, beginning $\llbracket \varnothing \vdash M \rrbracket \to^+ \llbracket \varnothing \vdash M_1 \rrbracket \to^+ \llbracket \varnothing \vdash M_2 \rrbracket \to^+ \cdots$. But this is a contradiction, because by Theorem 2.10 $\mu\nu\lambda 2$ is strongly normalising, so no such chain can exist. Therefore the theorem follows. ∎

Chapter 4

Operational precongruence

We will develop in the next chapter an entirely operational theory of the semantic meta-language $\mathcal{M}$. The purpose of the present chapter is to investigate how an operational equivalence can be defined on terms of $\mathcal{M}$. For the sake of simplicity we consider in this chapter operational preorders. Each such preorder induces an equivalence in the usual way.

The theory of $\mathcal{M}$ in Chapter 5 depends on $\mathcal{M}$ having an operationally adequate precongruence. An operationally adequate preorder is one that respects $\mathcal{M}$ evaluation in certain ways. A preorder $\lesssim$ is a precongruence iff whenever $M \lesssim N$ then $\mathcal{C}[M] \lesssim \mathcal{C}[N]$ for all contexts $\mathcal{C}$. Roughly speaking, a **context**, $\mathcal{C}$, is a term containing holes; the term $\mathcal{C}[M]$ is obtained by filling in each hole in context $\mathcal{C}$ with the term M.

We consider two candidate preorders: contextual order, $\lesssim^C$, and applicative similarity, $\lesssim^A$. §4.4 investigates contextual order, attributed by Abramsky [2] to Morris, and used by Plotkin [116, 117] and Milner [91]. If M and N are two $\mathcal{M}$ programs of the same type, then $M \lesssim^C N$ iff for all contexts $\mathcal{C}$, if $\mathcal{C}[M]$ converges then so does $\mathcal{C}[N]$. It is not hard to show that contextual order is a precongruence. We show that it is operationally adequate by defining an auxiliary preorder, experimental order, $\lesssim^E$, which is evidently operationally adequate, and showing that experimental and contextual order are the same. To do so, we use a variant of Milner's context lemma [91].

The other candidate preorder is **applicative similarity**, $\lesssim^A$, investigated in §4.5. This is a typed formulation of Abramsky's **applicative bisimulation**. Applicative similarity is the greatest fixpoint of a certain functional. Roughly speaking, if M and N are two $\mathcal{M}$ programs of the same type, then $M \lesssim^A N$ iff whenever $M \Downarrow V$, there is U with $N \Downarrow U$ such that U and V have the same outermost syntactic constructor, and their corresponding subterms are applicatively similar. It is not hard to prove that applicative similarity is operationally adequate. We show that it is a precongruence via a typed reworking of an ingenious method due to Howe [58].

In §4.6 we prove an **operational extensionality** result [14], that contextual order equals applicative similarity. Hence we have two independent characterisations of the same preorder. This preorder generates an equivalence in the usual way, which we refer to as **operational equivalence** or **applicative bisimilarity** in the remainder of the dissertation.

Mathematical material needed to do the work of the chapter is introduced at the beginning.
Contexts are defined in §4.1. Experiments were used to define the reduction semantics of
$\mathcal{M}$ in Chapter 3 and they are needed here to define experimental order. In §4.2 we recall
the definition of an experiment and define contextual-experiments, which are experiments
that act on contexts and terms. The detailed syntactic operations in §4.1 and §4.2 are
used here only in the study of contextual and experimental orders. The theory of $\mathcal{M}$ in
Chapter 5 is based on programs and confined terms, which were defined in Chapter 3. In
§4.3 we formulate certain properties of relations on confined terms or programs that are
needed later.

4.1   Contexts

Intuitively, a context is a term possibly containing holes, written $[]$. A **context** is produced from the grammar for $\mathcal{M}$ terms, with metavariables $\mathcal{C}$ and $\mathcal{D}$ instead of M and
N, augmented with an additional rule, $\mathcal{C} ::= []$. Contexts are not identified up to alpha-
conversion, unlike phrases of abstract syntax, such as terms, which are. Write $\mathcal{C} = \mathcal{C}'$ to
mean that contexts $\mathcal{C}$ and $\mathcal{C}'$ are literally the same. The sets of free and bound variables
of a context $\mathcal{C}$ are written $fv(\mathcal{C})$ and $bv(\mathcal{C})$ respectively. A **canonical context**, $\mathcal{V}$, is a
context generated from the grammar for $\mathcal{M}$ canonical terms, with metavariable $\mathcal{V}$ instead
of V, augmented with an additional rule, $\mathcal{V} ::= []$.

For any term M and context $\mathcal{C}$, define the **instantiation of M in $\mathcal{C}$, $\mathcal{C}[M]$,** to be the term
obtained by filling each hole $[]$ in $\mathcal{C}$ with the term M. Variables free in M may become
bound in $\mathcal{C}[M]$, such as x when $M \equiv \langle x, y \rangle$ and $\mathcal{C} = (\lambda x.\, [])$. If $\mathcal{V}$ is a canonical context,
then term $\mathcal{V}[M]$ is canonical, for any term M.

Suppose $\mathcal{C}$ and $\mathcal{D}$ are contexts, and x is a variable. If $bv(\mathcal{C}) \cap fv(\mathcal{D}, x) = \varnothing$, define
the **substitution** $\mathcal{C}[\mathcal{D}/x]$ to be the context obtained by replacing each occurrence of the
variable x in $\mathcal{C}$ with the context $\mathcal{D}$. This is a literal substitution; there is no renaming of
the variables bound in $\mathcal{C}$, which have been assumed to be distinct from the variables free
in $\mathcal{D}$.

We show that in certain circumstances, substitution and instantiation commute.

Lemma 4.1 *Suppose $\mathcal{C}$ and $\mathcal{D}$ are contexts, x is a variable and M is a term. If $bv(\mathcal{C}) \cap$
$fv(\mathcal{D}, x) = \varnothing$ and $x \notin fv(M)$ then $\mathcal{C}[\mathcal{D}/x][M] \equiv \mathcal{C}[M][\mathcal{D}[M]/x]$.*

Proof. By structural induction on context $\mathcal{C}$. We consider the following cases in detail.

Case $\mathcal{C} = []$. $lhs \equiv ([])[M] \equiv M$. $rhs \equiv M[\mathcal{D}[M]/x] \equiv M$ since $x \notin fv(M)$.

Case $\mathcal{C} = x$. $lhs \equiv \mathcal{D}[M]$. $rhs \equiv x[\mathcal{D}[M]/x] \equiv \mathcal{D}[M]$.

Case $\mathcal{C} = y \neq x$. $lhs \equiv (y)[M] \equiv y$. $rhs \equiv (y)[\mathcal{D}[M]/x] \equiv y$.

Case $C = (C_1 \, C_2)$.

$$
\begin{aligned}
lhs &\equiv (C_1 \, C_2)[\mathcal{P}\!/\!x][M] \\
&\equiv (C_1[\mathcal{P}\!/\!x][M]) \, (C_2[\mathcal{P}\!/\!x][M]) \\
&\equiv (C_1[M][\mathcal{P}[M]\!/\!x]) \, (C_2[M][\mathcal{P}[M]\!/\!x]) \quad \text{(IH)} \\
&\equiv (C_1[M] \, C_2[M])[\mathcal{P}[M]\!/\!x] \\
&\equiv (C_1 \, C_2)[M][\mathcal{P}[M]\!/\!x] \\
&\equiv rhs
\end{aligned}
$$

Case $C = (\lambda y. \, C')$. We have $y \neq x$ since $bv(C) \cap \{x\} = \varnothing$.

$$
\begin{aligned}
lhs &\equiv (\lambda y. \, C')[\mathcal{P}\!/\!x][M] \\
&\equiv (\lambda y. \, (C'[\mathcal{P}\!/\!x][M])) \\
&\equiv (\lambda y. \, (C'[M][\mathcal{P}[M]\!/\!x])) \quad \text{(IH)} \\
&\equiv (\lambda y. \, (C'[M]))[\mathcal{P}[M]\!/\!x] \\
&\equiv (\lambda y. \, C')[M][\mathcal{P}[M]\!/\!x] \\
&\equiv rhs
\end{aligned}
$$

The other cases follow similarly to the last two and are omitted. ∎

4.2 Experiments and contextual-experiments

Experiments were defined in Definition 3.4 and used in Table 3.3 as an economical notation for defining the reduction relation on programs of $\mathcal{M}$. Recall the defining grammar:

$$ E ::= \mathsf{Split}(\cdot, x. \, y. \, M) \mid \mathsf{Case}(\cdot, x_1. \, N_1, x_2. \, N_2) \mid (\cdot \, M) \mid \mathsf{Seq}(\cdot, x. \, N) \mid \mathsf{Elim}(\cdot) $$

We use experiments in this chapter to define experimental order on programs. When we come to prove that experimental order coincides with contextual order, we will use a variant of Milner's context lemma. In this variant, we need to extend the idea of an experiment to contexts. A **contextual-experiment**, $\mathcal{E}$, is given by the following grammar:

$$ \mathcal{E} ::= \mathsf{Split}(\cdot, x. \, y. \, C) \mid \mathsf{Case}(\cdot, x_1. \, C_1, x_2. \, C_2) \mid (\cdot \, C) \mid \mathsf{Seq}(\cdot, x. \, C) \mid \mathsf{Elim}(\cdot) $$

The symbol "$\cdot$" occurs once in each experiment or contextual-experiment. The term $E(M)$ and the context $\mathcal{E}(C)$ are obtained by replacing the occurrence of "$\cdot$" in E or $\mathcal{E}$ by the term M or context C respectively. Intuitively, an experiment wraps a destructor term around a term; similarly, a contextual-experiment wraps a destructor context around a context. Experiments are identified up to alpha-conversion; contextual-experiments are not. We define $fv(E)$ and $fv(\mathcal{E})$ to the sets of variables free in experiment E and contextual-experiment $\mathcal{E}$ respectively.

If $\tilde{E}$ is a possibly-empty list of experiments $E_1, \ldots, E_n$ then write $\tilde{E}(M)$ to mean the term $E_1(\cdots (E_n(M)) \cdots)$. Similarly, if $\tilde{\mathcal{E}}$ is a possibly-empty list of contextual-experiments $\mathcal{E}_1, \ldots, \mathcal{E}_n$ write $\tilde{\mathcal{E}}(C)$ to mean the context $\mathcal{E}_1(\cdots (\mathcal{E}_n(C)) \cdots)$.

Lemma 4.2

(1) *If M is a program, then there is a unique list of experiments $\tilde{E}$ such that either*

- $M \equiv \tilde{E}(V)$ *for some canonical program V, or*
- $M \equiv \tilde{E}(\mathsf{Fix}(x. \, N))$ *for some program $\mathsf{Fix}(x. \, N)$.*

(2) If C is a context, then there is a unique list of contextual-experiments $\tilde{\mathcal{E}}$ such that either

- $C = \tilde{\mathcal{E}}([])$ or
- $C = \tilde{\mathcal{E}}(x)$ for some variable x, or
- $C = \tilde{\mathcal{E}}(\mathcal{V})$ for some canonical context $\mathcal{V}$, or
- $C = \tilde{\mathcal{E}}(\mathsf{Fix}(x.\mathcal{C}))$ for some context $\mathsf{Fix}(x.\mathcal{C})$.

Proof. By structural inductions on program M and context C.   ∎

Experiments relate to reduction as follows:

Lemma 4.3 For any experiment E, list of experiments $\tilde{E}$, and programs M and N, such that terms $E(M)$, $E(N)$, $\tilde{E}(M)$ and $\tilde{E}(N)$ are programs:

(1) $E(M) \to E(N)$ if $M \to N$;

(2) $\tilde{E}(M) \to \tilde{E}(N)$ if $M \to N$;

(3) whenever $E(M) \Downarrow V$ there is U such that $M \Downarrow U$ and $E(U) \Downarrow V$;

(4) whenever $\tilde{E}(M) \Downarrow V$ there is U such that $M \Downarrow U$ and $\tilde{E}(U) \Downarrow V$.

Proof. (1) In Table 3.3 reduction is closed under this inference rule, so part (1) holds. Part (2) is a corollary of (1). Part (3) follows by an inspection of the five kinds of experiment, and the corresponding evaluation rules in Table 3.3. The proof of (4) is by induction on the size of the list $\tilde{E}$. The base case when the list is empty follows at once. Otherwise, suppose that $\tilde{E}(E'(M)) \Downarrow V$. By IH there is some U' such that $E'(M) \Downarrow U'$ and $\tilde{E}(U') \Downarrow V$. By (3) there is some U such that $M \Downarrow U$ and $E'(U) \Downarrow U'$. From (2) we have $\tilde{E}(E'(M)) \to^* \tilde{E}(E'(U)) \to^* \tilde{E}(U') \to^* V$, that is, $\tilde{E}(E'(M)) \Downarrow V$.   ∎

If $\mathcal{E}$ is an experimental context and M is a term, then the **instantiation of $\mathcal{E}$ with M**, $\mathcal{E}[M]$ is the experiment obtained by filling in each occurrence of a hole in $\mathcal{E}$ with the term M.

Lemma 4.4 For any contextual experiment $\mathcal{E}$, context C, term M, and list of contextual experiments $\tilde{\mathcal{E}}$ we have:

(1) $\mathcal{E}(C)[M] \equiv \mathcal{E}[M](C[M])$

(2) $\tilde{\mathcal{E}}(C)[M] \equiv \tilde{\mathcal{E}}[M](C[M])$

Proof. (1) Suppose $\mathcal{E} = \mathsf{Split}(\cdot, x.y.\mathcal{C}')$. Then $\mathcal{E}(C) = \mathsf{Split}(C, x.y.\mathcal{C}')$, and we have $\mathcal{E}[M] \equiv \mathsf{Split}(\cdot, x.y.\mathcal{C}'[M])$ so $\mathcal{E}(C)[M] \equiv \mathsf{Split}(C[M], x.y.\mathcal{C}'[M]) \equiv \mathcal{E}[M](C[M])$. The other four cases are similar. Part (2) is a corollary of (1).   ∎

Rules of $\widehat{\mathcal{R}}$

$$\Gamma \vdash x \, \widehat{\mathcal{R}} \, x$$

$$\frac{\Gamma \vdash M_i \mathcal{R} N_i \quad (i = 1, 2)}{\Gamma \vdash \langle M_1, M_2 \rangle \, \widehat{\mathcal{R}} \, \langle N_1, N_2 \rangle} \qquad \frac{\Gamma \vdash M_1 \mathcal{R} N_1 \qquad \Gamma, x{:}\sigma, y{:}\tau \vdash M_2 \mathcal{R} N_2}{\Gamma \vdash \mathsf{Split}(M_1, x.\, y.\, M_2) \, \widehat{\mathcal{R}} \, \mathsf{Split}(N_1, x.\, y.\, N_2)}$$

$$\frac{\Gamma \vdash M \mathcal{R} N}{\Gamma \vdash \mathsf{Inl}(M) \, \widehat{\mathcal{R}} \, \mathsf{Inl}(N)} \qquad \frac{\Gamma \vdash M \mathcal{R} N}{\Gamma \vdash \mathsf{Inr}(M) \, \widehat{\mathcal{R}} \, \mathsf{Inr}(N)}$$

$$\frac{\Gamma \vdash M_1 \mathcal{R} N_1 \qquad \Gamma, x_i{:}\sigma_i \vdash M_i \mathcal{R} N_i \quad (i = 2, 3)}{\Gamma \vdash \mathsf{Case}(M_1, x_2.\, M_2, x_3.\, M_3) \, \widehat{\mathcal{R}} \, \mathsf{Case}(N_1, x_2.\, N_2, x_3.\, N_3)}$$

$$\frac{\Gamma, x{:}\sigma \vdash M \mathcal{R} N}{\Gamma \vdash (\lambda x{:}\sigma.\, M) \, \widehat{\mathcal{R}} \, (\lambda x{:}\sigma.\, N)} \qquad \frac{\Gamma \vdash M_i \mathcal{R} N_i \quad (i = 1, 2)}{\Gamma \vdash (M_1 \, M_2) \, \widehat{\mathcal{R}} \, (N_1 \, N_2)}$$

$$\frac{\Gamma \vdash M \mathcal{R} N}{\Gamma \vdash \mathsf{Lift}(M) \, \widehat{\mathcal{R}} \, \mathsf{Lift}(N)} \qquad \frac{\Gamma \vdash M_1 \mathcal{R} N_1 \qquad \Gamma, x{:}\sigma \vdash M_2 \mathcal{R} N_2}{\Gamma \vdash \mathsf{Seq}(M_1, x.\, M_2) \, \widehat{\mathcal{R}} \, \mathsf{Seq}(N_1, x.\, N_2)}$$

$$\frac{\Gamma, x{:}\sigma_\bot \vdash M \, \widehat{\mathcal{R}} \, N}{\Gamma \vdash \mathsf{Fix}^\sigma(x.\, M) \mathcal{R} \, \mathsf{Fix}^\sigma(x.\, N)}$$

$$\frac{\Gamma \vdash M \mathcal{R} N}{\Gamma \vdash \mathsf{Intro}(M) \, \widehat{\mathcal{R}} \, \mathsf{Intro}(N)} \qquad \frac{\Gamma \vdash M \mathcal{R} N}{\Gamma \vdash \mathsf{Elim}(M) \, \widehat{\mathcal{R}} \, \mathsf{Elim}(N)}$$

Table 4.1: Definition of $\widehat{\mathcal{R}}$

4.3 Ground and confined relations in $\mathcal{M}$

Recall that we defined notions of programs and confined terms in Definition 3.3.

Definition 4.5

(1) A **ground relation**, $\mathcal{R}$, is a binary relation between programs of the same type.

(2) A **confined relation**, $\mathcal{R}$, is a binary relation between confined terms of the same type and environment. Write $\Gamma \vdash M \mathcal{R} N$ to mean that $(\Gamma \vdash M, \Gamma \vdash N) \in \mathcal{R}$.

We can immediately make precise the notion of operational adequacy, which we seek to prove for contextual order and applicative similarity. Let $\mathcal{M}$ program Ω be $\mathsf{Fix}(x.\, x)$, of type scheme $\sigma_\bot$ for any σ.

Definition 4.6 *A ground relation, $\mathcal{R}$, is **operationally adequate** iff for all programs M, N, and canonical programs V:*

(1) *If $M \to N$ then $N \mathcal{R} M$.*

(2) *If $M \Downarrow V$ then $V \mathcal{R} M$.*

(3) *$M\Uparrow$ iff $M \mathcal{R} \Omega$.*

$$\boxed{\begin{array}{c}
\textbf{Properties of Confined Relations} \\[4pt]
\textbf{Weak} \quad \dfrac{\Gamma \vdash M\mathcal{R}N}{\Gamma, \Gamma' \vdash M\mathcal{R}N} \\[16pt]
\textbf{Stren} \quad \dfrac{\Gamma, \Gamma' \vdash M\mathcal{R}N}{\Gamma \vdash M\mathcal{R}N} \\[16pt]
\textbf{Spec} \quad \dfrac{\Gamma, x{:}\sigma \vdash M_1\mathcal{R}M_2 \qquad \Gamma \vdash N : \sigma}{\Gamma \vdash M_1[N/x]\mathcal{R}M_2[N/x]} \\[16pt]
\textbf{Precong} \quad \dfrac{\Gamma \vdash M\mathcal{R}N}{\Gamma \vdash C[M]\mathcal{R}C[N]} \\[16pt]
\textbf{Comp} \quad \dfrac{\Gamma \vdash M\,\widehat{\mathcal{R}}\,N}{\Gamma \vdash M\mathcal{R}N} \\[16pt]
\textbf{Sub} \quad \dfrac{\Gamma, x{:}\sigma \vdash M_1\mathcal{R}N_1 \qquad \Gamma \vdash M_2\mathcal{R}N_2}{\Gamma \vdash M_1[M_2/x]\mathcal{R}N_1[N_2/x]}
\end{array}}$$

Table 4.2: Rules concerning confined relations.

(4) $M\!\Downarrow$ iff for some canonical V, $V\mathcal{R}M$.

Confined relations are important for the theory of $\mathcal{M}$ in Chapter 5. We formulate some useful operations and properties of confined relations, including precongruence.

Definition 4.7

(1) If $\mathcal{R}$ is a confined relation, let the confined relation $\widehat{\mathcal{R}}$ be defined by the rules in Table 4.1.

(2) We define inference rules **Weak, Stren, Spec, Precong, Comp** and **Sub** in Table 4.2. All these rules have the implicit side-condition that any sentence denoting a pair of confined terms is well-formed. A sentence $\Gamma \vdash M\mathcal{R}N$ is **well-formed** iff pairs $(\Gamma \vdash M)$ and $(\Gamma \vdash N)$ are confined terms of the same type.

(3) A confined relation is **natural** iff the rules **Weak, Stren** and **Spec** are valid.

(4) A confined relation is a **precongruence** iff the rule **Precong** is valid. A **congruence** is a confined relation that is both a precongruence and an equivalence relation.

Proposition 4.8

(1) If $\mathcal{R}$ is transitive and rules **Spec** and **Precong** are valid, then rule **Sub** is valid too.

(2) If $\mathcal{R}$ is a preorder, then rule **Precong** is valid iff rule **Comp** is valid.

Proof. (1) Suppose $\Gamma, x{:}\sigma \vdash M_1\mathcal{R}N_1$ and $\Gamma \vdash M_2\mathcal{R}N_2$. By **Precong** we have $\Gamma \vdash M_1[M_2/x]\mathcal{R}M_1[N_2/x]$ where we treat term M_1 as a context. By **Spec** we have $\Gamma \vdash M_1[N_2/x]\mathcal{R}N_1[N_2/x]$. By transitivity we have $\Gamma \vdash M_1[M_2/x]\mathcal{R}N_1[N_2/x]$.

(2) ($\Longrightarrow$) Given that $\mathcal{R}$ is a preorder and **Precong** is valid, we are to prove that $(\Gamma \vdash M\hat{\mathcal{R}}N)$ implies $(\Gamma \vdash M\mathcal{R}N)$. We proceed by an analysis of which rule from Table 4.1 derived $(\Gamma \vdash M\hat{\mathcal{R}}N)$. We examine the rule for Case-terms as a typical example. Given the inference

$$\frac{\Gamma \vdash M_1\mathcal{R}N_1 \qquad \Gamma, x_i{:}\sigma_i \vdash M_i\mathcal{R}N_i \quad (i = 2, 3)}{\Gamma \vdash \mathsf{Case}(M_1, x_2.\, M_2, x_3.\, M_3)\, \hat{\mathcal{R}}\, \mathsf{Case}(N_1, x_2.\, N_2, x_3.\, N_3)}$$

we are to show that $\Gamma \vdash \mathsf{Case}(M_1, x_2.\, M_2, x_3.\, M_3)\mathcal{R}\, \mathsf{Case}\,(N_1, x_2.\, N_2, x_3.\, N_3)$. From **Precong** we can calculate:

$$\Gamma \vdash \mathsf{Case}(M_1, x_2.\, M_2, x_3.\, M_3)\mathcal{R}\, \mathsf{Case}\,(N_1, x_2.\, M_2, x_3.\, M_3)$$
$$\Gamma \vdash \mathsf{Case}(N_1, x_2.\, M_2, x_3.\, M_3)\mathcal{R}\, \mathsf{Case}\,(N_1, x_2.\, N_2, x_3.\, M_3)$$
$$\Gamma \vdash \mathsf{Case}(N_1, x_2.\, N_2, x_3.\, M_3)\mathcal{R}\, \mathsf{Case}\,(N_1, x_2.\, N_2, x_3.\, N_3)$$

These together with the transitivity of $\mathcal{R}$ prove the result. The other cases are similar.

($\Longleftarrow$) Given that rule **Comp** is valid for preorder $\mathcal{R}$, we prove by induction on the structure of context $\mathcal{C}$ that for all Γ, M, and N, if $\Gamma \vdash M\mathcal{R}N$ then $\Gamma \vdash C[M]\,\mathcal{R}\,C[N]$. Consider any $\mathcal{C}$ and choose any Γ, M and N that satisfy the assumption $\Gamma \vdash M\mathcal{R}N$. We examine three cases.

Case $\mathcal{C} = []$. Goal $\Gamma \vdash C[M]\,\mathcal{R}\,C[N]$ is precisely $\Gamma \vdash M\mathcal{R}N$.

Case $\mathcal{C} = x$. $\Gamma \vdash x\mathcal{R}x$ follows from reflexivity of $\mathcal{R}$.

Case $\mathcal{C} = \mathsf{Case}(\mathcal{C}_1, x.\, \mathcal{C}_2, x.\, \mathcal{C}_3)$. By IH we have $\Gamma \vdash C_1[M]\mathcal{R}C_1[N]$, $\Gamma, x{:}\sigma_1 \vdash C_2[M]\mathcal{R}C_2[N]$ and $\Gamma, x{:}\sigma_1 \vdash C_3[M]\mathcal{R}C_3[N]$. These, together with the rule for Case-terms in Table 4.1 give $\Gamma \vdash C[M]\,\hat{\mathcal{R}}\,C[N]$ and hence $\Gamma \vdash C[M]\,\mathcal{R}\,C[N]$ as required.

The other cases are similar. ∎

We will often need to induce a confined relation from a ground relation, and vice versa.

Definition 4.9

(1) *Let Γ be an environment $x_1{:}\sigma_1, \ldots, x_n{:}\sigma_n$. Then a Γ-closure is an iterated substitution $\cdot[L_1/x_1] \cdots [L_n/x_n]$, where each L_i is a σ_i-program. (The order of substitution does not matter because the variables are disjoint and each L_i is closed.)*

(2) *The **confined extension** of a ground relation $\mathcal{R}_G$ is the confined relation $\mathcal{R}$ such that $\Gamma \vdash M\mathcal{R}N$ iff for all Γ-closures $\cdot[\tilde{L}/\tilde{x}]$, $M[\tilde{L}/\tilde{x}]\mathcal{R}_G N[\tilde{L}/\tilde{x}]$.*

(3) *If $\mathcal{R}$ is a confined relation, then its **ground restriction** is the ground relation $\{(M, N) \mid \varnothing \vdash M\mathcal{R}N\}$.*

(4) *If $\mathcal{R}$ is a confined relation, write $M\mathcal{R}N$ to mean that pair (M, N) is in the ground restriction of $\mathcal{R}$.*

We typically use the same symbol for a ground relation and its confined extension. If $\mathcal{R}_G$ is a ground relation, and $\mathcal{R}$ is its confined extension, we write $\widehat{\mathcal{R}_G}$ to mean $\hat{\mathcal{R}}$.

Proposition 4.10 *The confined extension of a ground relation is natural.*

Proof. We are to prove rule **Weak**, **Stren** and **Spec**. To begin with the first two, we must show the following inferences are valid,

$$\textbf{Weak} \quad \frac{\Gamma \vdash M\mathcal{R}N}{\Gamma,\Gamma' \vdash M\mathcal{R}N} \qquad \textbf{Stren} \quad \frac{\Gamma,\Gamma' \vdash M\mathcal{R}N}{\Gamma \vdash M\mathcal{R}N}$$

where $\mathcal{R}$ is the confined extension of a ground relation $\mathcal{R}_G$, for any given Γ, Γ', M and N, such that the sentences $\Gamma \vdash M\mathcal{R}N$ and $\Gamma,\Gamma' \vdash M\mathcal{R}N$ are well-formed. By definition of $\mathcal{R}$, these inferences would be valid if the following condition were true,

$$M[\tilde{L}/\tilde{x}]\mathcal{R}_G N[\tilde{L}/\tilde{x}] \quad \text{iff} \quad M[\tilde{L}/\tilde{x}][\tilde{L}'/\tilde{x}']\mathcal{R}_G N[\tilde{L}/\tilde{x}][\tilde{L}'/\tilde{x}'] \quad (*)$$

for all Γ-closures $\cdot[\tilde{L}/\tilde{x}]$ and Γ'-closures $\cdot[\tilde{L}'/\tilde{x}']$. But we know that $fv(M,N) \subseteq Dom(\Gamma)$ from the well-formedness of sentence $\Gamma \vdash M\mathcal{R}N$, and therefore we have $M[\tilde{L}/\tilde{x}][\tilde{L}'/\tilde{x}'] \equiv M[\tilde{L}/\tilde{x}]$ and $N[\tilde{L}/\tilde{x}][\tilde{L}'/\tilde{x}'] \equiv N[\tilde{L}/\tilde{x}]$. These equations immediately imply condition $(*)$, as required.

Finally, we are to prove the validity of the **Spec** rule.

$$\frac{\Gamma, x{:}\sigma \vdash M_1\mathcal{R}M_2 \qquad \Gamma \vdash N : \sigma}{\Gamma \vdash M_1[N/x]\mathcal{R}M_2[N/x]}$$

The sentence $\Gamma, x{:}\sigma \vdash M_1\mathcal{R}M_2$ means that $M_1[\tilde{L}/\tilde{x}][L'/x]\mathcal{R}_G N_1[\tilde{L}/\tilde{x}][L'/x]$ for any σ-program L' and suitably typed program list $\tilde{L}$. Let L' be $N[\tilde{L}/\tilde{x}]$, which we know to be a program since $fv(N) \subseteq Dom(\Gamma) = \tilde{x}$. Since $M_i[\tilde{L}/\tilde{x}][L'/x] \equiv M_i[\tilde{L}/\tilde{x}][N[\tilde{L}/\tilde{x}]/x] \equiv M_i[N/x][\tilde{L}/\tilde{x}]$ for each i, we have $M_1[N/x][\tilde{L}/\tilde{x}]\mathcal{R}_G M_2[N/x][\tilde{L}/\tilde{x}]$, which is to say that $\Gamma \vdash M_1[N/x]\mathcal{R}M_2[N/x]$, as required. ∎

4.4 Contextual and experimental order

We begin with a notion of operational ordering [116], which we call contextual order:

Definition 4.11 *Define* **contextual order** *to be the confined relation,* $\lesssim^C$, *such that* $\Gamma \vdash M \lesssim^C N$ *iff, for all contexts* C, *such that* $C[M]$ *and* $C[N]$ *are programs of the same type, if* $C[M]$ *converges so does* $C[N]$.

Programs $C[M]$ and $C[N]$ can be of any type; in Plotkin's formulation they must be of ground (integer) type.

Proposition 4.12 *Contextual order is a precongruence.*

Proof. It suffices to verify the **Precong** rule for $\lesssim^C$. Suppose that $\Gamma \vdash M \lesssim^C N$. For some particular context $\mathcal{D}$, we are to show that $\Gamma \vdash \mathcal{D}[M] \lesssim^C \mathcal{D}[N]$. This is to say that for all contexts C, such that $C[\mathcal{D}[M]]$ and $C[\mathcal{D}[N]]$ are programs of the same type, if $C[\mathcal{D}[M]]$ converges, then so does $C[\mathcal{D}[N]]$. This follows at once from $\Gamma \vdash M \lesssim^C N$ by definition. ∎

It is not so straightforward to prove that contextual order is operationally adequate. We do so by defining a second relation, experimental order, which is not hard to show operationally adequate, and then showing that contextual and experimental order coincide.

Definition 4.13 Ground experimental order, $\lesssim^E$, *is the ground relation such that* $M \lesssim^E N$ *iff whenever* $\tilde{E}$ *is a list of experiments with* $\tilde{E}(M)$ *and* $\tilde{E}(N)$ *programs of the same type, if* $\tilde{E}(M)$ *converges so does* $\tilde{E}(N)$. *The confined relation* **experimental order** *is the confined extension of ground experimental order.*

It is not hard to see that ground experimental order is reflexive and transitive, and hence that experimental order is a preorder. We prove operational adequacy.

Proposition 4.14 *Ground experimental order is operationally adequate.*

Proof. We are to show for all programs M, N, and canonical programs V:

(1) If $M \to N$ then $N \lesssim^E M$.

(2) If $M \Downarrow V$ then $V \lesssim^E M$.

(3) $M\Uparrow$ iff $M \lesssim^E \Omega$.

(4) $M\Downarrow$ iff for some canonical V, $V \lesssim^E M$.

(1) We are to show for all experiment lists $\tilde{E}$, if $\tilde{E}(N)\Downarrow$ then $\tilde{E}(M)\Downarrow$. Since $M \to N$ we have $\tilde{E}(M) \to \tilde{E}(N)$. So if the latter converges so must the former. (2) Corollary of (1) and the transitivity of $\lesssim^E$.

(3) For the forwards direction, suppose that $M\Uparrow$. To show $M \lesssim^E \Omega$, we need that for all $\tilde{E}$, if $\tilde{E}(M)$ converges then so does $\tilde{E}(\Omega)$. But for no $\tilde{E}$ does $\tilde{E}(M)$ converge. For the backwards direction, suppose that $M \lesssim^E \Omega$. So for all $\tilde{E}$, if $\tilde{E}(M)$ converges then so does $\tilde{E}(\Omega)$. Proceed by contradiction and suppose that M converges. Taking $\tilde{E}$ to be the empty list, we have that Ω converges since M does. Contradiction.

(4) For the forwards direction, $M\Downarrow$ means that $M \Downarrow V$ for some V. Then by part (2) we have $V \lesssim^E M$. For the backwards direction, suppose that $V \lesssim^E M$. From the definition of $\lesssim^E$ we have that if V converges, then so does M (take the list of experiments to be empty). But V converges, being canonical. ∎

It is not hard to show the following.

Proposition 4.15 *Contextual order implies experimental order.*

Proof. Suppose that $\Gamma \vdash M \lesssim^C N$ for some context $\Gamma = x_1{:}\sigma_1, \dots, x_n{:}\sigma_n$ and terms M and N. It is necessary to show for any Γ-closure $\cdot[\tilde{L}/\tilde{x}]$ that $\hat{M} \lesssim^E \hat{N}$, where $\hat{M} \equiv M[\tilde{L}/\tilde{x}]$ and $\hat{N} \equiv N[\tilde{L}/\tilde{x}]$. This is to say that for each suitably typed $\tilde{E}$, if $\tilde{E}(\hat{M})$ converges then so does $\tilde{E}(\hat{N})$. Pick some list $\tilde{E}$ and define context $\mathcal{C} = \tilde{E}((\lambda x_1{:}\sigma_1. \dots. \lambda x_n{:}\sigma_n. \, [])L_1 \dots L_n)$. We have $\mathcal{C}[M] \to^n \tilde{E}(\hat{M})$ and $\mathcal{C}[N] \to^n \tilde{E}(\hat{N})$. Then if $\tilde{E}(\hat{M})$ converges then so must $\mathcal{C}[M]$. If $\mathcal{C}[M]$ converges then so too does $\mathcal{C}[N]$, given that $\Gamma \vdash M \lesssim^C N$. But then $\tilde{E}(\hat{N})$ must converge, as required. ∎

The other direction is harder. The next two lemmas are needed to prove Proposition 4.18, that the ground restriction of contextual order coincides with ground experimental order.

Lemma 4.16 *Suppose context* $\mathcal{C} = \mathcal{E}(V)$ *for some contextual experiment* $\mathcal{E}$ *and canonical context* $\mathcal{V}$. *Then there is a context* $\mathcal{D}$ *such that for all programs* L *such that* $\mathcal{C}[L]$ *is a* program, $C[L] \to D[L]$.

Proof. We assume that all the bound variables in context C are distinct (if they are not we can easily find a context C' in which all bound variables are distinct such that for any program L, $C'[L]$ alpha-converts to $C[L]$). Since $C[L]$ is a program, $fv(C) = fv(\mathcal{E}) = fv(V) = \emptyset$. Given such a C, the context D can be defined as follows:

- if $V = \langle C_1, C_2 \rangle$ and $\mathcal{E} = \mathsf{Split}(\cdot, x.\, y.\, C_3)$ then $D = C_3[C_1/x][C_2/y]$;
- if $V = \mathsf{Inl}(C')$ and $\mathcal{E} = \mathsf{Case}(\cdot, x_1.C_1, x_2.C_2))$ then $D = C_1[C'/x_1]$;
- if $V = \mathsf{Inr}(C')$ and $\mathcal{E} = \mathsf{Case}(\cdot, x_1.C_1, x_2.C_2))$ then $D = C_2[C'/x_2]$;
- if $V = (\lambda x.\, C_1)$ and $\mathcal{E} = (\cdot\, C_2)$ then $D = C_1[C_2/x]$;
- if $V = \mathsf{Lift}(C_1)$ and $\mathcal{E} = \mathsf{Seq}(\cdot, x.\, C_2)$ then $D = C_2[C_1/x]$;
- if $V = \mathsf{Intro}(C')$ and $\mathcal{E} = \mathsf{Elim}(\cdot)$ then $D = C'$;

Given the assumptions we have made about context C, in each case we can check that the conditions hold for substitution of a context into another to be well-formed; we omit the details. From the type assignment rules in Table 3.2 all the cases when $C[L]$ is a program are covered above, and from the definition of one-step reduction, it is not hard to see that $C[L] \to D[L]$, given Lemma 4.1.   ■

The proof of the following lemma is based on a similar proof due to Allen Stoughton for the lazy λ-calculus, and based on Milner's context lemma [12, 91].

Lemma 4.17 (Context) *For any two programs M and N of the same type with $M \lesssim^E N$, and any context C such that $C[M]$ and $C[N]$ are both programs of the same type, if $C[M]$ converges, then $C[N]$ converges.*

Proof. Choose any two programs M and N of the same type, and assume $M \lesssim^E N$. We prove the following hypothesis by mathematical induction on n, that for any context C such that $C[M]$ and $C[N]$ are programs of the same type,

   if $C[M]$ converges in n steps, then $C[N]$ converges.

We proceed by a case analysis of C. According to Lemma 4.2(2) there is a possibly-empty list of contextual experiments, $\tilde{\mathcal{E}}$, such that one of four cases holds:

Case $C = \tilde{\mathcal{E}}(V)$. Either list $\tilde{\mathcal{E}}$ is empty—in which case both $C[M]$ and $C[N]$ are canonical, and hence converge—or the list takes the form $\tilde{\mathcal{E}}', \mathcal{E}$ and we have $C = \tilde{\mathcal{E}}'(\mathcal{E}(V))$. Let $C' = \mathcal{E}(V)$ and by Lemma 4.16 there is a context D' such that for any program L, if $C'[L]$ is a program, then $C'[L] \to D'[L]$. Let $D = \tilde{\mathcal{E}}'(D')$, and for any program L, we have $C[L] \equiv \tilde{\mathcal{E}}'(\mathcal{E}(V))[L] \equiv \tilde{\mathcal{E}}'[L](C'[L]) \to \tilde{\mathcal{E}}'[L](D'[L]) \equiv D[L]$ using Lemmas 4.3 and 4.4. Since M and N are programs we have $C[M] \to D[M]$ and $C[N] \to D[N]$. Now $D[M]$ must converge in $n-1$ steps, so by the induction hypothesis, $D[N]$ converges, and therefore so too does $C[N]$, as reduction is deterministic.

Case $C = \tilde{\mathcal{E}}(\mathsf{Fix}(x.\, C'))$. We may assume that all the bound variables in context C are distinct (if they are not, we could prove the hypothesis by working with a context C'' in which all bound variables are distinct and such that for any program L, $C''[L]$ alpha-converts to $C[L]$). Set $D = \tilde{\mathcal{E}}(C'[\mathsf{Fix}(x.\, C')/x])$. For any program L, we have $C[L] \equiv \tilde{\mathcal{E}}(\text{Fix}(x.\,C'))[L] \equiv \tilde{\mathcal{E}}[L](\text{Fix}(x.\,C'[L])) \to \tilde{\mathcal{E}}[L](C'[L][\text{Fix}(x.\,C'[L])/x]) \equiv \tilde{\mathcal{E}}[L](C'[\text{Fix}(x.\,C')/x][L]) \equiv \mathcal{D}[L]$ using Lemmas 4.1, 4.3 and 4.4. Hence we have $C[M] \to \mathcal{D}[M]$ and $C[N] \to \mathcal{D}[N]$. Just as in the previous case, since $\mathcal{D}[M]$ must converge in $n-1$ steps, by the induction hypothesis, $\mathcal{D}[N]$ converges, and therefore so too does $C[N]$.

Case $C = \tilde{\mathcal{E}}([\,])$. Let context $\mathcal{D} = \tilde{\mathcal{E}}(M)$ and then $\mathcal{D}[M] \equiv \tilde{\mathcal{E}}[M](M) \equiv C[M]$, so $\mathcal{D}[M]$ converges in n steps. But context $\mathcal{D}$ must take one of the forms already considered, so we can conclude that $\mathcal{D}[N] \equiv \tilde{\mathcal{E}}[N](M)$ converges. But we have $M \lesssim^E N$, so $\tilde{\mathcal{E}}[N](N)$ converges, and $\tilde{\mathcal{E}}[N](N) \equiv C[N]$.

Case $C = \tilde{\mathcal{E}}(x)$. Trivial because for no term L is $C[L]$ a program.

All cases considered, the hypothesis is proved for all n, and the lemma follows. ∎

A corollary of this lemma and Proposition 4.15 is that ground experimental order and the ground restriction of contextual order are the same.

Proposition 4.18 *For all programs M and N of the same type, $M \lesssim^C N$ iff $M \lesssim^E N$.*

Proof. The forwards direction is a special case of Proposition 4.15. For the backwards direction, suppose that $M \lesssim^E N$ and that $C[M]$ converges, where C is a context. Hence by the context lemma $C[N]$ converges too. ∎

We can extend this result to open terms via the next three lemmas.

Lemma 4.19 *If $M \widehat{\lesssim^E} N$ then $M \lesssim^E N$, where programs M and N are as follows:*

(1) $M \equiv \langle M_1, M_2 \rangle$ and $N \equiv \langle N_1, N_2 \rangle$;

(2) $M \equiv \text{Split}(M_1, x_1.\,x_2.\,L)$ and $N \equiv \text{Split}(N_2, x_1.\,x_2.\,L)$;

(3) $M \equiv \text{Inl}(M_1)$ and $N \equiv \text{Inl}(N_1)$;

(4) $M \equiv \text{Inr}(M_1)$ and $N \equiv \text{Inr}(N_1)$;

(5) $M \equiv \text{Case}(M_1, x_1.\,L_1, x_2.\,L_2)$ and $N \equiv \text{Case}(N_1, x_1.\,L_1, x_2.\,L_2)$;

(6) $M \equiv \text{Lift}(M_1)$ and $N \equiv \text{Lift}(N_1)$;

(7) $M \equiv \text{Seq}(M_1, x.\,L)$ and $N \equiv \text{Seq}(N_1, x.\,L)$;

(8) $M \equiv \text{Intro}(M_1)$ and $N \equiv \text{Intro}(N_1)$;

(9) $M \equiv \text{Elim}(M_1)$ and $N \equiv \text{Elim}(N_1)$;

(10) $M \equiv (M_1\, M_2)$ and $N \equiv (N_1\, N_2)$.

Proof. Since each M_i and N_i is a program and $M_i \lesssim^E N_i$, in each case we have $M_i \lesssim^C N_i$ by Proposition 4.18. Contextual order is a precongruence so $M \lesssim^C N$ in each case, and therefore $M \lesssim^E N$ by Proposition 4.15, as required. ∎

Lemma 4.20 *If $M \widehat{\lesssim^E} N$ then $M \lesssim^E N$, where programs M and N are as follows:*

(1) $M \equiv (\lambda x.\,M')$ and $N \equiv (\lambda x.\,N')$;

(2) $M \equiv \text{Split}(L, x_1.\,x_2.\,M')$ and $N \equiv \text{Split}(L, x_1.\,x_2.\,N')$;

(3) $M \equiv \mathsf{Case}(L, x_1. M_1, x_2. M_2)$ and $N \equiv \mathsf{Case}(L, x_1. N_1, x_2. N_2)$;

(4) $M \equiv \mathsf{Seq}(L, x. M')$ and $N \equiv \mathsf{Seq}(L, x. N')$.

Proof. (2) For any list $\tilde{E}$, suppose that $\tilde{E}(M)\Downarrow$. We are to show that $\tilde{E}(N)\Downarrow$. We have that $M\Downarrow$ by Lemma 4.3(4). Hence $L \Downarrow \langle L_1, L_2 \rangle$ and we have $M \to^+ M'[L_1/x_1][L_2/x_2]$ and $N \to^+ N'[L_1/x_1][L_2/x_2]$. From $M \stackrel{\widehat{E}}{\lesssim} N$ we can deduce $M'[L_1/x_1][L_2/x_2] \stackrel{E}{\lesssim} N'[L_1/x_1][L_2/x_2]$. Since $\tilde{E}(M)$ converges we have that $\tilde{E}(M'[L_1/x_1][L_2/x_2])$ converges, and so $\tilde{E}(N'[L_1/x_1][L_2/x_2])$ converges. Since $\tilde{E}(N) \to^+ \tilde{E}(N'[L_1/x_1][L_2/x_2])$ we have that $\tilde{E}(N)$ converges as required.

Parts (1), (3) and (4) follow by similar arguments, which we omit. ∎

Lemma 4.21 If $M \stackrel{\widehat{E}}{\lesssim} N$ then $M \stackrel{E}{\lesssim} N$, where program $M \equiv \mathsf{Fix}(x. M')$ and $N \equiv \mathsf{Fix}(x. N')$.

Proof. The proof is a generalisation of the argument in the context lemma. We prove the following hypothesis by mathematical induction on n, that for any context C such that $C[M]$ and $C[N]$ are programs of the same type,

if $C[M]$ converges in n steps, then $C[N]$ converges.

So we actually prove that $M \stackrel{C}{\lesssim} N$, from which $M \stackrel{E}{\lesssim} N$ follows by Proposition 4.15. Just as in the context lemma, Lemma 4.17, we proceed by a case analysis of C. There is a possibly-empty list of contextual experiments, $\tilde{E}$, such that one of four cases holds:

Case $C = \tilde{E}(\mathcal{V})$. The argument of the context lemma is valid here, because it took no account of the structure of programs M and N.

Case $C = \tilde{E}(\mathsf{Fix}(x. C'))$. For the same reason, the argument of the context lemma applies.

Case $C = \tilde{E}([])$. Let $\mathcal{D}$ be the context $\tilde{E}(M'[[]/x])$ (where term M' is being used as a context; we can assume that the bound variables in context M' are distinct from x). So $C[M] \equiv \tilde{E}[M](M) \to \tilde{E}[M](M'[M/x]) \equiv \tilde{E}(M'[[]/x])[M] \equiv \mathcal{D}[M]$ and hence $\mathcal{D}[M]$ converges in $n - 1$ steps. By IH we have that $\mathcal{D}[N] \equiv \tilde{E}[N](M'[N/x])$ converges. Since $M \stackrel{\widehat{E}}{\lesssim} N$ we have that $M'[N/x] \stackrel{E}{\lesssim} N'[N/x]$. Therefore, since $\tilde{E}[N](M'[N/x])$ converges, so does $\tilde{E}[N](N'[N/x])$. But $C[N] \to \tilde{E}[N](N'[N/x])$, so $C[N]$ converges.

Case $C = \tilde{E}(x)$. Trivial because for no term L is $C[L]$ a program.

Proposition 4.22 If $\Gamma \vdash M \stackrel{\widehat{E}}{\lesssim} N$ then $\Gamma \vdash M \stackrel{E}{\lesssim} N$.

Proof. By considering each rule from Table 4.1 in turn. We consider the rule for Case-terms in detail. We have $M \equiv \mathsf{Case}(M_1, x_2. M_2, x_3. M_3)$ and $N \equiv \mathsf{Case}(N_1, x_2. N_2, x_3. N_3)$:

$$\frac{\Gamma \vdash M_1 \stackrel{E}{\lesssim} N_1 \qquad \Gamma, x_i{:}\sigma_i \vdash M_i \stackrel{E}{\lesssim} N_i \quad (i = 2, 3)}{\Gamma \vdash M \stackrel{\widehat{E}}{\lesssim} N}$$

Let $\cdot[\tilde{L}/\tilde{x}]$ be any Γ-closure and for any term L, write $\hat{L}$ for $L[\tilde{L}/\tilde{x}]$. We are to prove that $\hat{M} \stackrel{E}{\lesssim} \hat{N}$, that is:

$$\mathsf{Case}(\hat{M}_1, x_2. \hat{M}_2, x_3. \hat{M}_3) \stackrel{E}{\lesssim} \mathsf{Case}(\hat{N}_1, x_2. \hat{N}_2, x_3. \hat{N}_3) \quad (*)$$

we have $C[L] \equiv \tilde{\mathcal{E}}(\mathsf{Fix}(x.\,C'))[L] \equiv \tilde{\mathcal{E}}[L](\mathsf{Fix}(x.\,C'[L])) \rightarrow \tilde{\mathcal{E}}[L](C'[L][\mathsf{Fix}(x.\,C'[L])/x]) \equiv \tilde{\mathcal{E}}[L](C'[\mathsf{Fix}(x.\,C')/x][L]) \equiv \mathcal{D}[L]$ using Lemmas 4.1, 4.3 and 4.4. Hence we have $C[M] \rightarrow \mathcal{D}[M]$ and $C[N] \rightarrow \mathcal{D}[N]$. Just as in the previous case, since $\mathcal{D}[M]$ must converge in $n-1$ steps, by the induction hypothesis, $\mathcal{D}[N]$ converges, and therefore so too does $C[N]$.

Case $C = \tilde{\mathcal{E}}([])$. Let context $\mathcal{D} = \tilde{\mathcal{E}}(M)$ and then $\mathcal{D}[M] \equiv \tilde{\mathcal{E}}[M](M) \equiv C[M]$, so $\mathcal{D}[M]$ converges in n steps. But context $\mathcal{D}$ must take one of the forms already considered, so we can conclude that $\mathcal{D}[N] \equiv \tilde{\mathcal{E}}[N](M)$ converges. But we have $M \lesssim^E N$, so $\tilde{\mathcal{E}}[N](N)$ converges, and $\tilde{\mathcal{E}}[N](N) \equiv C[N]$.

Case $C = \tilde{\mathcal{E}}(x)$. Trivial because for no term L is $C[L]$ a program.

All cases considered, the hypothesis is proved for all n, and the lemma follows. ∎

A corollary of this lemma and Proposition 4.15 is that ground experimental order and the ground restriction of contextual order are the same.

Proposition 4.18 *For all programs M and N of the same type, $M \lesssim^C N$ iff $M \lesssim^E N$.*

Proof. The forwards direction is a special case of Proposition 4.15. For the backwards direction, suppose that $M \lesssim^E N$ and that $C[M]$ converges, where C is a context. Hence by the context lemma $C[N]$ converges too. ∎

We can extend this result to open terms via the next three lemmas.

Lemma 4.19 *If $M \widehat{\lesssim^E} N$ then $M \lesssim^E N$, where programs M and N are as follows:*

(1) $M \equiv \langle M_1, M_2 \rangle$ and $N \equiv \langle N_1, N_2 \rangle$;

(2) $M \equiv \mathsf{Split}(M_1, x_1.\,x_2.\,L)$ and $N \equiv \mathsf{Split}(N_2, x_1.\,x_2.\,L)$;

(3) $M \equiv \mathsf{Inl}(M_1)$ and $N \equiv \mathsf{Inl}(N_1)$;

(4) $M \equiv \mathsf{Inr}(M_1)$ and $N \equiv \mathsf{Inr}(N_1)$;

(5) $M \equiv \mathsf{Case}(M_1, x_1.\,L_1, x_2.\,L_2)$ and $N \equiv \mathsf{Case}(N_1, x_1.\,L_1, x_2.\,L_2)$;

(6) $M \equiv \mathsf{Lift}(M_1)$ and $N \equiv \mathsf{Lift}(N_1)$;

(7) $M \equiv \mathsf{Seq}(M_1, x.\,L)$ and $N \equiv \mathsf{Seq}(N_1, x.\,L)$;

(8) $M \equiv \mathsf{Intro}(M_1)$ and $N \equiv \mathsf{Intro}(N_1)$;

(9) $M \equiv \mathsf{Elim}(M_1)$ and $N \equiv \mathsf{Elim}(N_1)$;

(10) $M \equiv (M_1\,M_2)$ and $N \equiv (N_1\,N_2)$.

Proof. Since each M_i and N_i is a program and $M_i \lesssim^E N_i$, in each case we have $M_i \lesssim^C N_i$ by Proposition 4.18. Contextual order is a precongruence so $M \lesssim^C N$ in each case, and therefore $M \lesssim^E N$ by Proposition 4.15, as required. ∎

Lemma 4.20 *If $M \widehat{\lesssim^E} N$ then $M \lesssim^E N$, where programs M and N are as follows:*

(1) $M \equiv (\lambda x.\,M')$ and $N \equiv (\lambda x.\,N')$;

(2) $M \equiv \mathsf{Split}(L, x_1.\,x_2.\,M')$ and $N \equiv \mathsf{Split}(L, x_1.\,x_2.\,N')$;

(3) $M \equiv \mathsf{Case}(L, x_1. M_1, x_2. M_2)$ and $N \equiv \mathsf{Case}(L, x_1. N_1, x_2. N_2)$;

(4) $M \equiv \mathsf{Seq}(L, x. M')$ and $N \equiv \mathsf{Seq}(L, x. N')$.

Proof. (2) For any list $\tilde{E}$, suppose that $\tilde{E}(M)\Downarrow$. We are to show that $\tilde{E}(N)\Downarrow$. We have that $M\Downarrow$ by Lemma 4.3(4). Hence $L \Downarrow \langle L_1, L_2 \rangle$ and we have $M \to^+ M'[L_1/x_1][L_2/x_2]$ and $N \to^+ N'[L_1/x_1][L_2/x_2]$. From $M \overset{\widehat{E}}{\lesssim} N$ we can deduce $M'[L_1/x_1][L_2/x_2] \overset{E}{\lesssim} N'[L_1/x_1][L_2/x_2]$. Since $\tilde{E}(M)$ converges we have that $\tilde{E}(M'[L_1/x_1][L_2/x_2])$ converges, and so $\tilde{E}(N'[L_1/x_1][L_2/x_2])$ converges. Since $\tilde{E}(N) \to^+ \tilde{E}(N'[L_1/x_1][L_2/x_2])$ we have that $\tilde{E}(N)$ converges as required.

Parts (1), (3) and (4) follow by similar arguments, which we omit. ∎

Lemma 4.21 If $M \overset{\widehat{E}}{\lesssim} N$ then $M \overset{E}{\lesssim} N$, where program $M \equiv \mathsf{Fix}(x. M')$ and $N \equiv \mathsf{Fix}(x. N')$.

Proof. The proof is a generalisation of the argument in the context lemma. We prove the following hypothesis by mathematical induction on n, that for any context C such that $C[M]$ and $C[N]$ are programs of the same type,

   if $C[M]$ converges in n steps, then $C[N]$ converges.

So we actually prove that $M \overset{C}{\lesssim} N$, from which $M \overset{E}{\lesssim} N$ follows by Proposition 4.15. Just as in the context lemma, Lemma 4.17, we proceed by a case analysis of C. There is a possibly-empty list of contextual experiments, $\tilde{E}$, such that one of four cases holds:

Case $C = \tilde{E}(\mathcal{V})$. The argument of the context lemma is valid here, because it took no account of the structure of programs M and N.

Case $C = \tilde{E}(\mathsf{Fix}(x. C'))$. For the same reason, the argument of the context lemma applies.

Case $C = \tilde{E}([])$. Let $\mathcal{D}$ be the context $\tilde{E}(M'[[]/x])$ (where term M' is being used as a context; we can assume that the bound variables in context M' are distinct from x). So $C[M] \equiv \tilde{E}[M](M) \to \tilde{E}[M](M'[M/x]) \equiv \tilde{E}(M'[[]/x])[M] \equiv \mathcal{D}[M]$ and hence $\mathcal{D}[M]$ converges in $n-1$ steps. By IH we have that $\mathcal{D}[N] \equiv \tilde{E}[N](M'[N/x])$ converges. Since $M \overset{\widehat{E}}{\lesssim} N$ we have that $M'[N/x] \overset{E}{\lesssim} N'[N/x]$. Therefore, since $\tilde{E}[N](M'[N/x])$ converges, so does $\tilde{E}[N](N'[N/x])$. But $C[N] \to \tilde{E}[N](N'[N/x])$, so $C[N]$ converges.

Case $C = \tilde{E}(x)$. Trivial because for no term L is $C[L]$ a program.

Proposition 4.22 If $\Gamma \vdash M \overset{\widehat{E}}{\lesssim} N$ then $\Gamma \vdash M \overset{E}{\lesssim} N$.

Proof. By considering each rule from Table 4.1 in turn. We consider the rule for Case-terms in detail. We have $M \equiv \mathsf{Case}(M_1, x_2. M_2, x_3. M_3)$ and $N \equiv \mathsf{Case}(N_1, x_2. N_2, x_3. N_3)$:

$$\frac{\Gamma \vdash M_1 \overset{E}{\lesssim} N_1 \qquad \Gamma, x_i{:}\sigma_i \vdash M_i \overset{E}{\lesssim} N_i \quad (i = 2, 3)}{\Gamma \vdash M \overset{\widehat{E}}{\lesssim} N}$$

Let $\cdot[\tilde{L}/\tilde{x}]$ be any Γ-closure and for any term L, write $\hat{L}$ for $L[\tilde{L}/\tilde{x}]$. We are to prove that $\hat{M} \overset{E}{\lesssim} \hat{N}$, that is:

$$\mathsf{Case}(\hat{M}_1, x_2. \hat{M}_2, x_3. \hat{M}_3) \overset{E}{\lesssim} \mathsf{Case}(\hat{N}_1, x_2. \hat{N}_2, x_3. \hat{N}_3) \quad (*)$$

Using Lemmas 4.19 and 4.20 we have:

$$\mathsf{Case}(\hat{M}_1, x_2.\,\hat{M}_2, x_3.\,\hat{M}_3) \precsim^E \mathsf{Case}(\hat{N}_1, x_2.\,\hat{M}_2, x_3.\,\hat{M}_3) \quad \text{from } \varnothing \vdash \hat{M}_1 \precsim^E \hat{N}_1$$
$$\mathsf{Case}(\hat{N}_1, x_2.\,\hat{M}_2, x_3.\,\hat{M}_3) \precsim^E \mathsf{Case}(\hat{N}_1, x_2.\,\hat{N}_2, x_3.\,\hat{M}_3) \quad \text{from } x_2{:}\sigma_2 \vdash \hat{M}_2 \precsim^E \hat{N}_2$$
$$\mathsf{Case}(\hat{N}_1, x_2.\,\hat{N}_2, x_3.\,\hat{M}_3) \precsim^E \mathsf{Case}(\hat{N}_1, x_2.\,\hat{N}_2, x_3.\,\hat{N}_3) \quad \text{from } x_3{:}\sigma_3 \vdash \hat{M}_3 \precsim^E \hat{N}_3$$

Then by transitivity of experimental order we have $(*)$ as required. Each of the other cases follows similarly. ∎

This proposition together with Proposition 4.15 establishes that experimental and contextual order are the same, and hence that contextual order is an operationally adequate precongruence.

4.5 Applicative and compatible similarity

We now define the ground preorder applicative similarity, which we will prove in §4.6 to be an independent characterisation of contextual order.

Definition 4.23 *Define function $[\cdot]$ over ground relations such that*

$$M[S]N \text{ iff whenever } M \Downarrow U \text{ there is } V \text{ with } N \Downarrow V \text{ and } U \,\hat{S}\, V.$$

An **applicative simulation** *is a relation S such that $S \subseteq [S]$. Define* **ground applicative similarity**, $\precsim^A$, *to be the union of all applicative simulations. Define* **applicative similarity**, $\precsim^A$, *to be the confined extension of ground applicative similarity.*

Proposition 4.24

(1) *Function $[\cdot]$ is monotone.*

(2) *The identity ground relation is an applicative simulation.*

(3) *If each S_i is an applicative simulation, then so is $S_1 S_2$.*

(4) *Ground applicative similarity is the greatest fixpoint of $[\cdot]$ and is the greatest applicative simulation.*

(5) *$M \precsim^A N$ iff there is an applicative simulation S such that MSN*

(6) *Ground applicative similarity is a preorder.*

Proof. Parts (1), (2) and (3) are easy to check from the definition. The remaining parts then follow from Proposition 1.1. ∎

Definition 4.25 *An* **applicative bisimulation** *is a relation S such that both S and S^{-1} are applicative simulations.* **Ground applicative bisimilarity**, $\simeq^A$, *is the ground relation such that $M \simeq^A N$ iff $M \precsim^A N$ and $N \precsim^A M$.* **Applicative bisimilarity**, $\simeq^A$, *is the confined extension of ground applicative bisimilarity.*

Clearly applicative bisimilarity is an equivalence relation. Furthermore, for any programs M and N, $M \simeq^A N$ iff for some applicative bisimulation S, $(M, N) \in S$.

Proposition 4.26 *Ground relations $\precsim^A$ and $\simeq^A$ are both operationally adequate.*

Proof. When $\mathcal{R}$ stands either for applicative similarity or bisimilarity, we need to prove each of the following properties.

(1) If $M \to N$ then $N\mathcal{R}M$.

(2) If $M \Downarrow V$ then $V\mathcal{R}M$.

(3) $M\Uparrow$ iff $M\mathcal{R}\Omega$.

(4) $M\Downarrow$ iff for some canonical V, $V\mathcal{R}M$.

To prove parts (1) and (2) it is sufficient to show that $\mathcal{S}_{12}$ is an applicative bisimulation, where $\mathcal{S}_{12}$ is given by:

$$\mathcal{S}_{12} \stackrel{\text{def}}{=} \{(N, M) \mid M \to^* N\}$$

Observe first that if $M \to^* N$ then for any U, $M \Downarrow U$ iff $N \Downarrow U$, from Proposition 3.5(6), and that $Id \subseteq \mathcal{S}_{12}$. Suppose $(N, M) \in \mathcal{S}_{12}$ and $N\Downarrow U$. Then $M\Downarrow U$ and $U \widehat{Id} U$. Similarly, suppose $(M, N) \in \mathcal{S}_{12}^{-1}$ and $M \Downarrow U$. Then $N \Downarrow U$ and $U \widehat{Id} U$.

For the forwards direction of part (3) we show that $\mathcal{S}_3$ below is an applicative bisimulation:

$$\mathcal{S}_3 \stackrel{\text{def}}{=} \{(M, \Omega) \mid \neg\exists U.\, M \Downarrow U\}$$

For any pair $(M, N) \in \mathcal{S}_3$, neither $M\Downarrow$ nor $N\Downarrow$, so $\mathcal{S}_3$ is trivially an applicative bisimulation. For the backwards direction of (3), either $M \simeq^A \Omega$ or $M \lesssim^A \Omega$ implies that pair (M, Ω) is contained in some applicative simulation. Hence, as Ω cannot converge, neither can M.

The forwards direction of part (4) follows immediately from the definition of $M\Downarrow$ and part (2). For the backwards direction, either $U \simeq^A M$ or $U \lesssim^A M$ implies that pair (U, M) is contained in some applicative simulation, so $M\Downarrow$ since $U\Downarrow$. ∎

We prove that applicative similarity for $\mathcal{M}$ is a precongruence by a typed reworking of Howe's method [58].

Definition 4.27 *Define the confined relation* **compatible similarity**, $\lesssim^*$, *to be the least set closed under the following rule.*

$$\frac{\Gamma \vdash L \widehat{\lesssim^*} M \qquad \Gamma \vdash M \lesssim^A N}{\Gamma \vdash L \lesssim^* N}$$

(Beware the ambiguous notation: the '*' in '$\lesssim^*$' does not denote reflexive transitive closure.)

Proposition 4.28

(1) *Applicative similarity is natural (that is, rules* **Spec**, **Weak** *and* **Stren** *are valid).*

(2) *Confined relations $\widehat{\lesssim^*}$ and $\lesssim^*$ are reflexive.*

(3) *Confined relations $\widehat{\lesssim^*}$ and $\lesssim^A$ both imply $\lesssim^*$*

(4) *If $\Gamma \vdash M_1 \lesssim^* M_2$ and $\Gamma \vdash M_2 \lesssim^A M_3$ then $\Gamma \vdash M_1 \lesssim^* M_3$.*

(5) *(***Sub***) If $\Gamma, x{:}\tau \vdash M_1 \lesssim^* N_1$ and $\Gamma \vdash M_2 \lesssim^* N_2$ then $\Gamma \vdash M_1[M_2/x] \lesssim^* N_1[N_2/x]$.*

(6) If $\varnothing \vdash U \lesssim^* M$ then there is V such that $M \Downarrow V$ and $\varnothing \vdash U \widehat{\lesssim}^* V$.

(7) If $\varnothing \vdash M \lesssim^* N$ and $M \Downarrow U$ then $\varnothing \vdash U \lesssim^* N$.

(8) If $\Gamma \vdash M \lesssim^* N$ then $\Gamma \vdash M \lesssim^A N$.

(9) Applicative similarity is a precongruence.

Proof. (1) Applicative similarity is natural because it is the confined extension of a ground relation (Proposition 4.10).

(2) By structural induction on M one can easily verify that $\Gamma \vdash M \lesssim^* M$, so $\lesssim^*$ is reflexive. A corollary is that $\widehat{\lesssim}^*$ is reflexive.

(3) Corollary of part (2) and the definition of compatible similarity.

(4) If $\Gamma \vdash M_1 \lesssim^* M_2$ then for some N, $\Gamma \vdash M_1 \widehat{\lesssim}^* N$ and $\Gamma \vdash N \lesssim^A M_2$. Since $\lesssim^A$ is transitive, we have $\Gamma \vdash N \lesssim^A M_3$. Then by definition we have $\Gamma \vdash M_1 \lesssim^* M_3$.

(5) The proof is by induction on the depth of inference of $\Gamma, x{:}\tau \vdash M_1 \lesssim^* N_1$. By definition, there is N_1' such that $\Gamma, x{:}\tau \vdash M_1 \widehat{\lesssim}^* N_1'$ and $\Gamma, x{:}\tau \vdash N_1' \lesssim^A N_1$. By **Spec** we have $\Gamma \vdash N_1'[N_2/x] \lesssim^A N_1[N_2/x]$. Proceed by a structural analysis of M_1 and show in each case, that $\Gamma \vdash M_1[M_2/x] \lesssim^* N_1'[N_2/x]$. The result will then follow by part (4). We show three cases. The other cases are similar.

Case $M_1 \equiv x$. So $N_1' \equiv x$. We have $\Gamma \vdash M_2 \lesssim^* N_2$ by assumption.

Case $M_1 \equiv y \neq x$. So $N_1' \equiv y$. We have $\Gamma \vdash y \lesssim^* y$ by reflexivity, part (2).

Case $M_1 \equiv \lambda y{:}\sigma. M_0$. So $N_1' \equiv \lambda y. N_0$ and $\Gamma, x{:}\tau, y{:}\sigma \vdash M_0 \lesssim^* N_0$. By IH $\Gamma, y{:}\sigma \vdash M_0[M_2/x] \lesssim^* N_0[N_2/x]$. So $\Gamma \vdash M_1[M_2/x] \widehat{\lesssim}^* N_1'[N_2/x]$ by definition. Then we have $\Gamma \vdash M_1[M_2/x] \lesssim^* N_1'[N_2/x]$ by part (3), as required.

(6) In each case there must be a program N such that $U \widehat{\lesssim}^* N$ and $N \lesssim^A M$. Proceed by a structural analysis of canonical program U:

Case $U \equiv \lambda x{:}\tau. M_1$. So $N \equiv \lambda x. N_1$ with $x{:}\tau \vdash M_1 \lesssim^* N_1$. Then $N \lesssim^A M$ implies that $M \Downarrow \lambda x. N_1'$ with $x{:}\tau \vdash N_1 \lesssim^A N_1'$. Therefore $x{:}\tau \vdash M_1 \lesssim^* N_1'$ by part (4), which implies $U \widehat{\lesssim}^* (\lambda x. N_1')$ as required.

Case $U \equiv \langle M_1, M_2 \rangle$. So $N \equiv \langle N_1, N_2 \rangle$ with $M_i \lesssim^* N_i$ for $i = 1, 2$. Then $N \lesssim^A M$ implies that $M \Downarrow \langle L_1, L_2 \rangle$ with $N_i \lesssim^A L_i$. So $M_i \lesssim^* L_i$ by part (4), and $U \equiv \langle M_1, M_2 \rangle$ so $U \widehat{\lesssim}^* \langle L_1, L_2 \rangle$ as required.

(7) By induction on the depth of inference of $M \Downarrow U$, proceeding by analysis of M:

Case M canonical. Immediate..

Case $M \equiv (M_1 M_2)$. We have $M_1 \Downarrow \lambda x{:}\tau. M_3$ and $M_3[M_2/x] \Downarrow U$. From $M \lesssim^* N$ there are N_1, N_2 such that each $M_i \lesssim^* N_i$ and $(N_1 N_2) \lesssim^A N$. Since $M_1 \Downarrow \lambda x{:}\tau. M_3$ and $M_1 \lesssim^* N_1$ we have $(\lambda x{:}\tau. M_3) \lesssim^* N_1$ by IH. By (6) there is N_3 with $N_1 \Downarrow \lambda x{:}\tau. N_3$ and $x{:}\tau \vdash M_3 \lesssim^* N_3$. By **Sub**, $M_3[M_2/x] \lesssim^* N_3[N_2/x]$, and then by IH we have $U \lesssim^* N_3[N_2/x]$. Since $(N_1 N_2) \rightarrow^+ N_3[N_2/x]$ we have $N_3[N_2/x] \lesssim^A (N_1 N_2)$ by operational adequacy.

From $(N_1 N_2) \lesssim^A N$ we have $N_3[N_2/x] \lesssim^A N$ by transitivity. Finally from $U \lesssim^* N_3[N_2/x]$ we have $U \lesssim^* N$ by (4).

The other cases follow the same pattern as the ones above.

(8) First we prove that the ground restriction of compatible similarity is an applicative simulation. Suppose for any programs M and N that $M \lesssim^* N$. We are to show that whenever $M \Downarrow U$ there is V such that $M \Downarrow V$ and $U \widehat{\lesssim^*} V$. Suppose that $M \Downarrow U$. By (7) we have $U \lesssim^* N$. By (6) there is V such that $N \Downarrow V$ and $U \widehat{\lesssim^*} V$.

Suppose now that $\Gamma \vdash M \lesssim^* N$. We are to prove that $\Gamma \vdash M \lesssim^A N$, which is to say that for all Γ-closures, $\cdot[\tilde{L}/\tilde{x}]$, programs $M[\tilde{L}/\tilde{x}]$ and $N[\tilde{L}/\tilde{x}]$ are paired in an applicative simulation. But by **Sub** and reflexivity we have $M[\tilde{L}/\tilde{x}] \lesssim^* N[\tilde{L}/\tilde{x}]$, and since the ground restriction of compatible similarity is an applicative simulation, we are done.

(9) A corollary of (3) and (8) is that applicative and compatible similarity are the same confined relation. We know applicative similarity is a preorder from Proposition 4.24(6). We know that rule **Comp** holds for compatible similarity from part (3). Therefore by Proposition 4.8(2) applicative similarity is a precongruence.   ∎

4.6   Contextual order and applicative similarity

Contextual order equals applicative similarity. Our proof is essentially a typed reworking of Howe's Theorem 3 [58].

Lemma 4.29 *Ground applicative similarity equals the ground restriction of contextual order.*

Proof. Let $\mathcal{S}$ be the ground restriction of contextual order.

$$\mathcal{S} \overset{\text{def}}{=} \{(M, N) \mid \varnothing \vdash M \lesssim^C N\}$$

To see why $\lesssim^A \subseteq \mathcal{S}$, it is enough to consider any $(M, N) \in \lesssim^A$ and show that $M \lesssim^C N$. If $C[M] \Downarrow$ for some context C, then $C[M] \lesssim^A C[M]$ (since $\lesssim^A$ is a precongruence) and therefore $C[M] \Downarrow$ as required.

For the reverse inclusion, it suffices by co-induction to show that symmetric $\mathcal{S}$ is an applicative simulation. Suppose then that $(M, N) \in \mathcal{S}$ and that $M \Downarrow V$. Since $M \lesssim^C N$ there must be U such that $N \Downarrow U$ (or else the trivial context $C = []$ would distinguish M and N). Based on the following case analysis of V we show that $V \widehat{\mathcal{S}} U$, as required for $\mathcal{S}$ to be an applicative simulation.

Case $V \equiv \mathsf{Inl}(M')$.   Since U and V have the same type, U must take one of the forms $\mathsf{Inl}(N')$ or $\mathsf{Inr}(N')$. We can rule out the latter, or else the context $C = \mathsf{Case}([], x. L, y. \Omega)$, where L is some convergent program such as $\mathsf{Lift}(\lambda x. x)$, would distinguish M and N. Let context $\mathcal{D}$ be $\mathsf{Case}([], x. x, y. M')$. We have $\mathcal{D}[M] \lesssim^C \mathcal{D}[N]$ since $\lesssim^C$ is a congruence. Moreover $\mathcal{D}[M] \to^+ M'$ and $\mathcal{D}[M] \to^+ N'$. By operational adequacy and determinacy the reduction relation $\to$ and its inverse $\to^{-1}$ are included in $\lesssim^A$. Hence we have $M' \lesssim^A \mathcal{D}[M]$ and $\mathcal{D}[M] \lesssim^A N'$. Since $\lesssim^A \subseteq \mathcal{S}$ we have

$(M', N') \in \mathcal{S}$ and therefore $V \, \widehat{\mathcal{S}} \, U$.

Case $V \equiv \lambda x{:}\sigma. \, M'$. This time U must take the form $\lambda x. \, N'$. To show $(\lambda x. \, M')\widehat{\mathcal{S}}(\lambda x. \, N')$, it suffices to prove that $(M'[L/x], N'[L/x]) \in \mathcal{S}$ for arbitrary σ-program L. Let context $\mathcal{D}$ be $([]\, L)$. We have $\mathcal{D}[M] \lesssim^C \mathcal{D}[N]$. Since $\mathcal{D}[M] \to^+ M'[L/x]$ and $\mathcal{D}[N] \to^+ N'[L/x]$ we may obtain $(M'[L/x], N'[L/x]) \in \mathcal{S}$ as in the previous case.

Case $V \equiv \mathsf{Lift}(M')$. Again we may conclude that U takes the form $\mathsf{Lift}(N')$. To show that $\mathsf{Lift}(M') \, \widehat{\mathcal{S}} \, \mathsf{Lift}(N')$, it suffices to prove that $M' \lesssim^C N'$. Suppose then for an arbitrary context $\mathcal{C}$, that $\mathcal{C}[M']$ and $\mathcal{C}[N']$ are programs of the same type, and that $\mathcal{C}[M']$ converges. We must show that $\mathcal{C}[N']$ converges too. We may suppose that $\mathcal{C}[M']$ and $\mathcal{C}[N']$ are of lifted type; otherwise by the convergence theorem for $\mathcal{M}$ it follows that both always converge. Set context $\mathcal{D}$ to be $\mathsf{Seq}([], x. \, \mathcal{C}[x])$. We have that $\mathcal{D}[M] \to^+ \mathcal{C}[M']$ and $\mathcal{D}[N] \to^+ \mathcal{C}[N']$. As before we have that $\mathcal{C}[M'] \lesssim^C \mathcal{D}[M]$ and $\mathcal{D}[N] \lesssim^C \mathcal{C}[N']$. Since $M \lesssim^C N$ we have also $\mathcal{D}[M] \lesssim^C \mathcal{D}[N]$ and therefore by transitivity that $\mathcal{C}[M'] \lesssim^C \mathcal{C}[N']$. Therefore if $\mathcal{C}[M']$ converges, so does $\mathcal{C}[N']$. Hence we have established $\mathsf{Lift}(M') \, \widehat{\mathcal{S}} \, \mathsf{Lift}(N')$, as required.

The other cases follow by similar reasoning. ∎

Theorem 4.30 (Operational Extensionality) $\lesssim^C \; = \; \lesssim^A$

Proof. We must show

$$\Gamma \vdash M \lesssim^C N \text{ iff } \Gamma \vdash M \lesssim^A N \quad (*)$$

for arbitrary Γ, M and N. The backwards direction follows by the same argument as used in the previous lemma to prove that $\lesssim^A \subseteq \mathcal{S}$. As for the forwards direction, we must show that

$$M[\tilde{L}/\tilde{x}] \lesssim^A N[\tilde{L}/\tilde{x}]$$

for any Γ-closure $\cdot[\tilde{L}/\tilde{x}]$. Set context $\mathcal{D}$ to be $(\lambda x_1 \cdots x_n. \, []) \, L_1 \cdots L_n$ and we have $\varnothing \vdash \mathcal{D}[M] \lesssim^C \mathcal{D}[N]$ by precongruence. By Lemma 4.29 we have $\varnothing \vdash \mathcal{D}[M] \lesssim^A \mathcal{D}[N]$ and since $\mathcal{D}[M] \to^+ M[\tilde{L}/\tilde{x}]$ and $\mathcal{D}[N] \to^+ N[\tilde{L}/\tilde{x}]$ we have $\varnothing \vdash M[\tilde{L}/\tilde{x}] \lesssim^A N[\tilde{L}/\tilde{x}]$, as required. ∎

In summary, this chapter considered two independent definitions of operational order, contextual order and applicative similarity, and proved that they are in fact the same relation, henceforth denoted by $\lesssim$. We use $\simeq$ for operational equivalence, equal to $\lesssim \cap \lesssim^{-1}$, also known as contextual equivalence or applicative bisimilarity. Both characterisations are of interest. By definition, contextual order is perhaps the simplest congruence induced by the evaluation relation. By definition, applicative similarity is a greatest fixpoint, giving rise to a powerful principle of co-induction used extensively in Chapter 5. Given operational extensionality, Howe's method and the context lemma method amount to the same thing: a proof that operational order is an operationally adequate precongruence. In a calculus where operational extensionality fails, the two methods would be of separate interest.

Chapter 5

Theory of the metalanguage

We conclude the three chapters on $\mathcal{M}$ by obtaining results about evaluation and equivalence needed in connection with the denotational semantics of $\mathcal{H}$ in the next chapter. We make extensive use in this chapter of the principal results obtained in Chapters 3 and 4: that no term of a certainly-convergent type can diverge and that operational equivalence (that is, contextual equivalence or applicative bisimilarity) is an operationally adequate congruence.

In §5.1 we prove basic facts about operational equivalence; these facts parallel the axioms of LCF [46, 105] but are simpler in that there are divergent terms only at lifted types. This is a consequence of the convergence theorem proved in Chapter 3 via Mendler's calculus developed in Chapter 2. §5.2 investigates empty and one-point types in $\mathcal{M}$, $0 \stackrel{\text{def}}{=} \mu X. X$ and $1 \stackrel{\text{def}}{=} 0 \to 0$ respectively. There are no programs of type 0. Any two programs of type 1 are operationally equivalent. §5.3 sketches the standard construction of iterated sum and product types from binary sums, binary products and the empty and one-point types. We conclude the chapter by investigating types of booleans and natural numbers in §5.4 and §5.5 respectively.

5.1 Laws of operational equivalence in $\mathcal{M}$

Recall that **operational equivalence** and **order**, $\simeq$ and $\lesssim$, equal the confined relations of applicative bisimilarity and similarity, $\simeq^A$ and $\lesssim^A$ respectively. We know that both these are operationally adequate precongruences. Let **ground equivalence** be the ground restriction of operational equivalence.

Proposition 5.1 *All the laws from Table 5.1 hold for operational equivalence:*

(1) *Exhaustion law;*

(2) *Congruence;*

(3) *Canonical Freeness;*

(4) *Beta, strictness and eta laws;*

(5) *Co-induction.*

Exhaustion Law

If M is a σ-program and σ is certainly-convergent then $(\exists V{:}\sigma.\, M \simeq V)$.
If M is a $(\sigma_{\perp})$-program then either $M \simeq \Omega$ or $(\exists N{:}\sigma.\, M \simeq \mathsf{Lift}(N))$.

Congruence

If $(\Gamma \vdash M \mathbin{\widehat{\simeq}} N)$ then $(\Gamma \vdash M \simeq N)$.

Canonical Freeness

If $(\Gamma \vdash U \simeq V)$ then $(\Gamma \vdash U \mathbin{\widehat{\simeq}} V)$.

Beta Laws

$$\Gamma \vdash \mathsf{Split}(\langle M_1, M_2 \rangle, x_1.\, x_2.\, N) \simeq N[M_1/x_1][M_2/x_2]$$
$$\Gamma \vdash \mathsf{Case}(\mathsf{Inl}(M), x_1.\, N_1, x_2.\, N_2) \simeq N_1[M/x_1]$$
$$\Gamma \vdash \mathsf{Case}(\mathsf{Inr}(M), x_1.\, N_1, x_2.\, N_2) \simeq N_2[M/x_2]$$
$$\Gamma \vdash ((\lambda x.\, M)\, N) \simeq M[N/x]$$
$$\Gamma \vdash \mathsf{Seq}(\mathsf{Lift}(M), x.\, N) \simeq N[M/x]$$
$$\Gamma \vdash \mathsf{Fix}(x.\, M) \simeq M[\mathsf{Fix}(x.\, M)/x]$$
$$\Gamma \vdash \mathsf{Elim}(\mathsf{Intro}(M)) \simeq M$$

Strictness Law

$$\Gamma \vdash \mathsf{Seq}(\Omega, x.\, N) \simeq \Omega$$

Eta Laws

$$\Gamma \vdash \mathsf{Split}(M, x_1.\, x_2.\, \langle x_1, x_2 \rangle) \simeq M$$
$$\Gamma \vdash \mathsf{Case}(M, x_1.\, \mathsf{Inl}\, (x_1), x_2.\, \mathsf{Inr}\, (x_2)) \simeq M$$
$$\Gamma \vdash (\lambda x.\, (M\, x)) \simeq M \qquad \text{if } x \notin fv(M)$$
$$\Gamma \vdash \mathsf{Seq}(M, x.\, \mathsf{Lift}\, (x)) \simeq M$$
$$\Gamma \vdash \mathsf{Intro}(\mathsf{Elim}(M)) \simeq M$$

Co-induction

A **bisimulation-up-to-$\simeq$** is a ground relation, S, such that whenever MSN, either $M \simeq N \simeq \Omega$ or there are canonical programs U and V such that $M \simeq U$, $N \simeq V$ and $U \mathbin{\widehat{S}} V$.

Any bisimulation-up-to-$\simeq$ is a subset of ground equivalence.

Table 5.1: Laws of equivalence in $\mathcal{M}$

Proof. (1) Suppose that M is a σ-program and that σ is certainly-convergent. By the convergence theorem, Theorem 3.11, $M\Downarrow$, which is to say, $(\exists V. M \Downarrow V)$. By operational adequacy, we have $M \simeq V$.

Suppose that M is a $(\sigma_\perp)$-program. Either $M\Uparrow$ or $M\Downarrow$. In the first case we are done. In the second case, there is some canonical program V such that $M \Downarrow V$. Since $V{:}\sigma_\perp$, by inspection of the typing rules there must be a σ-program N such that $V \equiv \mathsf{Lift}(N)$. By operational adequacy, we have $M \simeq V \simeq \mathsf{Lift}(N)$ as required.

(2) Congruence for applicative bisimilarity is a corollary of Proposition 4.28, in which we showed that applicative similarity and compatible similarity coincide. (The congruence rule in Table 5.1 is the same as the **Comp** rule in Table 4.2. The **Precong** rule in Table 4.2 is a common way to define precongruence. We showed in Proposition 4.7(3) that for any preorder, such as applicative similarity or bisimilarity, rule **Comp** is valid iff rule **Precong** is valid.)

(3) Note first a corollary of Proposition 4.28(6): for any canonical programs U and V, $U \lesssim V$ implies $U \hat{\lesssim} V$.

We are to show for any Γ-closure, $\cdot[\tilde{L}/\tilde{x}]$, that $U[\tilde{L}/\tilde{x}] \simeq V[\tilde{L}/\tilde{x}]$. We have $\Gamma \vdash U \simeq V$, which is to say that for all Γ-closures, $\cdot[\tilde{L}/\tilde{x}]$, $U[\tilde{L}/\tilde{x}] \simeq V[\tilde{L}/\tilde{x}]$. Since U and V are canonical, terms $U[\tilde{L}/\tilde{x}]$ and $V[\tilde{L}/\tilde{x}]$ are canonical programs. Therefore, the corollary of Proposition 4.28(6) applies, and we have $U[\tilde{L}/\tilde{x}] \hat{\lesssim} V[\tilde{L}/\tilde{x}]$, as required.

(4) Each law takes the form $\Gamma \vdash M_L \simeq M_R$. First, we show that each law holds for ground equivalence when Γ is empty. For each beta law we can check by inspection that $M_L \rightarrow^+ M_R$. In the strictness law $M_R \equiv \Omega$ and $M_L\Uparrow$. Therefore, by operational adequacy we have $M_L \simeq M_R$.

There are five eta laws. We can prove each law by a case analysis of program M_R based on the exhaustion law. In the law for Split, there must be programs M_i such that $M_R \simeq \langle M_1, M_2 \rangle$. By the beta law for Split we have $M_L \simeq \mathsf{Split}(\langle M_1, M_2 \rangle, x_1. x_2. \langle x_1, x_2 \rangle) \simeq \langle x_1, x_2 \rangle [M_1/x_1][M_2/x_2] \simeq M_R$. (Recall the general convention that bound variables, such as x_1 and x_2 in the table, are distinct.) In the law for λ-abstraction, there must be a term M' such that $M_R \simeq (\lambda y. M')$. We know that $x \notin fv(M_R)$. So by the beta law for λ-abstraction, $M_L \simeq ((\lambda x. M'[x/y]) \equiv M_R$. The other cases are similar.

Second, we prove each law for non-empty Γ. Suppose we are to prove a law of the form $\Gamma \vdash M_L \simeq M_R$. We are to show, for any Γ-closure $\cdot[\tilde{L}/\tilde{x}]$, that $M_L[\tilde{L}/\tilde{x}] \simeq M_R[\tilde{L}/\tilde{x}]$. Terms are identified up to alpha-conversion, so we may assume that any bound variable in M_L or M_R is distinct from $\tilde{x}$. Therefore the Γ-closure can be distributed into the bodies of terms M_L and M_R to obtain programs $\hat{M}_L$ and $\hat{M}_R$ to which the law with Γ empty can be applied.

(5) Suppose $\mathcal{S}$ is a bisimulation up-to-$\simeq$. We will prove $\mathcal{S}_\simeq \subseteq \simeq$, where $\mathcal{S}_\simeq$ is $\simeq\mathcal{S}\simeq$ (the relational composition of $\simeq$, $\mathcal{S}$ and $\simeq$). Since $\mathcal{S} \subseteq \mathcal{S}_\simeq$ we will have established $\mathcal{S} \subseteq \simeq$ as required.

We show that $\mathcal{S}_\simeq$ is an applicative simulation. Suppose then that $M \mathrel{\mathcal{S}_\simeq} N$ and that $M \Downarrow U$. We must find V such that $N \Downarrow V$ and $U \widehat{\mathcal{S}_\simeq} V$. Since $M \mathrel{\mathcal{S}_\simeq} N$ there must be programs M' and N' such that $M \simeq M'$, $M'\mathcal{S}N'$ and $N' \simeq N$. Since $M \Downarrow U$ and $M \simeq M'$

there must be a canonical program U' such that $M' \Downarrow U'$ and $U \cong U'$. Since $M' \Downarrow U'$ we have $M' \simeq U'$ which with $M'SN'$ implies there must be canonical U'' and V'' such that $M' \simeq U''$, $U'' \widehat{S} V''$ and $V'' \simeq N'$. Since $V'' \simeq N'$ there must be canonical V' such that $N' \Downarrow V'$ and $V'' \simeq V'$. From $N' \Downarrow V'$ and $N' \simeq N$ there must be a canonical V such that $N \Downarrow V$ and $V' \cong V$. In all we have

$$U \cong U' \simeq U'' \widehat{S} V'' \simeq V' \cong V$$

and therefore, by canonical freeness, that $U \widehat{\cong} \widehat{S} \widehat{\cong} V$. Now, for any confined relations $\mathcal{R}$ and $\mathcal{R}'$, it is not hard to verify that $\widehat{\mathcal{R}} \widehat{\mathcal{R}'} \subseteq \widehat{\mathcal{R}\mathcal{R}'}$. Hence we have $U \widehat{S_\sim} V$, which completes the proof that $S_\sim$ is an applicative simulation. Since $S_\sim$ is symmetric, we have shown that $S_\sim \subseteq \simeq$ as required.

5.2   Empty and one-point types in $\mathcal{M}$

Let type $0 \stackrel{\text{def}}{=} \mu X. X$ and $1 \stackrel{\text{def}}{=} 0 \to 0$; in the following propositions we prove that 0 is empty and that 1 has just one element.

Proposition 5.2   *There is no program of type 0.*

Proof. First, consider the relation $\rightsquigarrow$ on programs of type 0, inductively defined by the following two rules.

$$\frac{M \to N}{M \rightsquigarrow N} \qquad \frac{M \rightsquigarrow N}{\mathsf{Intro}^0(M) \rightsquigarrow \mathsf{Intro}^0(M)}$$

By definition $\rightsquigarrow$ includes the reduction relation $\to$, but also reduces beneath Intros. Since $\to$ is a partial function, so is $\rightsquigarrow$. In Proposition 3.10 we showed that each $\to$ reduction of an $\mathcal{M}$ program can be matched by one or more $\to$ reductions of its translation into $\mu\nu\lambda 2$. According to Table 3.4 the translation $[\![\mathsf{Intro}^0(M)]\!]$ is $\mu\nu\lambda 2$ program $\mathsf{Intro}^{[0]}[\![M]\!]$; we can strengthen Proposition 3.10 to the following.

If $\varnothing \vdash M : 0$ and $M \rightsquigarrow N$ in $\mathcal{M}$ then $[\![\varnothing \vdash M]\!] \to^+ [\![\varnothing \vdash N]\!]$ in $\mu\nu\lambda 2$.

Hence we have a corollary analogous to the normalisation result for $\mathcal{M}$, Theorem 3.11. Let an $\rightsquigarrow$-**normal form** be a program M of type 0 such that $M \not\rightsquigarrow$.

For each $\varnothing \vdash M : 0$ there is an $\rightsquigarrow$-normal form N such that $M \rightsquigarrow^* N$.

Any $\rightsquigarrow$-normal form is also an $\to$-normal form, so it must look like $\mathsf{Intro}^0(M)$ where M is also an $\rightsquigarrow$-normal form. So then each $\rightsquigarrow$-normal form contains another $\rightsquigarrow$-normal form that contains one less Intro^0. If there is an $\rightsquigarrow$-normal form it must contain a finite number of Intro^0's. Therefore if there is an $\rightsquigarrow$-normal form at all there must be one containing no Intro^0's. But this is impossible, as each $\rightsquigarrow$-normal form is also an $\to$-normal form, and hence must contain an outermost Intro^0. Hence there can be no $\rightsquigarrow$-normal forms, and therefore no programs of type 0 at all. ∎

Proposition 5.3   *There is a canonical program, $*$, of type 1 such that for any program M, of type 1, $M \simeq *$.*

Proof. Let $* \stackrel{\text{def}}{=} \lambda x{:}0.\,x$. To show that $*$ is unique up to $\simeq$, it suffices to show that relation S is a bisimulation.

$$S \stackrel{\text{def}}{=} \{(*, M) \mid \varnothing \vdash M : 1\}$$

Suppose that $(*, M) \in S$. Since 1 is certainly-convergent there must be some canonical term $\lambda x{:}0.\,N$ such that $M \Downarrow \lambda x{:}0.\,N$. Since $* \Downarrow * \equiv \lambda x{:}0.\,x$ we must show that $\varnothing \vdash * \hat{S} \lambda x{:}0.\,N$, that is, for all programs $L{:}0$ that $(x[^L\!/\!_x], N[^L\!/\!_x]) \in S$. But this is vacuously true, as there are no programs such as L. $\blacksquare$

5.3 Iterated products and sums in $\mathcal{M}$

Define iterated product and sum notations by induction on $n \geq 0$:

$$(\sigma_1 \times \cdots \times \sigma_n) \stackrel{\text{def}}{=} \begin{cases} 1 & \text{if } n = 0 \\ \sigma_1 & \text{if } n = 1 \\ \sigma_1 \times (\sigma_2 \times \cdots \times \sigma_n) & \text{if } n > 1 \end{cases}$$

$$(\sigma_1 + \cdots + \sigma_n) \stackrel{\text{def}}{=} \begin{cases} 0 & \text{if } n = 0 \\ \sigma_1 & \text{if } n = 1 \\ \sigma_1 + (\sigma_2 + \cdots + \sigma_n) & \text{if } n > 1 \end{cases}$$

Proposition 5.4 *Suppose* $\Pi = (\sigma_1 \times \cdots \times \sigma_n)$ *and* $\Sigma = (\sigma_1 + \cdots + \sigma_n)$. *Then there are canonical terms* $\langle M_1, \ldots, M_n \rangle^{\Pi}$ *and* $\mathsf{In}_i^{\Sigma}(M)$ *for* $1 \leq i \leq n$, *and terms* $\mathsf{Split}(M, x_1. \ldots x_n.\, N)$ *and* $\mathsf{Case}(M, x_1.\, N_1, \ldots, x_n.\, N_n)$ *such that:*

$$\frac{\Gamma \vdash M_i : \sigma_i \quad (1 \leq i \leq n)}{\Gamma \vdash \langle M_1, \ldots, M_n \rangle^{\Pi} : \Pi} \qquad \frac{\Gamma \vdash M : \Pi \quad \Gamma, x_1{:}\sigma_1, \ldots, x_n{:}\sigma_n \vdash N : \tau}{\Gamma \vdash \mathsf{Split}(M, x_1. \ldots x_n.\, N) : \tau}$$

$$\frac{\Gamma \vdash M : \sigma_i}{\Gamma \vdash \mathsf{In}_i^{\Sigma}(M) : \Sigma} \qquad \frac{\Gamma \vdash M : \Sigma \quad \Gamma, x_i{:}\sigma_i \vdash N_i : \tau \quad (1 \leq i \leq n)}{\Gamma \vdash \mathsf{Case}(M, x_1.\, N_1, \ldots, x_n.\, N_n) : \tau}$$

$$\frac{M \Downarrow \langle M_1, \ldots, M_n \rangle^{\Pi}}{\mathsf{Split}(M, x_1. \ldots x_n.\, N) \to^+ N[^{M_1}\!/\!_{x_1}] \cdots [^{M_n}\!/\!_{x_n}]}$$

$$\frac{M \Downarrow \mathsf{In}_i^{\Sigma}(M)}{\mathsf{Case}(M, x_1.\, N_1, \ldots, x_n.\, N_n) \to^+ N_i[^M\!/\!_{x_i}]}$$

Proof. We can define the canonical terms as follows.

$$\langle M_1, \ldots, M_n \rangle^{(\sigma_1 \times \cdots \times \sigma_n)} \stackrel{\text{def}}{=} \begin{cases} * & \text{if } n = 0 \\ M_1 & \text{if } n = 1 \\ \langle M_1, \langle M_2, \ldots, M_{n-1} \rangle^{(\sigma_2 \cdots \times \sigma_n)} \rangle & \text{if } n > 1 \end{cases}$$

$$\mathsf{In}_i^{(\sigma_1 + \cdots + \sigma_n)}(M) \stackrel{\text{def}}{=} \begin{cases} M & \text{if } n = 1 \\ \mathsf{Inl}^{(\sigma_2 + \cdots + \sigma_n)}(M) & \text{if } n > 1,\, i = 1 \\ \mathsf{Inr}^{\sigma_1}(\mathsf{In}_{i-1}^{(\sigma_2 + \cdots + \sigma_n)}(M)) & \text{if } n > 1,\, i > 1 \end{cases}$$

Given these definitions, it is straightforward to define terms $\mathsf{Split}(M, x_1. \ldots x_n. N)$ and $\mathsf{Case}(M, x_1. N_1, \ldots, x_n. N_n)$, and to prove the desired properties.   ■

5.4   Booleans in $\mathcal{M}$

We define a boolean type Bool and two Bool-programs $\lfloor tt \rfloor$ and $\lfloor ff \rfloor$.

$$\mathsf{Bool} \stackrel{\text{def}}{=} 1 + 1$$
$$\lfloor tt \rfloor \stackrel{\text{def}}{=} \mathsf{Inl}(*)$$
$$\lfloor ff \rfloor \stackrel{\text{def}}{=} \mathsf{Inr}(*)$$

Proposition 5.5   *Any program of type Bool either equals $\lfloor tt \rfloor$ or $\lfloor ff \rfloor$. Moreover, $\lfloor tt \rfloor$ does not equal $\lfloor ff \rfloor$.*

Proof. Suppose M is a program of type $1 + 1$. By the exhaustion law, M either equals $\mathsf{Inl}(N)$ or $\mathsf{Inr}(N)$ for some 1-program N. By Proposition 5.3, program N equals $*$, so M either equals $\mathsf{Inl}(*)$ or $\mathsf{Inr}(*)$, that is, $\lfloor tt \rfloor$ or $\lfloor ff \rfloor$.

To show that $\lfloor tt \rfloor$ does not equal $\lfloor ff \rfloor$, proceed by contradiction and suppose that $\mathsf{Inl}(*) \simeq \mathsf{Inr}(*)$. By canonical freeness, $\mathsf{Inl}(*) \mathbin{\hat{\simeq}} \mathsf{Inr}(*)$. But there is no rule in Table 4.1 which could derive $\mathsf{Inl}(*) \mathbin{\hat{\simeq}} \mathsf{Inr}(*)$, since the two terms have different outermost constructors, Inl and Inr. Contradiction.   ■

We define the notation if M then N_1 else N_2 to mean $\mathsf{Case}(M, u. N_1, u. N_2)$, where variable $u \notin fv(N_i)$. The if-notation has the following properties:

Proposition 5.6

(1)   *The following type assignment rule is valid:*

$$\frac{\Gamma \vdash M : \mathsf{Bool} \qquad \Gamma \vdash N_i : \tau \quad (i = 1, 2)}{\Gamma \vdash \text{if} M \text{ then } N_1 \text{ else } N_2 : \tau}$$

(2)   *The operational behaviour is characterised by the following rules:*

$$\frac{M \simeq \lfloor tt \rfloor}{\text{if} M \text{ then } N_1 \text{ else } N_2 \rightarrow^+ N_1} \qquad \frac{M \simeq \lfloor ff \rfloor}{\text{if} M \text{ then } N_1 \text{ else } N_2 \rightarrow^+ N_2}$$

(3)   *The following equational laws are valid:*

$$\Gamma \vdash (\text{if} \lfloor tt \rfloor \text{ then } N_1 \text{ else } N_2) \simeq N_1$$
$$\Gamma \vdash (\text{if} \lfloor ff \rfloor \text{ then } N_1 \text{ else } N_2) \simeq N_2$$
$$\Gamma \vdash (\text{if} M \text{ then } N \text{ else } N) \simeq N$$

Proof. (1) Immediate. (2) In the first rule, since $M \simeq \lfloor tt \rfloor$, we have $M \Downarrow \mathsf{Inl}(L)$ for some 1-program L. So $\mathsf{Case}(M, u. N_1, u. N_2) \rightarrow^* \mathsf{Case}(\mathsf{Inl}(L), u. N_1, u. N_2) \rightarrow N_1$. The second rule follows by a similar argument. (3) These equations are simple consequences of the beta and eta laws in Table 5.1.   ■

5.5 Natural numbers in $\mathcal{M}$

We define a type Num and a Num-program $\lfloor n \rfloor$ for each natural number $n \in \mathbb{N}$.

$$\text{Num} \overset{\text{def}}{=} \mu X. 1 + X$$
$$\lfloor 0 \rfloor \overset{\text{def}}{=} \text{Intro}(\text{Inl}(*))$$
$$\lfloor n+1 \rfloor \overset{\text{def}}{=} \text{Intro}(\text{Inr}(\lfloor n \rfloor))$$

Proposition 5.7 *Any* Num-*program equals* $\lfloor n \rfloor$ *for some natural number* $n \in \mathbb{N}$*. Moreover* $\lfloor n \rfloor$ *does not equal* $\lfloor n+1 \rfloor$*, for any* $n \in \mathbb{N}$*.*

Proof. The second part follows easily from canonical freeness. For the first part, we define another extension, $\leadsto$, of the reduction relation on Num programs.

$$\frac{M \to N}{M \leadsto N} \qquad \frac{M \to N}{\text{Intro}(M) \leadsto \text{Intro}(M)} \qquad \frac{M \leadsto N}{\text{Intro}(\text{Inr}(M)) \leadsto \text{Intro}(\text{Inr}(N))}$$

Evidently $\leadsto$ is a partial function and is contained in $\simeq$. It is normalising in the sense that if M is a Num-program, there exists an $\leadsto$-normal form N such that $M \leadsto^* N$. The proof is by appeal to the embedding of $\mathcal{M}$ in $\mu\nu\lambda 2$ from Chapter 3, similar to Proposition 5.3. If Num-program M is $\leadsto$-normal, then it either takes the form $\text{Intro}(\text{Inl}(N))$, where $N{:}1$, or $\text{Intro}(\text{Inr}(N))$ where N is also $\leadsto$-normal. Hence for any $\leadsto$-normal form M there is a number n such that $M \simeq \lfloor n \rfloor$, by induction on the number of Intro's in M. Moreover, for an arbitrary Num-program M there is an $\leadsto$-normal form N such that $M \simeq N$ and hence a number n such that $M \simeq \lfloor n \rfloor$. ∎

Let $\sigma \rightharpoonup \tau$ abbreviate the partial function $\sigma \to \tau_\perp$. The next proposition provides a general method for defining partial functions by recursion.

Proposition 5.8 *For each term F that satisfies*

$$\Gamma \vdash F : (\sigma \rightharpoonup \tau) \to (\sigma \rightharpoonup \tau)$$

there is a term Rec F *such that*

$$\Gamma \vdash \text{Rec } F : \sigma \rightharpoonup \tau$$

and, if F is a program

$$(\text{Rec } F)\, M \to^+ F\, (\text{Rec } F)\, M$$

for any program $M{:}\sigma$.

Proof. Let terms REC F and Rec F with types $(\sigma \rightharpoonup \tau)_\perp$ and $\sigma \rightharpoonup \tau$ respectively be as follows.

$$\text{REC } F \overset{\text{def}}{=} \text{Fix}(fx.\ \text{Lift}\ (\lambda x{:}\sigma.\ \text{Seq}\ (fx, g.\ F\, g\, x)))$$
$$\text{Rec } F \overset{\text{def}}{=} \lambda x{:}\sigma.\ \text{Seq}\ (\text{REC } F, g.\ F\, g\, x)$$

One can easily verify that $\mathsf{Rec}\,F$ is of the desired type. Now, suppose that M is a program of type $\sigma \rightharpoonup \tau$. We may calculate as follows.

$$
\begin{aligned}
\mathsf{REC}\,F &\equiv \mathsf{Fix}(fx.\ \mathsf{Lift}\,(\lambda x{:}\sigma.\ \mathsf{Seq}\,(fx, g.\,F\,g\,x))) \\
&\to \mathsf{Lift}(\lambda x{:}\sigma.\ \mathsf{Seq}\,(\mathsf{REC}\,F, g.\,F\,g\,x)) \\
&\equiv \mathsf{Lift}(\mathsf{Rec}\,F) \\
(\mathsf{Rec}\,F)\,M &\equiv (\lambda x{:}\sigma.\ \mathsf{Seq}\,(\mathsf{REC}\,F, g.\,F\,g\,x))\,M \\
&\to \mathsf{Seq}(\mathsf{REC}\,F, g.\,F\,g\,M) \\
&\to \mathsf{Seq}(\mathsf{Lift}(\mathsf{Rec}\,F), g.\,F\,g\,M) \\
&\to F\,(\mathsf{Rec}\,F)\,M
\end{aligned}
$$

Hence we have the desired reduction behaviour.   ∎

In order to define the elementary arithmetic operations needed in the denotational semantics of $\mathcal{H}$, we need the following programs.

$$
\begin{aligned}
\mathsf{Succ} &\overset{\text{def}}{=} \lambda x{:}\mathsf{Num}.\ \mathsf{Lift}\,(\mathsf{Intro}(\mathsf{Inr}(x))) \\
\mathsf{Pred} &\overset{\text{def}}{=} \lambda x{:}\mathsf{Num}.\ \mathsf{Case}\,(\mathsf{Elim}(x), u.\ \mathsf{Lift}\,\lfloor 0 \rfloor, y.\ \mathsf{Lift}\,(y)) \\
\mathsf{Iter}^{\sigma}(Z, F) &\overset{\text{def}}{=} \mathsf{Rec}(\lambda g{:}\mathsf{Num} \rightharpoonup \sigma.\ \lambda y{:}\mathsf{Num}. \\
&\qquad \mathsf{Case}(\mathsf{Elim}(y), u.\ \mathsf{Lift}\,(Z), y'.\ \mathsf{Seq}\,(g\,y', x.\,F\,x)))
\end{aligned}
$$

Proposition 5.9

(1) *The type assignments*

$$
\begin{aligned}
\mathsf{Succ} &:\ \mathsf{Num} \rightharpoonup \mathsf{Num} \\
\mathsf{Pred} &:\ \mathsf{Num} \rightharpoonup \mathsf{Num}
\end{aligned}
$$

and

$$
\frac{\Gamma \vdash Z : \sigma \qquad \Gamma \vdash F : \sigma \rightharpoonup \sigma}{\Gamma \vdash \mathsf{Iter}^{\sigma}(Z, F) : \mathsf{Num} \rightharpoonup \sigma}
$$

are valid.

(2) *These programs have the following reduction behaviour, where* $\varnothing \vdash Z : \sigma$ *and* $\varnothing \vdash F : \sigma \rightharpoonup \sigma$.

$$
\begin{aligned}
\mathsf{Succ}\,\lfloor n \rfloor &\Downarrow \mathsf{Lift}(\lfloor n + 1 \rfloor) \\
\mathsf{Pred}\,\lfloor 0 \rfloor &\Downarrow \mathsf{Lift}(\lfloor 0 \rfloor) \\
\mathsf{Pred}\,\lfloor n + 1 \rfloor &\Downarrow \mathsf{Lift}(\lfloor n \rfloor) \\
\mathsf{Iter}^{\sigma}(Z, F)\,\lfloor 0 \rfloor &\to^{+} \mathsf{Lift}(Z) \\
\mathsf{Iter}^{\sigma}(Z, F)\,\lfloor n + 1 \rfloor &\to^{+} \mathsf{Seq}(\mathsf{Iter}^{\sigma}(Z, F)\,\lfloor n \rfloor, x.\,F\,x)
\end{aligned}
$$

Proof. (1) By inspection. (2) From the beta rules of Table 5.1. We calculate the last two properties. For any m we have

$$
\mathsf{Iter}^{\sigma}(Z, F)\,\lfloor m \rfloor \to^{+} \mathsf{Case}(\mathsf{Elim}\,\lfloor m \rfloor, u.\ \mathsf{Lift}\,(Z), y'.\ \mathsf{Seq}\,(\mathsf{Iter}^{\sigma}(Z, F)\,y', x.\,F\,x)).
$$

When $m = 0$ we have

$$
\mathsf{Iter}^{\sigma}(Z, F)\,\lfloor m \rfloor \to^{+} \mathsf{Lift}(Z)
$$

and when $m = n + 1$

$$
\mathsf{Iter}^{\sigma}(Z, F)\,\lfloor m \rfloor \to^{+} \mathsf{Seq}(\mathsf{Iter}^{\sigma}(Z, F)\,\lfloor n \rfloor, x.\,F\,x)
$$

as required. The other equations are no harder to prove. ∎

We can define some simple arithmetic operations:

$$M\lfloor+\rfloor N \stackrel{\text{def}}{=} \text{Iter}^{\text{Num}}(M, \text{Succ})\, N$$
$$M\lfloor-\rfloor N \stackrel{\text{def}}{=} \text{Iter}^{\text{Num}}(M, \text{Pred})\, N$$
$$M\lfloor\times\rfloor N \stackrel{\text{def}}{=} \text{Iter}^{\text{Num}}(\lfloor 0\rfloor, \lambda x.\, x\lfloor+\rfloor M)\, N$$
$$\text{Iszero}(M) \stackrel{\text{def}}{=} \text{Case}(\text{Elim}(M), y_1.\, \lfloor tt\rfloor, y_2.\, \lfloor ff\rfloor)$$
$$M\lfloor<\rfloor N \stackrel{\text{def}}{=} \text{Seq}(N\lfloor-\rfloor M, x.\ \text{if Iszero}(x) \text{ then Lift}(\lfloor ff\rfloor) \text{ else Lift}(\lfloor tt\rfloor))$$
$$M\lfloor=\rfloor N \stackrel{\text{def}}{=} \text{Seq}(M\lfloor<\rfloor N, b.\ \text{if } b \text{ then Lift}(\lfloor ff\rfloor)\text{else}$$
$$\text{Seq}(N\lfloor<\rfloor M, b.\ \text{if } b \text{ then Lift}(\lfloor ff\rfloor) \text{ else Lift}(\lfloor tt\rfloor)))$$

Proposition 5.10

(1) $\lfloor m\rfloor\lfloor+\rfloor\lfloor n\rfloor \Downarrow \text{Lift}(\lfloor m+n\rfloor)$

(2) $\lfloor m\rfloor\lfloor-\rfloor\lfloor n\rfloor \Downarrow \text{Lift}(\lfloor m-n\rfloor)$

(3) $\lfloor m\rfloor\lfloor\times\rfloor\lfloor n\rfloor \Downarrow \text{Lift}(\lfloor m\times n\rfloor)$

(4) $\text{Iszero}(\lfloor 0\rfloor) \Downarrow \lfloor tt\rfloor$

(5) $\text{Iszero}(\lfloor n+1\rfloor) \Downarrow \lfloor ff\rfloor$

(6) $\lfloor m\rfloor\lfloor<\rfloor\lfloor n\rfloor \Downarrow \text{Lift}(\lfloor tt\rfloor)$ *if* $m < n$

(7) $\lfloor m\rfloor\lfloor<\rfloor\lfloor n\rfloor \Downarrow \text{Lift}(\lfloor ff\rfloor)$ *if* $n \leq m$

(8) $\lfloor m\rfloor\lfloor=\rfloor\lfloor m\rfloor \Downarrow \text{Lift}(\lfloor tt\rfloor)$

(9) $\lfloor m\rfloor\lfloor=\rfloor\lfloor n\rfloor \Downarrow \text{Lift}(\lfloor ff\rfloor)$ *if* $m \neq n$

Proof. From the previous proposition by inductive arguments. ∎

Chapter 6

An operational theory of functional programming

The second half of this dissertation, which begins with this chapter, examines a small functional language called $\mathcal{H}$, and considers how theories for various forms of functional I/O can be based on a theory of $\mathcal{H}$. This chapter shows how to develop an operational theory of programming for $\mathcal{H}$. Two parallel theories are developed: one based directly on an operational semantics of $\mathcal{H}$; the other based on a denotational semantics of $\mathcal{H}$ in $\mathcal{M}$. The former has been developed from first principles in this dissertation, whereas the latter depends ultimately on Mendler's result assumed in Chapter 2. This chapter is one of the most important in the dissertation because of its potential applications far beyond the study of functional I/O.

$\mathcal{H}$ is essentially a fragment of Haskell. $\mathcal{H}$ contains the basic data and control constructs of lazy functional programming—natural numbers, booleans, functions, recursion and lazy algebraic types—but is small enough that its theory can be developed in this chapter. We omit from $\mathcal{H}$ many constructs needed for practical programming but which are irrelevant to the study of functional I/O—such as polymorphic types, type inference, modules and realistic arithmetic.

In §6.1 we define syntax and typing rules for the object language $\mathcal{H}$. The abstract syntax of $\mathcal{H}$ is rather restrictive compared to Haskell notation. We show informally how certain Haskell notations may be interpreted as $\mathcal{H}$ programs. This interpretation allows us to use Haskell notation in Chapters 7 and 8 for $\mathcal{H}$ in our development of theories of functional I/O. In a study like this which is meant to be relevant to practical programming, it is good methodology to work with as realistic a notation as possible. Another merit of using Haskell notation is that programs can be type checked and executed.[1]

We follow the pattern set by Plotkin [120] and give two semantics for $\mathcal{H}$: a deterministic lazy operational semantics and a denotational semantics in terms of the metalanguage $\mathcal{M}$. The style of denotational semantics is greatly influenced by the work of Moggi [100, 101] and Pitts [112] on the computational λ-calculus as a semantic metalanguage. The most striking difference between the computational λ-calculus and $\mathcal{M}$ is that the former's se-

---

[1] We have used Mark Jones' Gofer system and also an implementation of $\mathcal{H}$ on top of Standard ML.

mantics is ultimately domain-theoretic whereas the latter's semantics is entirely operational. We finish §6.1 by proving a correspondence theorem between the operational and denotational semantics: that evaluation of any $\mathcal{H}$ term e is exactly matched by evaluation of its $\mathcal{M}$ denotation $[\![e]\!]$.

We base our theory of functional programming on equivalence of $\mathcal{H}$ terms. §6.2 develops notions of ground and confined relations. We develop two relations: operational equivalence and denotational equivalence. §6.3 develops operational equivalence directly from the operational semantics of $\mathcal{H}$. We prove that operational equivalence for $\mathcal{H}$ is a congruence using Howe's method, just as we proved the same result for $\mathcal{M}$ in Chapter 4. §6.4 defines denotational equivalence as the equivalence relation induced on $\mathcal{H}$ terms from the denotational semantics in $\mathcal{M}$. The main result of the section is a soundness theorem, that denotational equivalence implies operational equivalence. We leave open the converse, full abstraction.

In §6.5 we state a collection of basic programming laws, and show that they are valid for both operational and denotational equivalence. §6.6 shows how a further collection of laws and proof principles follow from the basic programming laws of the previous section. The theory of functional programming developed in §6.5 and §6.6 is entirely operational, in that it rests on operational equivalences defined from the operational semantics of either $\mathcal{M}$ or $\mathcal{H}$.

Finally, §6.7 considers what happens to the theory of functional programming if an exception mechanism is added to $\mathcal{H}$. The resulting language is called $\mathcal{HX}$ and is needed in Chapter 7 in the study of Landin-stream I/O.

6.1 $\mathcal{H}$, a small functional language

Table 6.1 shows the abstract syntax of $\mathcal{H}$, essentially a fragment of Haskell. The only construct of $\mathcal{H}$ not present in Haskell is call-by-value function application, $(e_1 \,\hat{}\, e_2)$. Call-by-value is included in $\mathcal{H}$ because of the control it gives over evaluation order; such control is useful when I/O is expressed using side-effects.

We assume countably infinite sets of type variables and term variables ranged over by metavariables X, Y, $Z \ldots$ and x, y, $z \ldots$ respectively. We assume there is a countably infinite set of **value constructors**, ranged over by metavariable K. There are six categories of abstract syntax: **types**, σ, τ, $\ldots$; **algebraic datatypes**, μ; **data-clauses**, dc; **canonical terms**, c; **terms**, e, p, q; and **case-clauses**, cc. Binding occurrences of type and value variables are indicated in Table 6.1. The notations and conventions concerning variables, substitution and alpha-conversion stated in §1.8 apply to $\mathcal{H}$.

We let metavariable ℓ ranges over the set of literals, $\{tt, f\!f\} \cup \mathbb{N}$. We use metavariable $\oplus$ to range over the arithmetic operators $\{+, -, \times, =, <\}$. An $\mathcal{H}$ literal or operator is written as ℓ or $\oplus$; the corresponding canonical program in the metalanguage is written $\lfloor \ell \rfloor$ or $\lfloor \oplus \rfloor$ respectively. The $\mathcal{H}$ type Int includes just the natural numbers; we call this type Int for the sake of compatibility with Haskell.

Suppose that μ is the algebraic type $(\mathsf{data}\, X = \mathsf{dc}_1 \mid \cdots \mid \mathsf{dc}_n)$. Then define functions

Syntax

$\sigma, \tau ::= $	X	(type variable)
	$\mathtt{Bool}$	(booleans)
	$\mathtt{Int}$	(natural numbers)
	$(\sigma_1 \mathtt{\,->\,} \sigma_2)$	(functions)
	μ	(algebraic datatype)
$\mu ::= $	$(\mathtt{data}\, X = \mathtt{dc}_1 \mid \cdots \mid \mathtt{dc}_n)$	(algebraic datatype, $n > 0$, $Con(\mathtt{dc}_i) = Con(\mathtt{dc}_j)$ iff $i = j$, X bound in each $\mathtt{dc}_i$)
$\mathtt{dc} ::= $	$(K\, \sigma_1 \cdots \sigma_m)$	(data-clause, $m \geq 0$)
$\mathtt{c} ::= $	ℓ	(literal, $\ell \in \{tt, f\!f\} \cup \mathbb{N}$)
	$(\backslash x{::}\sigma \mathtt{\,->\,} e)$	(abstraction, x bound in e)
	$(K^\mu\, e_1 \cdots e_m)$	(constructor application, $m \geq 0$)
$e ::= $	x	(value variable)
	c	(canonical expression)
	$(\mathtt{if}\, e_1 \,\mathtt{then}\, e_2 \,\mathtt{else}\, e_3)$	(conditional)
	$(e_1 \oplus e_2)$	(arithmetic, $\oplus \in \{+, -, \times, =, <\}$)
	$(e_1\, e_2)$	(call-by-name application)
	$(e_1 \,\hat{}\, e_2)$	(call-by-value application)
	$\mathtt{rec}^\sigma (x.\, e)$	(recursion, x bound in e)
	$(\mathtt{case}^\mu\, e \,\mathtt{of}\, cc_1 \mid \cdots \mid cc_n)$	(case-expression, $n > 0$)
$cc ::= $	$(K \mathtt{\,->\,} e)$	(case-clause)

Table 6.1: Syntax of $\mathcal{H}$

$Con(\mathtt{dc})$, $Rank(K, \mu)$ and $Arity(K, \mu)$ as follows:

$$Con(K\, \sigma_1 \cdots \sigma_m) \stackrel{\text{def}}{=} K$$
$$Rank(K, \mu) \stackrel{\text{def}}{=} i \quad \text{if } K = Con(\mathtt{dc}_i)$$
$$Arity(K, \mu) \stackrel{\text{def}}{=} m \quad \text{if } \mathtt{dc}_i \equiv (K\, \sigma_1 \cdots \sigma_m)$$

Operations $Rank$ and $Arity$ are well-defined functions because the side-condition on algebraic types in Table 6.1 requires that no two **data**-clauses contain the same constructor.

We place a further well-formedness condition on algebraic types: in any algebraic type $(\mathtt{data}\, X = \mathtt{dc}_1 \mid \cdots \mid \mathtt{dc}_n)$, for each clause $\mathtt{dc}_i \equiv (K\, \sigma_1 \cdots \sigma_m)$, in each type σ_j we insist that the type variable X occurs positively in each σ_j, and that the only type variable free in σ_j is X. A type variable X **occurs positively** in a type τ iff each occurrence of X in τ is to the left of an even number of function **->**'s. The only reason we make this restriction is so that the types of $\mathcal{H}$ can be mapped into well-formed types of $\mathcal{M}$. We implicitly assume that any $\mathcal{H}$ type we deal with is well-formed. Just as in $\mathcal{M}$, the set of well-formed types is closed under substitution.

Type assignment in $\mathcal{H}$

An **environment** Γ is a list of variables paired with closed types, written $x_1{::}\sigma_1, \ldots, x_n{::}\sigma_n$, where the variables are pairwise distinct.[2] We adopt the same no-

---

[2] We follow Haskell in using the symbol :: for type assignment.

Type Assignment

$$\ell \in \{T, F\} \qquad n \in \mathbb{N}$$

$$\frac{}{\Gamma, x{::}\sigma \vdash x :: \sigma} \qquad \frac{}{\Gamma \vdash \underline{\ell} :: \texttt{Bool}} \qquad \frac{}{\Gamma \vdash \underline{n} :: \texttt{Int}}$$

$$\frac{\Gamma \vdash e_1 :: \texttt{Bool} \qquad \Gamma \vdash e_2 :: \tau \qquad \Gamma \vdash e_3 :: \tau}{\Gamma \vdash (\texttt{if } e_1 \texttt{ then } e_2 \texttt{ else } e_3) :: \tau}$$

$$\frac{\Gamma \vdash e_1 :: \texttt{Int} \qquad \Gamma \vdash e_2 :: \texttt{Int}}{\Gamma \vdash (e_1 \oplus e_2) :: \texttt{Int}} \quad \oplus \in \{+, -, \times\}$$

$$\frac{\Gamma \vdash e_1 :: \texttt{Int} \qquad \Gamma \vdash e_2 :: \texttt{Int}}{\Gamma \vdash (e_1 \oplus e_2) :: \texttt{Bool}} \quad \oplus \in \{<, =\}$$

$$\frac{\Gamma, x{::}\sigma \vdash e :: \tau}{\Gamma \vdash (\backslash x{::}\sigma \texttt{ -> } e) :: (\sigma \texttt{ -> } \tau)} \qquad \frac{\Gamma \vdash e_1 :: (\sigma \texttt{ -> } \tau) \qquad \Gamma \vdash e_2 :: \sigma}{\Gamma \vdash (e_1 \, e_2) :: \tau}$$

$$\frac{\Gamma \vdash e_1 :: (\sigma \texttt{ -> } \tau) \qquad \Gamma \vdash e_2 :: \sigma}{\Gamma \vdash (e_1 \hat{\ } e_2) :: \tau} \qquad \frac{\Gamma, x{::}\sigma \vdash e :: \sigma}{\Gamma \vdash \texttt{rec}^\sigma(x.e) :: \sigma}$$

$$\frac{\Gamma \vdash e_j :: (\sigma_j[\mu/X]) \quad (1 \le j \le m)}{\Gamma \vdash (K^\mu \, e_1 \, \cdots \, e_m) :: \mu} \left\{ \begin{array}{l} \mu \equiv (\texttt{data } X = \texttt{dc}_1 \mid \cdots \mid \texttt{dc}_n) \\ \texttt{dc}_i \equiv (K \, \sigma_1 \cdots \sigma_m) \end{array} \right.$$

$$\frac{\Gamma \vdash e :: (\sigma_1 \texttt{ -> } \cdots \texttt{ -> } \sigma_m \texttt{ -> } \tau)}{\Gamma \vdash (K \texttt{ -> } e), (K \, \sigma_1 \cdots \sigma_m) :: \tau} \quad (*)$$

$$\frac{\Gamma \vdash e :: \mu \qquad \Gamma \vdash \texttt{cc}_i, (\texttt{dc}_i[\mu/X]) :: \tau \quad (1 \le i \le n)}{\Gamma \vdash (\texttt{case}^\mu e \texttt{ of } \texttt{cc}_1 \mid \cdots \mid \texttt{cc}_n) :: \tau} \quad \mu \equiv (\texttt{data } X = \texttt{dc}_1 \mid \cdots \mid \texttt{dc}_n)$$

Canonical Terms

If $c{::}\texttt{Bool}$ then $\exists b \in \{tt, ff\}. c \equiv \underline{b}$.

If $c{::}\texttt{Int}$ then $\exists n \in \mathbb{N}. c \equiv \underline{n}$.

If $c{::}(\sigma \texttt{ -> } \tau)$ then $\exists e. c \equiv (\backslash x \texttt{ -> } e)$.

If $c{::}\mu$ then $\exists K, e_1, \ldots, e_m. c \equiv (K \, e_1 \, \cdots \, e_m)$.

Table 6.2: Type assignment rules for $\mathcal{H}$

tational conventions as defined for $\mathcal{M}$ environments at the beginning of §3.2.

Definition 6.1 *The $\mathcal{H}$ type assignment relation, $\Gamma \vdash e :: \sigma$, is inductively defined by the rules in Table 6.2, which make use of an auxiliary relation $\Gamma \vdash cc, dc :: \sigma$ defined in the rule marked with $(*)$. Each rule bears the implicit side-condition that any environments appearing in the rule are well-formed.*

Proposition 6.2

(1) *If $\Gamma \vdash e :: \tau$ and $\Gamma \vdash e :: \sigma$ then $\tau \equiv \sigma$.*

(2) *If $\Gamma \vdash e :: \tau$ and $\Gamma \subseteq \Gamma'$ then $\Gamma' \vdash e :: \tau$.*

(3) *If $\Gamma, x::\sigma \vdash e_1 :: \tau$ and $\Gamma \vdash e_2 :: \sigma$ then $\Gamma \vdash e_1[e_2/x] :: \tau$.*

(4) *If $\Gamma \vdash e :: \tau$ then $fv(e) \subseteq Dom(\Gamma)$.*

(5) *The statements about canonical terms in Table 6.2 are true.*

(6) *If $\Gamma \vdash e :: \tau$ then $ftv(e, \tau) = \varnothing$.*

Proof. Easy rule inductions. Part (6) depends on the fact that no type variable can occur free in a type in the range of an environment, and that the environments used to derive the type assignment relation must be well-formed. ∎

We define classes of programs and confined terms:

Definition 6.3

(1) *A **program** is a term e such that $\varnothing \vdash e :: \tau$ for some (necessarily unique) type τ. The type τ is called the **type of** e, which is called a τ-**program**.*

(2) *A **confined term** is a pair $(\Gamma \vdash e)$ such that there is a (necessarily unique) type τ such that $\Gamma \vdash e :: \tau$. The type τ is called the **type of** $(\Gamma \vdash e)$ and Γ is called the **environment of** $(\Gamma \vdash e)$.*

Just as in $\mathcal{M}$, the syntax of $\mathcal{H}$ carries enough type information that any program has a unique type. We often omit type information from terms.

Interpreting Haskell in $\mathcal{H}$

We show in this section how some Haskell notations absent from $\mathcal{H}$ can nevertheless be interpreted as derived forms of $\mathcal{H}$. For tutorial and reference material on Haskell we refer the reader to the Haskell report [59] and to Fasel and Hudak's tutorial [37]. We shall use a Haskell-like notation for the programming examples in the remainder of this dissertation. We do not attempt a formal description of how Haskell can be interpreted in $\mathcal{H}$, but instead give a series of illustrative examples. Descriptions of similar interpretations are well-known; for instance, Peyton Jones' textbook [109] discusses in detail how Miranda can be translated into a λ-calculus notation of about the same level as $\mathcal{H}$.

We will use the letters a, b and c to stand for closed types of $\mathcal{H}$. Type and value definitions in Haskell may be polymorphic: that is, they may depend on one or more type parameters. We interpret such definitions in $\mathcal{H}$ as defining families of closed types or terms indexed by the type parameters. Here are three examples, the second of which also illustrates how

```
id              :: a -> a
id x             = x

fst             :: (a,b) -> a
fst (a,b)        = a

snd             :: (a,b) -> b
snd (a,b)        = b

const           :: a -> b -> a
const a b        = a

curry           :: ((a,b) -> c) -> a -> b -> c
curry f a b      =  f (a,b)

uncurry         :: (a -> b -> c) -> (a,b) -> c
uncurry f ab     = f (fst ab) (snd ab)

(.)             :: (b -> c) -> (a -> b) -> (a -> c)
(f . g) x        = f (g x)

head            :: [a] -> a
head (x:xs)      = x

tail            :: [a] -> [a]
tail (x:xs)      = xs

(++)            :: [a] -> [a] -> [a]
[]      ++ ys    = ys
(x:xs) ++ ys     = x:(xs++ys)

map             :: (a -> b) -> [a] -> [b]
map f []         = []
map f (x:xs)     = f x : map f xs

iterate         :: (a -> a) -> a -> [a]
iterate f x      = x : iterate f (f x)

foldr             :: (a -> b -> b) -> b -> [a] -> b
foldr f z []        = z
foldr f z (x:xs)  = f x (foldr f z xs)
```

Table 6.3: Some standard functions

$$
\begin{aligned}
\text{id} &\overset{\text{def}}{=} (\backslash x \mathbin{\text{-}\!\!>} x) \\
\text{fst} &\overset{\text{def}}{=} (\backslash ab \mathbin{\text{-}\!\!>} \text{case } ab \text{ of } \text{Tuple2 } a\, b \mathbin{\text{-}\!\!>} a) \\
\text{snd} &\overset{\text{def}}{=} (\backslash ab \mathbin{\text{-}\!\!>} \text{case } ab \text{ of } \text{Tuple2 } a\, b \mathbin{\text{-}\!\!>} b) \\
\text{const} &\overset{\text{def}}{=} (\backslash a \mathbin{\text{-}\!\!>} \backslash b \mathbin{\text{-}\!\!>} a) \\
\text{curry} &\overset{\text{def}}{=} (\backslash f \mathbin{\text{-}\!\!>} \backslash a \mathbin{\text{-}\!\!>} \backslash b \mathbin{\text{-}\!\!>} f\,(a,b)) \\
\text{uncurry} &\overset{\text{def}}{=} (\backslash f \mathbin{\text{-}\!\!>} \backslash ab \mathbin{\text{-}\!\!>} f\,(\text{fst } ab)\,(\text{snd } ab)) \\
(.) &\overset{\text{def}}{=} (\backslash f \mathbin{\text{-}\!\!>} \backslash g \mathbin{\text{-}\!\!>} \backslash x \mathbin{\text{-}\!\!>} f(g\,x))
\end{aligned}
$$

head $\overset{\text{def}}{=}$ (\xs -> case xs of
      Nil -> Ω
      Cons x xs -> x)

tail $\overset{\text{def}}{=}$ (\xs -> case xs of
      Nil -> Ω
      Cons x xs -> xs)

(++) $\overset{\text{def}}{=}$ rec(app. \xs -> \ys -> case xs of
         Nil -> ys
         Cons x xs -> Cons x (app xs ys))

map $\overset{\text{def}}{=}$ rec(map. \f -> \xs -> case xs of
         Nil -> Nil
         Cons x xs -> Cons (f x) (map f xs))

iterate $\overset{\text{def}}{=}$ rec(iterate. \f -> \x -> Cons x (iterate f (f x)))

foldr $\overset{\text{def}}{=}$ rec(foldr. \f -> \z -> \xs -> case xs of
         Nil -> z
         Cons x xs -> f x (foldr f z xs))

Table 6.4: Interpretations of Haskell functions in ℋ

Haskell-style algebraic datatypes are interpreted in $\mathcal{H}$:

Polymorphic Haskell definition	Interpretation in $\mathcal{H}$
`type Endo a = a -> a`	$\text{Endo}^{\text{a}} \stackrel{\text{def}}{=} (\text{a -> a})$
`data List a = Nil	Cons a (List a)`	$\text{List}^{\text{a}} \stackrel{\text{def}}{=} (\text{data}\, X = \text{Nil} \mid \text{Cons}\, \text{a}\, X)$
`id :: a -> a`	$\text{id}^{\text{a}} \stackrel{\text{def}}{=} (\text{\textbackslash x::a -> x})$
`id = (\x -> x)`	

We use notation in typewriter font for $\mathcal{H}$ literals: for instance, interpret `True`, `False`, `563`, `1441` and `+` as the boolean literals $\underline{tt}$ and $\underline{ff}$, the numeric literals $\underline{563}$ and $\underline{1441}$ and the addition operator $\underline{+}$, respectively.

Write `[a]` as an abbreviation for `List a`. Define:

$$[] \stackrel{\text{def}}{=} \text{Nil} \qquad \text{(empty list)}$$
$$[e_1, \ldots, e_{n+1}] \stackrel{\text{def}}{=} (\text{Cons}\, e_1\, [e_2, \ldots, e_{n+1}]) \quad \text{(non-empty list)}$$
$$(e : e') \stackrel{\text{def}}{=} (\text{Cons}\, e\, e') \qquad \text{(infix cons)}$$

Define a series of polymorphic tuple types, indexed by $m \neq 1$:

```
data Tuplem a1 ... am = Tuplem a1 ... am
```

Define the following abbreviations for tuples, where $m \neq 1$:

$$(a_1, \ldots, a_m) \stackrel{\text{def}}{=} (\text{Tuplem}\, a_1 \cdots a_m) \qquad (m\text{-tuple type})$$
$$(e_1, \ldots, e_m) \stackrel{\text{def}}{=} (\text{Tuplem}\, e_1 \ldots e_m) \qquad \text{(tuple)}$$
$$(\text{\textbackslash}(x_1, \ldots, x_m) \text{-> e}) \stackrel{\text{def}}{=} (\text{\textbackslash}y \text{-> case } y \text{ of} \qquad \text{(tupled abstraction,)}$$
$$\text{Tuplem}\, x_1 \cdots x_m \text{-> e}) \qquad y \notin fv(e))$$

The 0-tuple type, (), is called the unit type.

To discuss teletype I/O we need to support the Haskell type `Char` of ASCII characters. For the benefit of simplicity (at the cost of cavalier software engineering) we define `Char` to be `Int`. We interpret any Haskell character notation to be $\underline{n}$, where n is the ASCII code for the character. For instance, `'a'`, `'0'` and `'\n'` are interpreted as $\underline{65}$, $\underline{48}$ and $\underline{10}$ respectively. We interpret the Haskell functions `ord:Char -> Int` and `chr:Int -> Char` as the identity function, `id`. We define a type of strings as in Haskell:

```
type String = [Char]
```

To illustrate how Haskell function definitions are to be interpreted in $\mathcal{H}$, we show in Table 6.3 some standard function definitions. Each of these function definitions can be interpreted as an $\mathcal{H}$ definition as shown in Table 6.4. Let $\mathcal{H}$ program $\Omega^\sigma \stackrel{\text{def}}{=} \text{rec}^\sigma(x.x)$. We use Ω to represent undefined values (as in `head` or `tail`). The `case`-clauses in Table 6.4 use a derived syntax:

$$(K\, x_1 \ldots x_n \text{-> e}) \stackrel{\text{def}}{=} (K \text{-> \textbackslash} x_1 \text{-> } \ldots \text{\textbackslash} x_n \text{-> e})$$

Indentation is used instead of | symbols to separate multiple `case`-clauses. Using the theory developed later in this chapter, one can check that any of the definitions in Table 6.3, when treated as an equation between programs, is provable from the corresponding $\mathcal{H}$ definition in Table 6.4.

Expressions in Haskell may contain local definitions. An expression (e where $x = $ e′) is to be interpreted as the $\mathcal{H}$ expression $(\backslash x \texttt{->} \text{e})(\text{e}')$. A Haskell list-comprehension of the form [e | x -> e′] is interpreted in $\mathcal{H}$ as $(\texttt{map}\,(\backslash x \texttt{->} \text{e})\,\text{e}')$.

Operational semantics of $\mathcal{H}$

The operational semantics of $\mathcal{H}$ is deterministic, and lazy in the sense that constructors of algebraic types do not evaluate their arguments.

Definition 6.4 **Left** and **right experiments**, *LE and RE respectively, are functions from terms to terms defined by the grammar at the top of Table 6.5. A left experiment defines the leftmost position in a term where a reduction may occur. A right experiment defines a position in a term where a reduction may occur provided terms to its left are canonical. These are analogous to experiments in $\mathcal{M}$, Definition 3.4.*

*The **reduction** and **evaluation relations** for $\mathcal{H}$ are the binary relations on $\mathcal{H}$ programs, $\rightarrow$ and $\Downarrow$ respectively, defined inductively by the rules Table 6.5.*

Proposition 6.5

(1) *If $\varnothing \vdash$ e :: τ and e $\rightarrow$ e′ then $\varnothing \vdash$ e′ :: τ.*

(2) *If $\varnothing \vdash$ e :: τ and e $\Downarrow$ e′ then $\varnothing \vdash$ e′ :: τ.*

(3) *If e $\rightarrow$ e′ and e $\rightarrow$ e″ then e′ $\equiv$ e″.*

(4) *If e $\Downarrow$ c and e $\Downarrow$ c′ then c $\equiv$ c′.*

(5) *The canonical terms are the normal forms of reduction.*

(6) *If e $\Downarrow$ c then e $\rightarrow^*$ c.*

(7) *Suppose e $\rightarrow$ e′. Then for any c, e′ $\Downarrow$ c implies e $\Downarrow$ c.*

(8) *e $\rightarrow^*$ c iff e $\Downarrow$ c.*

Proof. Similar to the proof of Proposition 3.5. ∎

We define terminology for termination of evaluation:

Definition 6.6 *Suppose e is a program. Say that e **converges** and write e$\Downarrow$ iff there is a (necessarily unique) canonical program c such that e $\Downarrow$ c. Conversely, say that e **diverges** and write e$\Uparrow$ iff e does not converge.*

Recall the program Ω^{a} defined earlier to be $\textbf{rec}^{\text{a}}(x.\,x)$, at each closed type **a**. We have $\Omega^{\text{a}} \rightarrow \Omega^{\text{a}}$; hence there is a divergent program at every closed type of $\mathcal{H}$.

Denotational semantics of $\mathcal{H}$

The denotational semantics of the object language $\mathcal{H}$ is given using $\mathcal{M}$ as a metalanguage. The semantics is based on that of TINY-ML given by Pitts [112]. Classical domain-theoretic semantics [118, 134] use explicit environments to model the binding of object variables to their values. (These environments are typically denoted by the metavariable ρ, and are not to be confused with the environments denoted by Γ here.) Following

Reduction Semantics

$$LE ::= (\text{if} \cdot \text{then} e_2 \text{ else } e_2) \mid (\cdot \oplus e) \mid (\cdot \; e) \mid (\cdot \hat{} \; e) \mid (\text{case} \cdot \text{of} cc_1 \mid \cdots \mid cc_n)$$

$$RE ::= (\ell \oplus \cdot) \mid ((\backslash x \to e)\hat{}\cdot)$$

$$(\text{if } \underline{tt} \text{ then } e_2 \text{ else } e_3) \to e_2$$

$$(\text{if } \underline{ff} \text{ then } e_2 \text{ else } e_3) \to e_3$$

$$(\underline{\ell_1} \oplus \underline{\ell_2}) \to \underline{\ell_1 \oplus \ell_2}$$

$$(\backslash x{::}\sigma \to e_1) \, e_2 \to e_1[e_2/x]$$

$$(\backslash x{::}\sigma \to e)\hat{} \, c \to e[c/x]$$

$$rec(x.\,e) \to e[rec(x.\,e)/x]$$

$$\frac{cc_{Rank(K,\mu)} \equiv (K \to e')}{(\text{case}(K^\mu \, e_1 \cdots e_m) \text{ of } cc_1 \mid \cdots \mid cc_n) \to (e' \, e_1 \cdots e_m)}$$

$$\frac{e \to e'}{LE(e) \to LE(e')} \qquad \frac{e \to e'}{RE(e) \to RE(e')}$$

Evaluation Semantics

$$c \Downarrow c$$

$$\frac{e_1 \Downarrow \underline{tt} \qquad e_2 \Downarrow c}{(\text{if } e_1 \text{ then } e_2 \text{ else } e_3) \Downarrow c} \qquad \frac{e_1 \Downarrow \underline{ff} \qquad e_3 \Downarrow c}{(\text{if } e_1 \text{ then } e_2 \text{ else } e_3) \Downarrow c}$$

$$\frac{e_1 \Downarrow \underline{\ell_1} \qquad e_2 \Downarrow \underline{\ell_2}}{(e_1 \oplus e_2) \Downarrow \underline{\ell_1 \oplus \ell_2}}$$

$$\frac{e_1 \Downarrow (\backslash x \to e_3) \qquad e_3[e_2/x] \Downarrow c}{(e_1 \, e_2) \Downarrow c}$$

$$\frac{e_1 \Downarrow (\backslash x \to e_3) \qquad e_2 \Downarrow c_2 \qquad e_3[c_2/x] \Downarrow c}{(e_1 \hat{} \, e_2) \Downarrow c}$$

$$\frac{e[rec(x.\,e)/x] \Downarrow c}{rec(x.\,e) \Downarrow c}$$

$$\frac{e \Downarrow (K^\mu \, e_1 \cdots e_m) \qquad cc_{Rank(K,\mu)} \equiv (K \to e') \qquad (e' \, e_1 \cdots e_m) \Downarrow c}{(\text{case } e \text{ of } cc_1 \mid \cdots \mid cc_n) \Downarrow c}$$

Table 6.5: Operational semantics of $\mathcal{H}$

Pitts, we can take advantage of variable binding in the metalanguage and do without such environments by mapping object variables to metavariables.

We structure the denotational semantics to reflect the distinction made by the operational semantics between canonical and non-canonical terms. Computation is characterised operationally either as a series of reductions or as a single evaluation. Canonical terms, which are not reducible, are the answers from computation. Non-canonical terms, which are reducible, represent a computation, which depending on the object language, may terminate and return an answer or may diverge or may engage in other activity such as I/O. We parameterise the denotational semantics on a metalanguage type constructor, T, with associated operations Let and Val that obey the following typing rules.

$$\frac{\Gamma \vdash M : \sigma}{\Gamma \vdash \mathsf{Val}(M) : T\sigma} \qquad \frac{\Gamma \vdash M : T\sigma \qquad \Gamma, v{:}\sigma \vdash N : T\tau}{\Gamma \vdash (\mathsf{Let}\, v \Leftarrow M \text{ in } N) : T\tau}$$

Free occurrences of v in N become bound in $(\mathsf{Let}\, v \Leftarrow M \text{ in } N)$. Type $T\sigma$ represents computations of type σ. To compute $\mathsf{Val}(N)$ simply return the answer N. To compute $(\mathsf{Let}\, v \Leftarrow M \text{ in } N)$, first compute M. If M returns an answer L, proceed to compute $N[L/v]$ to obtain the answer from the whole computation. In principle, the benefit of this parametric approach is that the same translation rules can be used with different interpretations of the structure $(T, \mathsf{Val}, \mathsf{Let})$. For instance, in §6.7 we give an interpretation where computations may raise an exception instead of returning an answer.

This parametric approach to denotational semantics was pioneered by Moggi [100, 101], who defined a metalanguage, called **computational λ-calculus**, into which object languages are translated, and whose own semantics is given by a **computational model**, a category with a strong monad and other properties. Pitts [112] proposes the development of **evaluation logic** for reasoning about the denotations of object programs in computational λ-calculus. Crole and Pitts [24, 25] investigate how to obtain the power of general recursion in computational λ-calculus. We have adopted Moggi's parametric approach but instead of using a metalanguage with a general categorical model, we use $\mathcal{M}$, a metalanguage based on Plotkin's [120] but with a specific operational semantics and effectively a term model. Rather than work in a general categorical framework we work in a pragmatic operational framework in order to study a particular programming language and its extensions for I/O.

We now give a denotational semantics of $\mathcal{H}$ in which computations may either diverge or return an answer, to reflect the operational semantics of Table 6.5.

Definition 6.7 *Make the following definitions of parameters T, Val and Let:*

$$T\sigma \overset{\text{def}}{=} \sigma_\perp$$
$$\mathsf{Val}(N) \overset{\text{def}}{=} \mathsf{Lift}(N)$$
$$\mathsf{Let}\, v \Leftarrow M \text{ in } N \overset{\text{def}}{=} \mathsf{Seq}(M, v.\, N)$$

Given these parameters define denotations for the abstract syntax of $\mathcal{H}$ inductively according to the rules in Table 6.6:

- *to each type σ, an $\mathcal{M}$ type $[\sigma]$;*
- *to each data-clause dc, an $\mathcal{M}$ type $[\text{dc}]$;*

Types

$$[\![X]\!] \stackrel{\text{def}}{=} X$$

$$[\![\texttt{Bool}]\!] \stackrel{\text{def}}{=} \texttt{Bool}$$

$$[\![\texttt{Int}]\!] \stackrel{\text{def}}{=} \texttt{Num}$$

$$[\![\sigma \texttt{ -> } \tau]\!] \stackrel{\text{def}}{=} T[\![\sigma]\!] \to T[\![\tau]\!]$$

$$[\![\texttt{data } X = \texttt{dc}_1 \mid \cdots \mid \texttt{dc}_n]\!] \stackrel{\text{def}}{=} (\mu X.\, [\![\texttt{dc}_1]\!] + \cdots + [\![\texttt{dc}_n]\!])$$

Data-clauses

$$[\![K\, \sigma_1 \cdots \sigma_m]\!] \stackrel{\text{def}}{=} T[\![\sigma_1]\!] \times \cdots \times T[\![\sigma_m]\!]$$

Canonical terms

$$|\backslash x :: \sigma \texttt{ -> } \texttt{e}| \stackrel{\text{def}}{=} \lambda x{:}T[\![\sigma]\!].\, [\![\texttt{e}]\!]$$

$$|\underline{\ell}| \stackrel{\text{def}}{=} \lfloor \ell \rfloor$$

$$|K^\mu\, \texttt{e}_1 \cdots \texttt{e}_m| \stackrel{\text{def}}{=} \mathsf{Intro}^{[\![\mu]\!]}(\mathsf{In}_{Rank(K,\mu)}(\langle [\![\texttt{e}_1]\!], \ldots, [\![\texttt{e}_m]\!]\rangle))$$

Terms

$$[\![x]\!] \stackrel{\text{def}}{=} x$$

$$[\![c]\!] \stackrel{\text{def}}{=} \mathsf{Val}(|c|)$$

$$[\![\texttt{if } \texttt{e}_1 \texttt{ then } \texttt{e}_2 \texttt{ else } \texttt{e}_3]\!] \stackrel{\text{def}}{=} \mathsf{Let}\, v \Leftarrow [\![\texttt{e}_1]\!] \texttt{ in if } v \texttt{ then } [\![\texttt{e}_2]\!] \texttt{ else } [\![\texttt{e}_3]\!]$$

$$[\![\texttt{e}_1 \oplus \texttt{e}_2]\!] \stackrel{\text{def}}{=} \mathsf{Let}\, v_1 \Leftarrow [\![\texttt{e}_1]\!] \texttt{ in } \mathsf{Let}\, v_2 \Leftarrow [\![\texttt{e}_2]\!] \texttt{ in}$$
$$\mathsf{Seq}(v_1 \lfloor \oplus \rfloor v_2, x.\, \mathsf{Val}\,(x))$$

$$[\![\texttt{e}_1\, \texttt{e}_2]\!] \stackrel{\text{def}}{=} [\![\texttt{e}_1]\!] \bullet [\![\texttt{e}_2]\!]$$

$$[\![\texttt{e}_1\,\hat{}\,\texttt{e}_2]\!] \stackrel{\text{def}}{=} \mathsf{Let}\, v_1 \Leftarrow [\![\texttt{e}_1]\!] \texttt{ in } \mathsf{Let}\, v_2 \Leftarrow [\![\texttt{e}_2]\!] \texttt{ in } v_1(\mathsf{Val}(v_2))$$

$$[\![\texttt{rec}(x.\,\texttt{e})]\!] \stackrel{\text{def}}{=} \mathsf{Fix}(x.\, [\![\texttt{e}]\!])$$

$$[\![\texttt{case}^\mu \texttt{e of } \texttt{cc}_1 \mid \cdots \mid \texttt{cc}_n]\!] \stackrel{\text{def}}{=} \mathsf{Let}\, v \Leftarrow [\![\texttt{e}]\!] \texttt{ in}$$
$$\mathsf{Case}(\mathsf{Elim}\, v, (v_1.\, [\![\texttt{cc}_1]\!]^\mu_{v_1}), \ldots, (v_n.\, [\![\texttt{cc}_n]\!]^\mu_{v_n}))$$

Case-clauses

$$[\![K \texttt{ -> } \texttt{e}]\!]^\mu_v \stackrel{\text{def}}{=} \mathsf{Split}(v, u_1 \ldots u_m.\, [\![\texttt{e}]\!] \bullet u_1 \bullet \cdots \bullet u_m) \quad \text{where } m = Arity(K, \mu)$$

Table 6.6: Denotational semantics of $\mathcal{H}$

- to each canonical term c, an $\mathcal{M}$ term $|c|$;
- to each term e, an $\mathcal{M}$ term $[\![e]\!]$;
- to each case-clause cc, an $\mathcal{M}$ term $[\![cc]\!]$.

The bound variables v, v_i, u_i used to construct $\mathcal{M}$ denotations are assumed to be distinct from any variables occurring free in object language terms. We use a derived notation for function application.

$$M \bullet N \stackrel{\text{def}}{=} \text{Let } f \Leftarrow M \text{ in } f N$$

The notation associates to the left, that is, $M_1 \bullet M_2 \bullet M_3$ means $(M_1 \bullet M_2) \bullet M_3$. Finally, if $\mathcal{H}$ environment $\Gamma = x_1{::}\sigma_1, \ldots, x_n{::}\sigma_n$, then $[\![\Gamma]\!]$ is the $\mathcal{M}$ environment $x_1{:}T[\![\sigma_1]\!], \ldots, x_n{:}T[\![\sigma_n]\!]$.

Operations Val and Let are simply an alternative syntax for primitives Lift and Seq of $\mathcal{M}$; we use these abstract operations so that the rules of Table 6.6 can be re-used with other interpretations of T, Val and Let.

The only rules to make any assumptions about the type constructor T in the denotational semantics rules in Table 6.5 are the ones for recursion and arithmetic. By translating rec to Fix and using Seq in the translation of arithmetic we are assuming that T has the property that for any σ, $T\sigma$ is a lifted type.

Proposition 6.8

(1) If τ is an $\mathcal{H}$ type, then $[\![\tau]\!]$ is a well-formed $\mathcal{M}$ type.

(2) If $\Gamma \vdash e :: \tau$ then $[\![\Gamma]\!] \vdash [\![e]\!] : T[\![\tau]\!]$.

(3) If $\Gamma, x{::}\sigma \vdash e_1 :: \tau$ and $\Gamma \vdash e_2 :: \sigma$ then $[\![e_1]\!][[\![e_2]\!]/x] \equiv [\![e_1[e_2/x]]\!]$.

(4) $[\![e_0]\!] \bullet \cdots \bullet [\![e_n]\!] \equiv [\![e_0 \ldots e_n]\!]$.

Proof. Part (1) follows by structural induction on τ, given the restriction on the form of algebraic types in $\mathcal{H}$. Part (2) is by induction on the depth of inference of $\Gamma \vdash e :: \tau$. Part (3) is by induction on the depth of inference of $\Gamma, x{::}\sigma \vdash e_1 :: \tau$, and is straightforward since the denotational semantics is compositional. Part (4) follows by an induction on n. ∎

Example denotations

We repeat the definition in $\mathcal{H}$ of the function head from Table 6.4.

$$cc_1 \stackrel{\text{def}}{=} \text{Nil} \rightarrow \Omega$$
$$cc_2 \stackrel{\text{def}}{=} \text{Cons} \rightarrow \backslash x \rightarrow \backslash xs \rightarrow x$$
$$\text{head} \stackrel{\text{def}}{=} \backslash xs \rightarrow \text{case } xs \text{ of } cc_1 \mid cc_2$$

To illustrate the denotational semantics, we calculate the following denotations:

$$[\![\sigma]\!] \equiv (\mu X.\, 1 + (T[\![\sigma]\!] \times TX))$$
$$[\![\texttt{[1583]}]\!] \equiv [\![\texttt{Cons 1583 Nil}]\!]$$
$$\equiv \mathsf{Val}(\mathsf{Intro}(\mathsf{Inr}\langle[\![\texttt{1583}]\!], [\![\texttt{Nil}]\!]\rangle))$$
$$\equiv \mathsf{Val}(\mathsf{Intro}(\mathsf{Inr}\langle\mathsf{Val}\lfloor 1583\rfloor, \mathsf{Val}(\mathsf{Intro}(\mathsf{Inl}\,*))\rangle)))$$
$$[\![\texttt{head}]\!] \equiv \mathsf{Val}(\lambda\texttt{xs}.\,[\![\texttt{case xs of } cc_1 \mid cc_2]\!])$$
$$\equiv \mathsf{Val}(\lambda\texttt{xs}.\,\mathsf{Let}\, v \Leftarrow [\![\texttt{xs}]\!]\,\mathsf{in}$$
$$\mathsf{Case}(\mathsf{Elim}\, v, v_1.\,[\![cc_1]\!]_{v_1}^{[\![\texttt{[Int]}]\!]}, v_2.\,[\![cc_2]\!]_{v_2}^{[\![\texttt{[Int]}]\!]}))$$
$$[\![cc_1]\!]_{v_1}^{[\![\texttt{[Int]}]\!]} \equiv \mathsf{Split}(v_1, [\![\Omega]\!])$$
$$\equiv \Omega$$
$$[\![cc_2]\!]_{v_2}^{[\![\texttt{[Int]}]\!]} \equiv \mathsf{Split}(v_2, u_1.\, u_2.\,([\![\texttt{\textbackslash x -> \textbackslash xs -> x}]\!] \bullet u_1 \bullet u_2))$$
$$[\![\texttt{\textbackslash x -> \textbackslash xs -> xs}]\!] \equiv \mathsf{Val}(\lambda\texttt{x}.\,\mathsf{Val}\,(\lambda\texttt{xs}.\,\texttt{x}))$$

We will return to these examples when we look at denotational equivalence in §6.4.

Operational correspondence between the semantics

First we show operational properties of the denotational constants—that is, the $\mathcal{M}$ type constructor T and operations Val, Let—used in the denotational semantics.

Lemma 6.9

(1) *For any $T\sigma$-program M, either $M\Uparrow$ or $M \Downarrow \mathsf{Val}(N)$ for some σ-program N.*

(2) *The operational behaviour of the denotational constants obeys the following rules:*

$$\frac{M\Uparrow}{(\mathsf{Let}\, v \Leftarrow M \text{ in } N)\Uparrow} \qquad \frac{M \Downarrow \mathsf{Val}(L)}{(\mathsf{Let}\, v \Leftarrow M \text{ in } N)\to^+ N[L/v]}$$

Proof. From the definitions of Val and Let.   ∎

We conclude this section on the definition of $\mathcal{H}$ with the proof of a close correspondence between the operational behaviour of each $\mathcal{H}$ program and its denotation:

Proposition 6.10 *For any $\mathcal{H}$ program e, canonical $\mathcal{H}$ program c, and canonical $\mathcal{M}$ program V, we have:*

(1) *If e $\Downarrow$ c then $[\![\texttt{e}]\!] \Downarrow [\![\texttt{c}]\!]$.*

(2) *If $[\![\texttt{e}]\!] \Downarrow V$ then there is c such that $V \equiv [\![\texttt{c}]\!]$ and e $\Downarrow$ c.*

Therefore e $\Downarrow$ c iff $[\![\texttt{e}]\!] \Downarrow [\![\texttt{c}]\!]$.

Proof. Part (1) is proved by induction on the depth of inference of e $\Downarrow$ c. We show two example cases.

Case e $\Downarrow$ e where e $\equiv$ c is canonical. We have $[\![\texttt{e}]\!] \equiv \mathsf{Val}\lfloor\texttt{c}\rfloor$ which is canonical, so $[\![\texttt{e}]\!]\Downarrow[\![\texttt{e}]\!]$.

Case e $\equiv$ (e$_1\times$e$_2$). We have c $\equiv m_1 \times m_2$ where each e$_i \Downarrow m_i$. By appeal to the induction hypothesis and Proposition 5.10 we have the following.

$$
\begin{aligned}
[\![e]\!] \quad &\equiv \quad \mathsf{Let}\, v_1 \Leftarrow [\![e_1]\!] \text{ in } \mathsf{Let}\, v_2 \Leftarrow [\![e_2]\!] \text{ in } \mathsf{Seq}(v_1 \lfloor \times \rfloor v_2, x.\ \mathsf{Val}\,(x)) \\
&\to^+ \quad \mathsf{Let}\, v_1 \Leftarrow \mathsf{Val}(\lfloor m_1 \rfloor) \text{ in } \mathsf{Let}\, v_2 \Leftarrow [\![e_2]\!] \text{ in } \mathsf{Seq}(v_1 \lfloor \times \rfloor v_2, x.\ \mathsf{Val}\,(x)) \\
&\to \quad \mathsf{Let}\, v_2 \Leftarrow [\![e_2]\!] \text{ in } \mathsf{Seq}(\lfloor m_1 \rfloor \lfloor \times \rfloor v_2, x.\ \mathsf{Val}\,(x)) \\
&\to^+ \quad \mathsf{Let}\, v_2 \Leftarrow \mathsf{Val}(\lfloor m_2 \rfloor) \text{ in } \mathsf{Seq}(\lfloor m_1 \rfloor \lfloor \times \rfloor v_2, x.\ \mathsf{Val}\,(x)) \\
&\to \quad \mathsf{Seq}(\lfloor m_1 \rfloor \lfloor \times \rfloor \lfloor m_2 \rfloor, x.\ \mathsf{Val}\,(x)) \\
&\to^+ \quad \mathsf{Seq}(\lfloor m_1 \times m_2 \rfloor, x.\ \mathsf{Val}\,(x)) \\
&\to \quad \mathsf{Val}(\lfloor m_1 \times m_2 \rfloor) \\
&\equiv \quad [\![c]\!]
\end{aligned}
$$

Part (2) is proved by induction on the depth of inference of $[\![e]\!] \Downarrow V$, proceeding by a structural analysis of e. Again we show two example cases.

Case e is canonical. We have $[\![e]\!] \Downarrow V$ where $V \equiv [\![e]\!]$, and $e \Downarrow e$.

Case $e \equiv (e_1 \underline{\times} e_2)$. We have:

$$[\![e]\!] \equiv \mathsf{Let}\, v_1 \Leftarrow [\![e_1]\!] \text{ in } \mathsf{Let}\, v_2 \Leftarrow [\![e_2]\!] \text{ in } \mathsf{Seq}(v_1 \lfloor \times \rfloor v_2, x.\ \mathsf{Val}\,(x))$$

Proceed by a case analysis of the evaluation behaviour of $[\![e_1]\!]$ and $[\![e_2]\!]$. From Lemma 6.9(1), either $[\![e_i]\!]\Uparrow$ or $(\exists N_i.\ [\![e_i]\!] \Downarrow \mathsf{Val}(N_i))$ for each i. But neither $[\![e_1]\!]$ nor $[\![e_2]\!]$ can diverge or else by Lemma 6.9(2) $[\![e]\!]$ would diverge. So there are N_i such that $[\![e_i]\!] \Downarrow \mathsf{Val}(N_i)$. By IH, we have $e_i \Downarrow m_i$ and $[\![e_i]\!] \Downarrow \mathsf{Val}(\lfloor m_i \rfloor)$. Then by a calculation similar to the one given for part (1) we have that $[\![e]\!] \Downarrow \mathsf{Val}(\lfloor m_1 \times m_2 \rfloor)$ and also that $e \Downarrow m_1 \times m_2$ as required. $\blacksquare$

6.2 Ground and confined relations in $\mathcal{H}$

Before developing operational and denotational equivalence, we need several preliminary definitions. This section reworks basic notions of ground and confined relations developed first in §4.3. Recall the notions of program and confined term from Definition 6.3.

Definition 6.11

(1) A **ground relation**, $\mathcal{R}$, is a binary relation between programs of the same type.

(2) A **confined relation**, $\mathcal{R}$, is a binary relation between confined terms of the same type and environment. Write $\Gamma \vdash e \mathcal{R} e'$ to mean that $(\Gamma \vdash e, \Gamma \vdash e') \in \mathcal{R}$.

We state a sense in which a ground relation respects the operational semantics. Recall from §6.1 that program Ω of any type equals $\mathsf{rec}(x.\, x)$.

Definition 6.12 A ground relation, $\mathcal{R}$, is **operationally adequate** iff for all programs e, e', and canonical programs c:

(1) If $e \to e'$ then $e' \mathcal{R} e$.

(2) If $e \Downarrow c$ then $c \mathcal{R} e$.

(3) $e\Uparrow$ iff $e \mathcal{R} \Omega$.

(4) $e\Downarrow$ iff for some canonical c, $c \mathcal{R} e$.

The first half of Table 6.7 shows inference rules for constructing the confined relation $\widehat{\mathcal{R}}$ from any confined relation $\mathcal{R}$. The second half of the table shows six inference rules that

Rules of $\widehat{\mathcal{R}}$

$$\Gamma \vdash x \,\widehat{\mathcal{R}}\, x \qquad \Gamma \vdash \ell \,\widehat{\mathcal{R}}\, \ell$$

$$\frac{\Gamma \vdash e_i \mathcal{R} e_i' \quad (i = 1, 2)}{\Gamma \vdash (e_1 \oplus e_2) \,\widehat{\mathcal{R}}\, (e_1' \oplus e_2')} \qquad \frac{\Gamma \vdash e_i \mathcal{R} e_i' \quad (i = 1, 2, 3)}{\Gamma \vdash (\text{if } e_1 \text{ then } e_2 \text{ else } e_3) \,\widehat{\mathcal{R}}\, (\text{if } e_1' \text{ then } e_2' \text{ else } e_3')}$$

$$\frac{\Gamma, x{::}\tau \vdash e \mathcal{R} e'}{\Gamma \vdash (\backslash x{::}\tau \rightarrow e) \,\widehat{\mathcal{R}}\, (\backslash x{::}\tau \rightarrow e')} \qquad \frac{\Gamma \vdash e_i \mathcal{R} e_i' \quad (i = 1, 2)}{\Gamma \vdash (e_1 \, e_2) \,\widehat{\mathcal{R}}\, (e_1' \, e_2')}$$

$$\frac{\Gamma, x{::}\sigma \vdash e \mathcal{R} e'}{\Gamma \vdash \text{rec}^\sigma(x.\,e) \,\widehat{\mathcal{R}}\, \text{rec}^\sigma(x.\,e')} \qquad \frac{\Gamma \vdash e_i \mathcal{R} e_i' \quad (1 \le i \le n)}{\Gamma \vdash (K \, e_1 \cdots e_n) \,\widehat{\mathcal{R}}\, (K \, e_1' \cdots e_n')}$$

$$\frac{\Gamma \vdash e \mathcal{R} e' \quad cc_i = (K_i \rightarrow e_i) \quad cc_i' = (K_i \rightarrow e_i') \quad \Gamma \vdash e_i \mathcal{R} e_i' \quad (1 \le i \le n)}{\Gamma \vdash (\text{case } e \text{ of } cc_1 \mid \cdots \mid cc_n) \,\widehat{\mathcal{R}}\, (\text{case } e' \text{ of } cc_1' \mid \cdots \mid cc_n')}$$

Properties of Confined Relations

$$\text{Weak} \quad \frac{\Gamma \vdash e \mathcal{R} e'}{\Gamma, \Gamma' \vdash e \mathcal{R} e'}$$

$$\text{Stren} \quad \frac{\Gamma, \Gamma' \vdash e \mathcal{R} e'}{\Gamma \vdash e \mathcal{R} e'}$$

$$\text{Spec} \quad \frac{\Gamma, x{::}\sigma \vdash e_1 \mathcal{R} e_2 \quad \Gamma \vdash e' :: \sigma}{\Gamma \vdash e_1[e'/x] \mathcal{R} e_2[e'/x]}$$

$$\text{Precong} \quad \frac{\Gamma \vdash e \mathcal{R} e'}{\Gamma \vdash C[e] \mathcal{R} C[e']}$$

$$\text{Comp} \quad \frac{\Gamma \vdash e \,\widehat{\mathcal{R}}\, e'}{\Gamma \vdash e \mathcal{R} e'}$$

$$\text{Sub} \quad \frac{\Gamma, x{::}\sigma \vdash e_1 \mathcal{R} e_1' \quad \Gamma \vdash e_2 \mathcal{R} e_2'}{\Gamma \vdash e_1[e_2/x] \mathcal{R} e_1'[e_2'/x]}$$

Table 6.7: Definition of $\widehat{\mathcal{R}}$ and rules concerning confined relations.

may be valid for a confined relation.

Definition 6.13

(1) If $\mathcal{R}$ is a confined relation, then confined relation $\widehat{\mathcal{R}}$ is defined by the rules in the first half of Table 6.7.

(2) The inference rules **Weak, Stren, Spec, Precong, Comp** and **Sub** are defined in the second half of Table 6.7.

(3) A confined relation is **natural** iff the rules **Weak, Stren** and **Spec** are valid.

(4) A confined relation is a **precongruence** iff the rule **Precong** is valid. A **congruence** is a confined relation that is both a precongruence and an equivalence relation.

As usual, the rules in Table 6.7 bear the implicit side-condition that any sentence in a rule is well-formed. In rule **Stren** for instance, from the lower sentence $(\Gamma \vdash e\mathcal{R}e')$ we may deduce that $fv(e, e') \subseteq Dom(\Gamma)$, and then from the upper sentence $(\Gamma, \Gamma' \vdash e\mathcal{R}e')$ that $Dom(\Gamma) \cap Dom(\Gamma') = \varnothing$, and hence that $fv(e, e') \cap Dom(\Gamma') = \varnothing$.

Proposition 6.14

(1) If rules **Spec** and **Precong** are valid for a transitive confined relation, then rule **Sub** is valid too.

(2) If $\mathcal{R}$ is a preorder, rule **Comp** is valid iff rule **Precong** is valid.

Proof. Similar to that of Proposition 4.8.   ∎

We will often need to induce a confined relation from a ground relation, and vice versa, as follows.

Definition 6.15

(1) Let Γ be an environment $x_1 {::} \sigma_1, \ldots, x_n {::} \sigma_n$. Then a Γ-**closure** is an iterated substitution $\cdot[\mathsf{p}_1/x_1] \cdots [\mathsf{p}_n/x_n]$, where each p_i is a σ_i-program. (The order of substitution does not matter because the variables are disjoint and each p_i is closed.)

(2) The **confined extension** of a ground relation $\mathcal{R}_G$ is the confined relation $\mathcal{R}$ such that:

$$(\Gamma \vdash e\mathcal{R}e') \text{ iff for all } \Gamma\text{-closures } \cdot[\tilde{\mathsf{p}}/\tilde{x}], \ e[\tilde{\mathsf{p}}/\tilde{x}]\mathcal{R}_Ge'[\tilde{\mathsf{p}}/\tilde{x}].$$

(3) If $\mathcal{R}$ is a confined relation, then its **ground restriction** is the ground relation $\{(\mathsf{p}, \mathsf{q}) \mid \varnothing \vdash \mathsf{p}\mathcal{R}\mathsf{q}\}$.

(4) If $\mathcal{R}$ is a confined relation, write $\mathsf{p}\mathcal{R}\mathsf{q}$ to mean that pair (p, q) is in the ground restriction of $\mathcal{R}$.

Proposition 6.16 The confined extension of a ground relation is natural (that is, rules **Weak, Stren** and **Spec** are valid).

Proof. Similar to that of Proposition 4.10.   ∎

We typically use the same symbol for a ground relation and its confined extension. If $\mathcal{R}_G$ is a ground relation and $\mathcal{R}$ is its confined extension, we sometimes write $\widehat{\mathcal{R}_G}$ for $\widehat{\mathcal{R}}$.

6.3   Operational equivalence for $\mathcal{H}$

In this section we define a notion of applicative bisimilarity directly from the operational semantics of $\mathcal{H}$. In §6.4 we will develop a second notion of equivalence from the denotational semantics. This operational theory of $\mathcal{H}$ parallels the theory of applicative bisimilarity for $\mathcal{M}$ developed in Chapter 4. Just as in that chapter, one can also develop a theory of contextual equivalence for $\mathcal{H}$, and establish an operational extensionality result, but for the purpose of studying functional I/O applicative bisimilarity is sufficient. We begin with applicative similarity, the ground preorder from which we shall define operational equivalence.

Definition 6.17 *Define function $[\cdot]$ over ground relations such that*

$$\text{p}[\mathcal{S}]\text{q iff whenever p} \Downarrow \text{c}_p \text{ there is c}_q \text{ with q} \Downarrow \text{c}_q \text{ and c}_p \, \widehat{\mathcal{S}} \, \text{c}_q.$$

An **applicative simulation** *is a relation $\mathcal{S}$ such that $\mathcal{S} \subseteq [\mathcal{S}]$. Define* **ground applicative similarity**, $\sqsubseteq$, *to be the union of all applicative simulations. Define* **applicative similarity**, $\sqsubseteq$, *to be the confined extension of ground applicative similarity.*

We can restate the definition of $[\cdot]$ as follows:

Lemma 6.18 *For any ground relation $\mathcal{S}$, $\text{p}[\mathcal{S}]\text{q}$ iff*

(1) *whenever $\text{p} \Downarrow \ell$ then $\text{q} \Downarrow \ell$;*

(2) *whenever $\text{p} \Downarrow (\backslash x{::}\tau \rightarrow \text{e}_1)$, then $\text{q} \Downarrow (\backslash x{::}\tau \rightarrow \text{e}_2)$ and for all τ-programs p, $(\text{e}_1[\text{P}/x], \text{e}_2[\text{P}/x]) \in \mathcal{S}$;*

(3) *whenever $\text{p} \Downarrow (K\,\text{p}_1 \ldots \text{p}_n)$, then $\text{q} \Downarrow (K\,\text{q}_1 \ldots \text{q}_n)$ and $(\text{p}_i, \text{q}_i) \in \mathcal{S}$ for each i.*

Proposition 6.19

(1) *Function $[\cdot]$ is monotone.*

(2) *The identity ground relation is an applicative simulation.*

(3) *If each $\mathcal{S}_i$ is an applicative simulation, then so is $\mathcal{S}_1\mathcal{S}_2$.*

(4) *Ground applicative similarity is the greatest fixpoint of $[\cdot]$ and is the greatest applicative simulation.*

(5) *$M \sqsubseteq N$ iff there is an applicative simulation $\mathcal{S}$ such that $M\mathcal{S}N$*

(6) *Ground applicative similarity is a preorder.*

Proof. Parts (1), (2) and (3) are easy to check from the definition. The remaining parts then follow from Proposition 1.1.   ∎

Definition 6.20 *An* **applicative bisimulation** *is a relation $\mathcal{S}$ such that both $\mathcal{S}$ and $\mathcal{S}^{-1}$ are applicative simulations.* **Ground applicative bisimilarity**, $=$, *is the ground relation $(\sqsubseteq \cap \sqsubseteq^{-1})$.* **Applicative bisimilarity**, $=$, *is the confined extension of ground applicative bisimilarity.*

Clearly applicative bisimilarity is an equivalence relation. We have: for any programs e and e', e = e' iff for some applicative bisimulation $\mathcal{S}$, $e\mathcal{S}e'$.

Proposition 6.21 *Ground relations $\sqsubseteq$ and $=$ are both operationally adequate.*

Proof. Similar to the proof of Proposition 4.26. ∎

We adopt $\sqsubseteq$ and $=$ as operational order and equivalence respectively on $\mathcal{H}$.

Applicative similarity is a precongruence

We prove that applicative similarity for $\mathcal{H}$ is a precongruence by a typed reworking of Howe's method, just as we proved that applicative similarity for $\mathcal{M}$ was a precongruence in Chapter 4.

Definition 6.22 *Define the confined relation* **compatible similarity,** $\sqsubseteq^*$ *to be the least set closed under the rule:*

$$\frac{\Gamma \vdash e \,\widehat{\sqsubseteq}^* e'' \qquad \Gamma \vdash e'' \sqsubseteq e'}{\Gamma \vdash e \sqsubseteq^* e'}$$

Again, despite the notational ambiguity, $\sqsubseteq^*$ is not defined to be the reflexive transitive closure of $\sqsubseteq$.

Proposition 6.23

(1) *Applicative similarity is natural (that is, rules* **Spec**, **Weak** *and* **Stren** *are valid).*

(2) *Confined relations $\widehat{\sqsubseteq}^*$ and $\sqsubseteq^*$ are reflexive.*

(3) *Confined relations $\widehat{\sqsubseteq}^*$ and $\sqsubseteq$ both imply $\sqsubseteq^*$.*

(4) *If $\Gamma \vdash e_1 \sqsubseteq^* e_2$ and $\Gamma \vdash e_2 \sqsubseteq e_3$ then $\Gamma \vdash e_1 \sqsubseteq^* e_3$.*

(5) **(Sub)** *If $\Gamma, x::\tau \vdash e_1 \sqsubseteq^* e_1'$ and $\Gamma \vdash e_2 \sqsubseteq^* e_2'$ then $\Gamma \vdash e_1[e_2/x] \sqsubseteq^* e_1'[e_2'/x]$.*

(6) *If $\varnothing \vdash c \sqsubseteq^* e$ then there is c' such that $e \Downarrow c'$ and $c \,\widehat{\sqsubseteq}^* c'$.*

(7) *If $\varnothing \vdash e \sqsubseteq^* e'$ and $e \Downarrow c$ then $\varnothing \vdash c \sqsubseteq^* e'$.*

(8) *If $\Gamma \vdash e \sqsubseteq^* e'$ then $\Gamma \vdash e \sqsubseteq e'$.*

(9) *Applicative similarity is a precongruence.*

Proof. The proof takes exactly the same form as Proposition 4.28. We omit the details of parts (1) to (5), which are almost identical to the corresponding parts of Proposition 4.28.

(6) In each case there must be a program e' such that $c \,\widehat{\sqsubseteq}^* e'$ and $\varnothing \vdash e' \sqsubseteq e$. Proceed by a structural analysis of canonical program c:

Case $c \equiv \ell$. So $e' \equiv \ell$. Then $\ell \sqsubseteq e$ implies that $e \Downarrow \ell$, as required.

Case $c \equiv (\lambda x::\tau \rightarrow e_1)$. So $e' \equiv (\lambda x \rightarrow e_1')$ with $(x::\tau \vdash e_1 \sqsubseteq^* e_1')$. Then $e' \sqsubseteq e$ implies that $e \Downarrow (\lambda x \rightarrow e_1'')$ with $(x::\tau \vdash e_1' \sqsubseteq e_1'')$. Therefore $(x::\tau \vdash e_1 \sqsubseteq^* e_1'')$ by part (4), which implies $c \,\widehat{\sqsubseteq}^* (\lambda x \rightarrow e_1'')$ as required.

Case $c \equiv (K\,p_1 \ldots p_n)$. So $e' \equiv (K\,q_1 \ldots q_n)$ with $p_i \sqsubseteq^* q_i$ for each i. Then $e' \sqsubseteq e$ implies that $e \Downarrow (K\,q_1' \ldots q_n')$ with $q_i \sqsubseteq q_i'$ for each i. By part (4) we have $p_i \sqsubseteq^* q_i'$

for each i, and therefore $c \sqsubseteq^* (K q'_1 \ldots q'_n)$ as required.

(7) By induction on the depth of inference of $e \Downarrow c$, proceeding by analysis of e:

Case e canonical. Immediate.

Case $e \equiv (e_1 \oplus e_2)$. We have $e_i \Downarrow \ell_i$ with $c \equiv \ell_1 \oplus \ell_2$. From $(e_1 \oplus e_2) \sqsubseteq^* e'$ there are e'_i $(i = 1, 2)$ such that $e_i \sqsubseteq^* e'_i$ and $(e'_1 \oplus e'_2) \sqsubseteq e'$. By IH we have $\ell_i \sqsubseteq^* e'_i$, hence $(\ell_1 \oplus \ell_2) \sqsubseteq^* e'$. From $(\ell_1 \oplus \ell_2) \sqsubseteq^* e'$ by definition there are e''_i such that $\ell_i \sqsubseteq^* e''_i$ and $(e''_1 \oplus e''_2) \sqsubseteq e'$. By (6) we have $e''_i \Downarrow \ell_i$. So $(e''_1 \oplus e''_2) \Downarrow \ell_1 \oplus \ell_2$, and $\ell_1 \oplus \ell_2 \sqsubseteq (e''_1 \oplus e''_2)$ by operational adequacy. Therefore $c \sqsubseteq e'$ by transitivity, and $c \sqsubseteq^* e'$ by (3).

Case $e \equiv (e_1 e_2)$. We have $e_1 \Downarrow (\lambda x {::} \tau \rightarrow e_3)$ and $e_3[e_2/x] \Downarrow c$. From $e \sqsubseteq^* e'$ there are e'_i $(i = 1, 2)$ such that $e_i \sqsubseteq^* e'_i$ and $(e'_1 e'_2) \sqsubseteq e'$. Since $e_1 \Downarrow (\lambda x {::} \tau \rightarrow e_3)$ and $e_1 \sqsubseteq^* e'_1$ we have $(\lambda x {::} \tau \rightarrow e_3) \sqsubseteq^* e'_1$ by IH. By (6) there is e'_3 with $e'_1 \Downarrow (\lambda x {::} \tau \rightarrow e'_3)$ and $(x {::} \tau \vdash e_3 \sqsubseteq^* e'_3)$. By **Sub**, $e_3[e_2/x] \sqsubseteq^* e'_3[e'_2/x]$, then by IH we have $c \sqsubseteq^* e'_3[e'_2/x]$. Since $(e'_1 e'_2) \rightarrow^+ e'_3[e'_2/x]$ we have $e'_3[e'_2/x] \sqsubseteq (e'_1 e'_2)$ by operational adequacy. From $(e'_1 e'_2) \sqsubseteq e'$ we have $e'_3[e'_2/x] \sqsubseteq e'$ by transitivity. Finally from $c \sqsubseteq^* e'_3[e'_2/x]$ we have $c \sqsubseteq^* e'$ by (4).

Case $e \equiv (e_1 \hat{\ } e_2)$. We have $e_1 \Downarrow (\lambda x {::} \tau \rightarrow e_3)$, $e_2 \Downarrow c_2$ and $e_3[c_2/x] \Downarrow c$. From $e \sqsubseteq^* e'$ there are e'_i $(i = 1, 2)$ such that $e_i \sqsubseteq^* e'_i$ and $(e'_1 \hat{\ } e'_2) \sqsubseteq e'$. Since $e_1 \Downarrow (\lambda x {::} \tau \rightarrow e_3)$ and $e_1 \sqsubseteq^* e'_1$ we have $(\lambda x {::} \tau \rightarrow e_3) \sqsubseteq^* e'_1$ by IH. Since $e_2 \Downarrow c_2$ and $e_2 \sqsubseteq^* e'_2$ we have $c_2 \sqsubseteq^* e'_2$ by IH. By (6) there is e'_3 with $e'_1 \Downarrow (\lambda x {::} \tau \rightarrow e'_3)$ and $(x {::} \tau \vdash e_3 \sqsubseteq^* e'_3)$. By (6) there is c'_2 with $e'_2 \Downarrow c'_2$ and $c_2 \widehat{\sqsubseteq}^* c'_2$. Therefore $c_2 \sqsubseteq^* c'_2$ by (3). By **Sub**, $e_3[c_2/x] \sqsubseteq^* e'_3[c'_2/x]$, then by IH we have $c \sqsubseteq^* e'_3[c'_2/x]$. Since $(e'_1 \hat{\ } e'_2) \rightarrow^+ e'_3[c'_2/x]$ we have $e'_3[c'_2/x] \sqsubseteq (e'_1 \hat{\ } e'_2)$ by operational adequacy. From $(e'_1 \hat{\ } e'_2) \sqsubseteq e'$ we have $e'_3[c'_2/x] \sqsubseteq e'$ by transitivity. Finally from $c \sqsubseteq^* e'_3[c'_2/x]$ we have $c \sqsubseteq^* e'$ by (4).

Case $e \equiv (\text{case } e_1 \text{ of } \cdots \mid K_i \rightarrow e_i \mid \cdots)$. We have $e_1 \Downarrow (K_j p_1 \ldots p_n)$, for some j, and $(e_j p_1 \ldots p_n) \Downarrow c$. From $e \sqsubseteq^* e'$ there are e'_i such that $e_i \sqsubseteq^* e'_i$ and $(\text{case } e'_1 \text{ of } \cdots \mid K_i {\rightarrow} e'_i \mid \cdots) \sqsubseteq e'$. Since $e_1 \Downarrow (K_j p_1 \ldots p_n)$ and $e_1 \sqsubseteq^* e'_1$ we have $(K_j p_1 \ldots p_n) \sqsubseteq^* e'_1$ by IH. By (6) there are p'_i such that $e'_1 \Downarrow (K_j p'_1 \ldots p'_n)$ and $p_i \sqsubseteq^* p'_i$. By **Sub** we have $(e_j p_1 \ldots p_n) \sqsubseteq^* (e'_j p'_1 \ldots p'_n)$, so since $(e_j p_1 \ldots p_n) \Downarrow c$ we have $c \sqsubseteq^* (e'_j p'_1 \ldots p'_n)$ by IH. Since $(\text{case } e'_1 \text{ of } \cdots \mid K_i \rightarrow e'_i \mid \cdots) \rightarrow^+ (e'_j p'_1 \ldots p'_n)$ we have $(e'_j p'_1 \ldots p'_n) \sqsubseteq (\text{case } e'_1 \text{ of } \cdots \mid K_i \rightarrow e'_i \mid \cdots)$ by operational adequacy. By transitivity and (4) we have $c \sqsubseteq^* e'$.

We omit the case for conditionals, which has the same structure as the cases above.

(8) First we prove that the ground restriction of compatible similarity is an applicative simulation. Suppose for any programs e and e' that $e \sqsubseteq^* e'$. We are to show that whenever $e \Downarrow c$ there is c' such that $e \Downarrow c'$ and $c \widehat{\sqsubseteq}^* c'$. Suppose that $e \Downarrow c$. By (7) we have $c \sqsubseteq^* e'$. By (6) there is c' such that $e' \Downarrow c'$ and $c \widehat{\sqsubseteq}^* c'$.

Suppose now that $(\Gamma \vdash e \sqsubseteq^* e')$. We are to prove that $(\Gamma \vdash e \sqsubseteq e')$, which is to say that for all Γ-closures, $\cdot[\tilde{p}/\tilde{x}]$, programs $e[\tilde{p}/\tilde{x}]$ and $e'[\tilde{p}/\tilde{x}]$ are paired in an applicative simulation. But by **Spec** and reflexivity we have $e[\tilde{p}/\tilde{x}] \sqsubseteq^* e'[\tilde{p}/\tilde{x}]$, and since the ground restriction of compatible similarity is an applicative simulation, we are done.

(9) A corollary of (3) and (8) is that applicative and compatible similarity are the same confined relation, just as in Proposition 4.28. ∎

To summarise this section, we have taken operational equivalence on $\mathcal{H}$ to be applicative bisimilarity shown it to be an operationally adequate congruence.

6.4 Denotational equivalence for $\mathcal{H}$

Two object terms are denotationally equal just when their denotations in the metalanguage are equal. We take equivalence in the metalanguage to be a operational equivalence on $\mathcal{M}$, $\simeq$, the equivalence characterised as contextual equivalence and applicative bisimilarity in Chapter 5.

Definition 6.24 *Define **denotational equivalence**, $\simeq$, to be the confined relation:*

$$(\Gamma \vdash e \simeq e') \overset{\text{def}}{=} (\llbracket \Gamma \rrbracket \vdash \llbracket e \rrbracket \simeq \llbracket e' \rrbracket)$$

Since operational equivalence on $\mathcal{M}$ is a natural equivalence relation, so is denotational equivalence on $\mathcal{H}$. Next we prove that denotational equivalence respects the operational semantics of $\mathcal{H}$.

Proposition 6.25 *Denotational equivalence is operationally adequate.*

Proof. There are four parts to the definition of operational adequacy, Definition 6.12, to establish. We appeal to operational adequacy for ground applicative bisimilarity in $\mathcal{M}$, Proposition 4.26, and the correspondence theorem between the operational and denotational semantics of $\mathcal{H}$, Proposition 6.10. We leave part (1) to the end of the proof.

Part (2). Suppose $e \Downarrow c$. Then $\llbracket e \rrbracket \Downarrow \llbracket c \rrbracket$ from the correspondence theorem. So $\llbracket e \rrbracket \simeq \llbracket c \rrbracket$ from operational adequacy of $\mathcal{M}$. Then $e \simeq c$ by definition.

Part (3). We have been using the symbol Ω to stand for $\text{Fix}(x.\,x)$ in $\mathcal{M}$ and $\text{rec}(x.\,x)$ in $\mathcal{H}$. Note that $\llbracket \Omega \rrbracket \equiv \Omega$, where Ω is interpreted in $\mathcal{H}$ and $\mathcal{M}$ in the left- and right-hand sides respectively.

$$
\begin{aligned}
e\Uparrow \ &\text{iff} \ (\neg \exists c.\, e \Downarrow c) \\
&\text{iff} \ (\neg \exists c.\, \llbracket e \rrbracket \Downarrow \llbracket c \rrbracket) \ \text{(Correspondence)} \\
&\text{iff} \ \llbracket e \rrbracket\Uparrow \\
&\text{iff} \ \llbracket e \rrbracket \simeq \Omega \qquad \text{(Operational adequacy for } \mathcal{M}) \\
&\text{iff} \ \llbracket e \rrbracket \simeq \llbracket \Omega \rrbracket \qquad \text{(since } \llbracket \Omega \rrbracket \simeq \Omega) \\
&\text{iff} \ e \simeq \Omega
\end{aligned}
$$

Part (4)

$$
\begin{aligned}
e\Downarrow \ &\text{iff} \ (\exists c.\, e \Downarrow c) \\
&\text{iff} \ (\exists c.\, \llbracket e \rrbracket \Downarrow \llbracket c \rrbracket) \ \text{(Correspondence)} \\
&\text{iff} \ (\exists c.\, \llbracket e \rrbracket \simeq \llbracket c \rrbracket) \ \text{(Operational adequacy for } \mathcal{M}) \\
&\text{iff} \ (\exists c.\, e \simeq c)
\end{aligned}
$$

Finally, part (1). Suppose $e \to e'$. Either $e'\Uparrow$ or for some c, $e' \Downarrow c$. In the former case, $e\Uparrow$ too, so $e \simeq e' \simeq \Omega$ by part (3). In the latter case, $e \Downarrow c$ too, and $e \simeq e' \simeq c$ by part (4). ∎

Moggi [100] defines a notion of computational model, based on a categorical strong monad, as a general framework for reasoning with denotational semantics. We make an analogous definition of a **computational monad** in the context of $\mathcal{M}$:

Definition 6.26 *A* **computational monad** *is a structure* $(T, \mathsf{Val}, \mathsf{Let})$ *where* T *maps any* $\mathcal{M}$ *type* σ, *to an* $\mathcal{M}$ *type* $T\sigma$, *and* Val *and* Let *are* $\mathcal{M}$ *operations that obey the typing rules:*

$$\frac{\Gamma \vdash M : \sigma}{\Gamma \vdash \mathsf{Val}(M) : T\sigma} \qquad \frac{\Gamma \vdash M : T\sigma \qquad \Gamma, v{:}\sigma \vdash N : T\tau}{\Gamma \vdash (\mathsf{Let}\, v \Leftarrow M \text{ in } N) : T\tau}$$

together with the equations

$$\frac{\Gamma \vdash M : T\sigma \qquad \Gamma, v{:}\sigma \vdash N : T\sigma'}{\Gamma \vdash (\mathsf{Let}\, v \Leftarrow \mathsf{Val}(M) \text{ in } N) \simeq N[M/v]}$$

$$\frac{\Gamma \vdash M : T\sigma}{\Gamma \vdash (\mathsf{Let}\, v \Leftarrow M \text{ in } \mathsf{Val}(v)) \simeq M}$$

$$\frac{\Gamma \vdash M_1 : T\sigma_1 \qquad \Gamma, v_1{:}\sigma_1 \vdash M_2 : T\sigma_2 \qquad \Gamma, v_2{:}\sigma_2 \vdash M_3 : T\sigma_3}{\Gamma \vdash (\mathsf{Let}\, v_2 \Leftarrow (\mathsf{Let}\, v_1 \Leftarrow M_1 \text{ in } M_2) \text{ in } M_3) \simeq}{(\mathsf{Let}\, v_1 \Leftarrow M_1 \text{ in } (\mathsf{Let}\, v_2 \Leftarrow M_2 \text{ in } M_3))}$$

and the injectivity requirement that $\Gamma \vdash \mathsf{Val}(M) \simeq \mathsf{Val}(N)$ *iff* $\Gamma \vdash M \simeq N$.

Lemma 6.9 stated properties of the evaluation behaviour of the operations used in the denotational semantics as a preliminary to proving the correspondence theorem between the operational and denotational semantics for $\mathcal{H}$. In the following lemma we prove equational properties of the operations used in the denotational semantics as a preliminary to proving the main result of this section: that denotational equivalence implies operational equivalence.

Lemma 6.27 *The structure* $(T, \mathsf{Val}, \mathsf{Let})$ *that parameterised the denotational semantics of* $\mathcal{H}$ *in Definition 6.7, is a computational monad.*

Proof. The typing rules in Definition 6.26 follow by inspection. The first two equations follow from the beta and eta laws for lifting in Table 5.1. Associativity of Let follows from proving the following equation:

$$\Gamma \vdash \mathsf{Seq}(\mathsf{Seq}(M_1, v_1. M_2), v_2. M_3)) \simeq \mathsf{Seq}(M_1, v_1. \mathsf{Seq}\,(M_2, v_2. M_3))$$

It suffices to prove the equation for Γ empty, from which case the non-empty case follows. By the exhaustion law in Table 5.1, either $M_1 \simeq \Omega$ or $M_1 \simeq \mathsf{Lift}(L)$ for some program L. In the first case, both sides equal Ω by the strictness law in Table 5.1. In the second case, by the beta law from we have $lhs \simeq \mathsf{Seq}(M_2[L/v_1], v_2. M_3)$ and $rhs \simeq \mathsf{Seq}(M_2, v_2. M_3)[L/v_1] \simeq lhs$ since $v_1 \notin fv(M_3)$. Finally, the injectivity requirement follows from canonical freeness in Table 5.1. ∎

An example calculation

Before proceeding, we show an example calculation. Recall the denotations calculated on page 77. We show that $[\![\mathsf{head}[1583]]\!] \simeq [\![1583]\!]$ by calculating as follows, where we use only the laws of $\mathcal{M}$ from Chapter 5, the equational laws of a computational monad and substitution properties from Proposition 6.8.

$$\begin{aligned}
[\![\mathtt{head}[1583]]\!] &\equiv \mathsf{Let}\, v \Leftarrow [\![\mathtt{head}]\!]\, \mathsf{in}\, v\,[\![[1583]]\!] \\
&\equiv \mathsf{Let}\, v \Leftarrow \mathsf{Val}(\lambda\mathtt{xs}.[\![\mathtt{case\ xs\ of}\ cc_1\ |\ cc_2]\!])\, \mathsf{in}\, v\,[\![[1583]]\!] \\
&\simeq (\lambda\mathtt{xs}.[\![\mathtt{case\ xs\ of}\ cc_1\ |\ cc_2]\!])\,[\![[1583]]\!] \\
&\equiv (\lambda\mathtt{xs}.\ \mathsf{Let}\, v \Leftarrow \mathtt{xs}\, \mathsf{in} \\
&\qquad \mathsf{Case}(\mathsf{Elim}\, v, v_1.[\![cc_1]\!]_{v_1}, v_2.[\![cc_2]\!]_{v_2}))\,[\![[1583]]\!] \\
&\simeq \mathsf{Let}\, v \Leftarrow [\![[1583]]\!]\, \mathsf{in} \\
&\qquad \mathsf{Case}(\mathsf{Elim}\, v, v_1.[\![cc_1]\!]_{v_1}, v_2.[\![cc_2]\!]_{v_2}) \\
&\equiv \mathsf{Let}\, v \Leftarrow \mathsf{Val}(\mathsf{Intro}(\mathsf{Inr}\langle[\![1583]\!],[\![\mathtt{Nil}]\!]\rangle))\, \mathsf{in} \\
&\qquad \mathsf{Case}(\mathsf{Elim}\, v, v_1.[\![cc_1]\!]_{v_1}, v_2.[\![cc_2]\!]_{v_2}) \\
&\simeq \mathsf{Case}(\mathsf{Inr}\langle[\![1583]\!],[\![\mathtt{Nil}]\!]\rangle, v_1.[\![cc_1]\!]_{v_1}, v_2.[\![cc_2]\!]_{v_2})) \\
&\simeq [\![cc_2]\!]_{v_2}[\langle[\![1583]\!],[\![\mathtt{Nil}]\!]\rangle/v_2] \\
&\equiv \mathsf{Split}(\langle[\![1583]\!],[\![\mathtt{Nil}]\!]\rangle, u_1.u_2.[\![\backslash \mathtt{x} \mathtt{->} \backslash \mathtt{xs} \mathtt{->} \mathtt{xs}]\!] \bullet u_1 \bullet u_2) \\
&\simeq [\![\backslash \mathtt{x} \mathtt{->} \backslash \mathtt{xs} \mathtt{->} \mathtt{x}]\!] \bullet [\![1583]\!] \bullet [\![\mathtt{Nil}]\!] \\
&\equiv \mathsf{Let}\, v_1 \Leftarrow [\![\backslash \mathtt{x} \mathtt{->} \backslash \mathtt{xs} \mathtt{->} \mathtt{x}]\!] \bullet [\![1583]\!]\, \mathsf{in}\, v_1\,[\![\mathtt{Nil}]\!] \\
&\equiv \mathsf{Let}\, v_1 \Leftarrow (\mathsf{Let}\, v_2 \Leftarrow [\![\backslash \mathtt{x} \mathtt{->} \backslash \mathtt{xs} \mathtt{->} \mathtt{x}]\!]\, \mathsf{in}\, v_2\,[\![1583]\!])\, \mathsf{in}\, v_1\,[\![\mathtt{Nil}]\!] \\
&\simeq \mathsf{Let}\, v_1 \Leftarrow ((\lambda \mathtt{x}.[\![\backslash \mathtt{xs} \mathtt{->} \mathtt{x}]\!])\,[\![1583]\!])\, \mathsf{in}\, v_1\,[\![\mathtt{Nil}]\!] \\
&\simeq \mathsf{Let}\, v_1 \Leftarrow [\![\backslash \mathtt{xs} \mathtt{->} 1583]\!]\, \mathsf{in}\, v_1\,[\![\mathtt{Nil}]\!] \\
&\simeq (\lambda \mathtt{xs}.[\![1583]\!])[\![\mathtt{Nil}]\!] \\
&\simeq [\![1583]\!]
\end{aligned}$$

The calculation is extremely detailed but each step is trivial. A more tractable way to reason about $\mathcal{H}$ programs is to appeal to a set of laws formulated at the object level, such as those we develop in §6.5. Such laws can be proved correct by translation into the metalanguage, and then used for object level reasoning.

The other point to make about this calculation is that it holds for any computational monad, not just the one in Definition 6.7. An important reason for parameterising the semantics is so that program calculations that do not depend on the detail of a particular computational monad can be proved once and for all.

Denotational implies operational equivalence

We prove a soundness theorem: that denotational implies operational equivalence. Completeness or full abstraction—whether operational implies denotational equivalence—is left as an open problem.

Proposition 6.28

(1) If $(\Gamma \vdash c \simeq c')$ then $(\Gamma \vdash c \mathrel{\widehat{\simeq}} c')$.

(2) For all programs e, e', if $e \simeq e'$ then $e = e'$.

(3) If $(\Gamma \vdash e \simeq e')$ then $(\Gamma \vdash e = e')$.

Proof. Part (1). We have $[\![\Gamma]\!] \vdash \mathsf{Val}|c| \simeq \mathsf{Val}|c'|$, and therefore by the monadic injectivity requirement, we have $[\![\Gamma]\!] \vdash |c| \simeq |c'|$. By analysis of the type of c and c' there are three cases to consider:

Case $c \equiv \ell, c' \equiv \ell'$. We have $[\![\Gamma]\!] \vdash \lfloor \ell \rfloor \simeq \lfloor \ell' \rfloor$, therefore $\ell = \ell'$ as required.

Case $c \equiv (\backslash x{::}\tau \mathrel{-}{>} e), c' \equiv (\backslash x{::}\tau \mathrel{-}{>} e')$. We have $[\![\Gamma]\!] \vdash (\lambda x. [\![e]\!]) \simeq (\lambda x. [\![e']\!])$ and therefore $[\![\Gamma]\!], x{:}T[\![\tau]\!] \vdash [\![e]\!] \simeq [\![e']\!]$ by canonical freeness in $\mathcal{M}$, as required.

Case $c \equiv (K\, e_1 \ldots e_m), c' \equiv (K'\, e'_1 \ldots e'_n)$. Suppose c and c' are of type μ in environment Γ. We have

$$[\![\Gamma]\!] \vdash \mathsf{Intro}^{[\mu]}(in_{Rank(K,\mu)}(\langle [\![e_1]\!], \ldots, [\![e_m]\!] \rangle)) \simeq \mathsf{Intro}^{[\mu]}(in_{Rank(K',\mu)}(\langle [\![e'_1]\!], \ldots, [\![e'_n]\!] \rangle))$$

Therefore we have $K = K'$ and $m = n$ and for each i, $[\![\Gamma]\!] \vdash [\![e_i]\!] \simeq [\![e'_i]\!]$ by canonical freeness in $\mathcal{M}$, as required.

For part (2) we prove that the ground restriction, $\mathcal{S}$, of denotational equivalence is an applicative bisimulation:

$$\mathcal{S} \stackrel{\text{def}}{=} \{(e, e') \mid [\![e]\!] \simeq [\![e']\!]\}$$

Since $\mathcal{S}$ is symmetric we need only prove that it is an applicative simulation. Suppose then that $e \Downarrow c$. By the correspondence theorem we have $[\![e]\!] \Downarrow [\![c]\!]$. Since $[\![e]\!] \simeq [\![e']\!]$ there is a V such that $[\![e']\!] \Downarrow V$ and $[\![c]\!] \simeq V$ by operational adequacy for $\mathcal{M}$. By correspondence there is a canonical c' such that $e' \Downarrow c'$ and $V \equiv [\![c']\!]$. We have that $[\![c]\!] \simeq [\![c']\!]$, and hence that $c \simeq c'$. Hence by (1) we have $c \mathrel{\widehat{\simeq}} c'$, which is to say $c\,\widehat{\mathcal{S}}\,c'$ as required.

Part (3). We are to show for any Γ-closure, $\cdot[\bar{P}/x]$, that $e[\bar{P}/x] = e'[\bar{P}/x]$. But from $[\![\Gamma]\!] \vdash [\![e]\!] \simeq [\![e']\!]$ and **Spec** we have $[\![e]\!][[\![\bar{P}]\!]/x] \simeq [\![e']\!][[\![\bar{P}]\!]/x]$. By substitution lemma we have $[\![e[\bar{P}/x]]\!] \simeq [\![e'[\bar{P}/x]]\!]$. Then by part (2) we are done. ∎

6.5   A theory of $\mathcal{H}$ programming

We state a collection of programming laws in Table 6.8. In his seminal study of programming languages [138], Strachey begins his discussion of expressions and evaluation with the definition that the "characteristic feature of an expression is that it has a **value**." What we have called canonical expressions correspond to what Strachey calls values. Expressions in $\mathcal{H}$ are more expressive than Strachey's in that the former include recursive expressions and hence non-termination. Nonetheless what we have named Strachey's property in Table 6.8 conveys the essence of Strachey's view: that every $\mathcal{H}$ program either equals Ω or some canonical program.

We show in this section that all these laws hold for both operational and denotational equivalence, except the principle of bisimulation-up-to-=, which has only been proved for operational equivalence. We conjecture without proof that it holds also for denotational equivalence. We begin with operational equivalence.

Proposition 6.29 *All the laws from Table 6.8 hold for operational equivalence:*

(1) *Strachey's property;*

(2) *congruence;*

(3) *canonical freeness;*

(4) *beta, strictness and eta laws;*

(5) *co-induction.*

Proof. The proof is similar to that of Proposition 5.1. ∎

We prove the same results, apart from the co-induction principle, for denotational equivalence.

Proposition 6.30 *All the laws from Table 6.8 hold for denotational equivalence (with $\simeq$ in place of $=$):*

(1) *Strachey's property;*

(2) *congruence;*

(3) *canonical freeness;*

(4) *beta, strictness and eta laws.*

Proof. (1) By definition of evaluation, any program e either diverges or evaluates to some canonical program c. Then by operational adequacy, in the first case $e \simeq \Omega$, and in the second, $e \simeq c$.

(2) Given $(\Gamma \vdash e \cong e')$ we are to show $(\Gamma \vdash e \simeq e')$. Proceed by an analysis of which rule in Table 6.7 derived $(\Gamma \vdash e \cong e')$. In each case from the rule's antecedents, we can use the denotational semantics rules in Table 6.6 to prove $(\llbracket \Gamma \rrbracket \vdash \llbracket e \rrbracket \simeq \llbracket e' \rrbracket)$ as required.

(3) Canonical freeness for denotational equivalence was proved as Proposition 6.28(1).

(4) Each law takes the form $\Gamma \vdash e_L \simeq e_R$. By definition we are to show, for all $\llbracket \Gamma \rrbracket$-closures, $\cdot [\tilde{L}/\tilde{x}]$, that $\llbracket e_L \rrbracket [\tilde{L}/\tilde{x}] \simeq \llbracket e_R \rrbracket [\tilde{L}/\tilde{x}]$. Terms are identified up to alpha-conversion so we may assume that any bound variable in $\llbracket e_L \rrbracket$ or $\llbracket e_R \rrbracket$ is distinct from variables in the list $\tilde{x}$. For each beta law we can check by inspection that $\llbracket e_L \rrbracket [\tilde{L}/\tilde{x}] \rightarrow^+ \llbracket e_R \rrbracket [\tilde{L}/\tilde{x}]$. For each eta law we can check the same property, but with appeal also to the laws of canonical programs in Table 6.2. For each strictness law $e_R \equiv \Omega$ we can check that $\llbracket e_L \rrbracket [\tilde{L}/\tilde{x}] \Uparrow$. Therefore for any one of the strictness laws the required equation follows from operational adequacy of $\mathcal{M}$. ∎

As a simple example of co-induction, here is a proof of an equivalence (of two streams) used by Paulson to illustrate Scott induction [105]. Since the two streams are unbounded, structural induction would fail on this example.

Proposition 6.31 *For any* f::σ -> σ *and* x::σ,

$$\text{iterate f (f x)} = \text{map f (iterate f x)}.$$

(Definitions of iterate *and* map *are shown in Table 6.3.)*

Proof. Consider relation S defined as follows.

$$S = \{(\text{iterate f (f x)}, \text{map f (iterate f x)}) \mid \text{f}::\sigma \text{ -> } \sigma, \text{x}::\sigma\}$$

We shall prove that the union $S \cup \equiv$ is a bisimulation-up-to-$=$, and hence that $S \subseteq =$. Suppose then that e and e' are arbitrary programs such that eSe'. Set

$$e_0 \equiv \text{iterate f (f (f x))}$$
$$e_0' \equiv \text{map f (iterate f (f x))}$$

Strachey's Property

Any program e either equals Ω or some canonical term c.

Congruence

If $(\Gamma \vdash e \mathrel{\hat{=}} e')$ then $(\Gamma \vdash e = e')$.

Canonical Freeness

If $(\Gamma \vdash c = c')$ then $(\Gamma \vdash c \mathrel{\hat{=}} c')$.

Beta Laws

$$\Gamma \vdash (\ell_1 \oplus \ell_2) = \ell_1 \oplus \ell_2$$
$$\Gamma \vdash (\text{if}\underline{T} \text{ then } e_1 \text{ else } e_2) = e_1$$
$$\Gamma \vdash (\text{if}\underline{F} \text{ then } e_1 \text{ else } e_2) = e_2$$
$$\Gamma \vdash ((\backslash x{::}\sigma \rightarrow e_1) \, e_2) = e_1[e_2/x]$$
$$\Gamma \vdash ((\backslash x{::}\sigma \rightarrow e)\hat{\,}c) = e[c/x]$$
$$\Gamma \vdash (\text{case}^\mu (K_i \, e_1 \cdots e_m) \text{ of } (K_1 \rightarrow e_1') \mid \cdots \mid (K_n \rightarrow e_n')) = (e_i' \, e_1 \cdots e_m)$$
$$\Gamma \vdash \text{rec}(x.\, e) = e[\text{rec}(x.\, e)/x]$$

Strictness Laws

$$\Gamma \vdash LE(\Omega) = \Omega$$
$$\Gamma \vdash RE(\Omega) = \Omega$$

Eta Laws

$$\Gamma \vdash (\text{if } c \text{ then } e \text{ else } e) = e$$
$$\Gamma \vdash (\backslash x{::}\sigma \rightarrow c \, x) = c \qquad \text{if } x \notin fv(c)$$
$$\Gamma \vdash (\text{case}^\mu c \text{ of } \cdots \mid (K_i \, x_1 \ldots x_{Arity(K_i,\mu)} \rightarrow e) \mid \cdots) = e \quad \text{if no } x_i \in fv(e)$$

Co-induction

A **bisimulation-up-to-=** is a ground relation, $\mathcal{S}$, such that whenever $e \mathcal{S} e'$, either $e = e' = \Omega$, or there are canonical programs c, c' such that $e = c$, $e' = c'$ and $c \mathrel{\widehat{\mathcal{S}}} c'$.

Any bisimulation-up-to-= is a subset of ground equivalence.

Table 6.8: Laws of equivalence in $\mathcal{H}$

and we can calculate as follows.

$$e \equiv \texttt{iterate f (f x)}$$
$$\quad = \texttt{f x} : e_0$$
$$e' \equiv \texttt{map f (iterate f x)}$$
$$\quad = \texttt{map f (x : iterate f (f x))}$$
$$\quad = \texttt{f x} : e_0'$$

Since $(\texttt{f x}) \equiv (\texttt{f x})$ and $e_0 \mathcal{S} e_0'$ we have $(\texttt{f x} : e_0) \,\widehat{\mathcal{S} \cup {\equiv}}\, (\texttt{f x} : e_0')$. Since e and e' were arbitrary we have established that $\mathcal{S} \cup {\equiv}$ is a bisimulation-up-to-=. Hence $\mathcal{S} \subseteq {=}$ and the proposition follows.   ∎

6.6   Derived laws of programming

In this section we derive further laws of program equivalence. Their derivations depend only on the laws in Table 6.8 (not including co-induction) so they hold for both operational and denotational equivalence. It is reassuring that these familiar results, functional extensionality and structural induction, can be derived simply from the theory of $\mathcal{H}$.

Functional extensionality

Two canonical functions are equal if whenever they are applied to the same argument they yield the same answer.

Proposition 6.32   *If* $(\Gamma, x{::}\sigma \vdash c\,x = c'\,x)$ *then* $(\Gamma \vdash c = c' :: (\sigma \texttt{ -> } \tau))$.

Proof. We may assume that the canonical terms c and c' take the forms $(\backslash x \texttt{ -> } e)$ and $(\backslash x \texttt{ -> } e')$. We have $(\Gamma, x{::}\sigma \vdash (\backslash x \texttt{ -> } e)\,x = (\backslash x \texttt{ -> } e')\,x)$. Therefore by the beta law for functions we have $(\Gamma, x{::}\sigma \vdash e = e')$. Then by precongruence $(\Gamma \vdash c = c')$.   ∎

This principle does not extend to non-canonical functions. Counterexample: let programs $\texttt{f}$ and $\texttt{g}$ of type $\sigma \texttt{ -> } \tau$ be Ω and $(\backslash x \texttt{ -> } \Omega)$ respectively. Then $(x{::}\sigma \vdash \texttt{f } x = \texttt{g} x)$ yet $\texttt{f} \neq \texttt{g}$ since $\texttt{f}{\Uparrow}$ whereas $\texttt{g}{\Downarrow}$.

Structural induction for sum-of-product types

We can derive a familiar structural induction principle for a class of sum-of-product types.

Definition 6.33   *A* **sum-of-products** *type is an algebraic datatype* μ *such that* $\mu \equiv (\texttt{data}\,X = \texttt{dc}_1 | \cdots | \texttt{dc}_n)$ *and each clause* $\texttt{dc}_i$ *takes the form* $(K\,\sigma_1 \cdots \sigma_m)$ *where each* σ_i *is either the variable* X *or is closed.*

For each such type μ, *define a program* $\texttt{size}^\mu$:

$$\texttt{size}^\mu \;::\; \mu \texttt{ -> Int}$$
$$\texttt{size}^\mu \;\overset{\text{def}}{=}\; \texttt{rec(size.} \backslash x \texttt{ -> case } x \texttt{ of cc}_1 | \cdots | \texttt{cc}_n)$$

where for each i, if $\mathrm{dc}_i \equiv (K\, \sigma_1 \cdots \sigma_m)$ we define cc_i to be:

$$\mathrm{cc}_i \stackrel{\mathrm{def}}{=} (K\, x_1 \cdots x_m \mathrel{-\!\!>} 1 + \mathrm{t}_1 + \cdots + \mathrm{t}_m)$$

$$\text{where each } \mathrm{t}_j \stackrel{\mathrm{def}}{=} \begin{cases} \mathtt{size}(x_j) & \text{if } \sigma_j = X \\ 0 & \text{otherwise} \end{cases}$$

Define $Finite^\mu$ to be the following set of μ-programs:

$$Finite^\mu \stackrel{\mathrm{def}}{=} \{\mathrm{e} \mid \mathrm{e} \text{ is a } \mu\text{-program and } \exists n \in \mathbb{N}.\ \mathtt{size}^\mu\, \mathrm{e} = \underline{n}\}$$

*Finally, say that a μ-program e is **finite** iff $\mathrm{e} \in Finite^\mu$.*

Proposition 6.34 *Suppose μ is a sum-of-product type $(\mathtt{data}\, X = \mathrm{dc}_1 | \cdots | \mathrm{dc}_n)$. If ϕ is a predicate on finite μ-programs, that is, $\phi \subseteq Finite^\mu$, then the following induction principle is valid:*

$$\text{for each clause } \mathrm{dc}_i \equiv (K\, \sigma_1 \cdots \sigma_m), \quad \forall \mathrm{e}_1 \in \psi_1. \ldots \forall \mathrm{e}_m \in \psi_m.\, (K\, \mathrm{e}_1 \cdots \mathrm{e}_m) \in \phi$$

$$\text{where each set } \psi_j \stackrel{\mathrm{def}}{=} \begin{cases} \phi & \text{if } \sigma_j = X \\ \{\mathrm{e} \mid \mathrm{e}{::}\sigma_j\} & \text{otherwise} \end{cases}$$

$$\rule{9cm}{0.4pt}$$

$$Finite^\mu \subseteq \phi$$

Proof. Suppose that the rule hypothesis holds. By mathematical induction on n we prove for all μ-programs e that if $\mathtt{size}(\mathrm{e}) = \underline{n}$ then $\mathrm{e} \in \phi$. This amounts to a proof that $Finite^\mu \subseteq \phi$ as required.

Suppose then that $\mathtt{size}(\mathrm{e}) = \underline{n}$ for some e. By Strachey's property we have that either $\mathrm{e} = \Omega$ or e equals a canonical program. But $\mathtt{size}(\Omega) = \Omega$ by the strictness law for **case**-expressions, so e must be canonical. So there must be a clause $(K\, \sigma_1 \cdots \sigma_m)$ such that $\mathrm{e} = (K\, \mathrm{e}_1 \cdots \mathrm{e}_m)$. From $\mathtt{size}(K\, \mathrm{e}_1 \cdots \mathrm{e}_m) = \underline{n}$ we have:

$$(1 + \mathrm{t}_1 + \cdots + \mathrm{t}_m) = \underline{n} \text{ where for each } j,\ \mathrm{t}_j = \begin{cases} \mathtt{size}(\mathrm{e}_j) & \text{if } \sigma_j = X \\ 0 & \text{otherwise} \end{cases}.$$

We can show that each $\mathrm{e}_j \in \psi_j$. Either $\sigma_j = X$ or not. If $\sigma_j = X$, from the equation above we have that $\mathtt{size}(\mathrm{e}_j) = \underline{m}$ for some $m < n$. So by IH we have $\mathrm{e}_j \in \phi = \psi_j$. Otherwise, we know that $\mathrm{e}_j{::}\sigma_j$ since $\mathrm{e} = (K\, \mathrm{e}_1 \cdots \mathrm{e}_m)$, and hence $\mathrm{e}_j \in \psi_j$.

Since each $\mathrm{e}_j \in \psi_j$ we can conclude that $\mathrm{e} \in \phi$ from the rule's hypothesis. Hence we have that every program $\mathrm{e}{:}\mu$ of any size is contained in ϕ. So $Finite^\mu \subseteq \phi$ and we have verified the induction principle.   ∎

The list type is a sum-of-products type in the sense of Definition 6.33. Given a closed type a of list elements, the general definition of $\mathtt{size}$ given there specialises to the following:

```
size[a]  ::  [a] -> Int
size[a]  def  rec(size.\x -> case x of
                  Nil -> 1
                  Cons x xs -> 1 + 0 + size(xs))
```

The set $Finite^{[a]}$ consists of those $[a]$-programs xs such that $(\mathtt{size}\, \mathrm{xs}) = \underline{n}$, for some n. We call such a list **finite**. Lists $[1, 2, 3]$ or $[]$ are finite; lists Ω, $[\Omega]$, $(1 : \Omega)$, rec(xs.1 : xs) (which are all distinct, since Cons is lazy) are not finite, in this sense. Proposition 6.34 yields the following structural induction principle for finite lists,

$$\frac{\text{Nil} \in \phi \qquad \forall x::a.\, \forall xs \in \phi.\, (\text{Cons } x\, xs) \in \phi}{Finite^{[a]} \subseteq \phi}$$

where $\phi \subseteq Finite^{[a]}$ is a predicate on lists.

6.7 $\mathcal{HX}$, an extension of $\mathcal{H}$ with exceptions

We develop our theory of functional programming by considering what happens when we add an exception mechanism to $\mathcal{H}$. Languages such as Standard ML and Modula-3 have an exception mechanism, which is typically used by programmers to express error conditions. We use exceptions in Chapter 7 to model the demand for function arguments during evaluation. In $\mathcal{HX}$, a computation of type σ can either return a value of type σ, diverge, or raise an exception. For the sake of simplicity, we consider a language with just one exception, the canonical term bang. Raising an exception is represented by a program evaluating to bang, which is present at every type. For the sake of brevity, we say the program has **banged**. Program bang bangs. In general, if a program needs to evaluate several subterms before terminating, and evaluation of any one of the subterms bangs, then the whole program bangs. The only exemptions from this rule are programs of the form (e_1 ?? e_2). If evaluation of e_1 returns an answer or diverges, then evaluation of the whole program does so too. But if evaluation of e_1 bangs, then the whole program behaves the same as e_2. The operator, ??, called **biased choice**, is a new primitive in $\mathcal{HX}$; it is a version without parameters of exception handling mechanisms found in Standard ML and Modula-3.

Definition 6.35

- *The abstract syntax of $\mathcal{HX}$ is based on the same syntactic categories as $\mathcal{H}$, defined by the $\mathcal{H}$ rules from Table 6.1 augmented by the two new syntactic rules from Table 6.9.*

- *Define the predicate Mute(c) on canonical terms, to hold iff for no type τ does $c \equiv \text{bang}^\tau$.*

- *The type assignment relation, ($\Gamma \vdash e :: \tau$), is inductively defined by the $\mathcal{H}$ rules from Table 6.2, together with the new type assignment rules from Table 6.9.*

- *The reduction and evaluation relations for $\mathcal{HX}$ are the binary relations on $\mathcal{HX}$ programs, $\rightarrow$ and $\Downarrow$ respectively, defined inductively by the reduction and evaluation rules respectively, from Tables 6.5 and 6.9. The rule for call-by-value reduction in Table 6.5 is to apply only when Mute(c), and the rule for call-by-value evaluation only when Mute(c_2).*

- *Make the following definitions of parameters T, Val and Let:*

$$T\sigma \overset{\text{def}}{=} (\sigma + 1)_\perp$$
$$\text{Val}(N) \overset{\text{def}}{=} \text{Lift}(\text{Inl}(N))$$
$$(\text{Let } v \Leftarrow M \text{ in } N) \overset{\text{def}}{=} \text{Seq}(x, u.\, \text{Case}\,(u, v.\, N, w.\, \text{Lift}\,(\text{Inr}(*))))$$

Syntax

$$c ::= \text{bang} \quad (\text{exception})$$
$$e ::= (e_1 \text{ ?? } e_2) \quad (\text{biased choice})$$

Type Assignment

$$\Gamma \vdash \text{bang}^\sigma :: \sigma \qquad \frac{\Gamma \vdash e_1 :: \sigma \qquad \Gamma \vdash e_2 :: \sigma}{\Gamma \vdash (e_1 \text{ ?? } e_2) :: \sigma}$$

Reduction Semantics

$$\frac{e_1 \to e_1'}{(e_1 \text{ ?? } e_2) \to (e_1' \text{ ?? } e_2)} \qquad (\text{bang}^\sigma \text{ ?? } e) \to e$$

$$(c \text{ ?? } e) \to c \qquad \text{if } Mute(c)$$

$$LE(\text{bang}^\sigma) \to \text{bang}^\tau \qquad \text{if } \varnothing \vdash LE[\text{bang}^\sigma] :: \tau$$
$$RE(\text{bang}^\sigma) \to \text{bang}^\tau \qquad \text{if } \varnothing \vdash RE[\text{bang}^\sigma] :: \tau$$

Evaluation Semantics

$$e \Downarrow \text{bang}^\sigma \qquad \varnothing \vdash LE(e) :: \tau \qquad\qquad e_1 \Downarrow \ell \quad e_2 \Downarrow \text{bang}^\sigma \quad \varnothing \vdash e_1 \oplus e_2 :: \tau$$
$$\frac{}{LE(e) \Downarrow \text{bang}^\tau} \qquad\qquad\qquad \frac{}{(e_1 \oplus e_2) \Downarrow \text{bang}^\tau}$$

$$\frac{e_1 \Downarrow (\backslash x \text{ -> } e) \quad e_2 \Downarrow \text{bang}^\sigma \quad \varnothing \vdash e_1{\hat{\ }}e_2 :: \tau}{(e_1{\hat{\ }}e_2) \Downarrow \text{bang}^\tau}$$

$$\frac{e_1 \Downarrow c \qquad Mute\,(c)}{(e_1 \text{ ?? } e_2) \Downarrow c} \qquad \frac{e_1 \Downarrow \text{bang}^\sigma \qquad e_2 \Downarrow c}{(e_1 \text{ ?? } e_2) \Downarrow c}$$

Denotational Semantics

$$\begin{aligned}
\text{bang} \;&:\; T\sigma \\
\text{alt} \;&:\; T\sigma \to T\sigma \to T\sigma \\
\text{bang} \;&\stackrel{\text{def}}{=}\; \text{Lift}(\text{Inr}(*)) \\
\text{alt} \;&\stackrel{\text{def}}{=}\; \lambda x.\, \lambda y.\, \text{Seq}\,(x, u.\ \text{Case}\,(u, v.\ \text{Val}\,(v), w.\, y))
\end{aligned}$$

$$[\![\text{bang}^\sigma]\!] \stackrel{\text{def}}{=} \text{bang}^{[\![\sigma]\!]}$$
$$[\![e_1 \text{ ?? } e_2]\!] \stackrel{\text{def}}{=} \text{alt}[\![e_1]\!][\![e_2]\!]$$

Table 6.9: $\mathcal{HX}$, an extension of $\mathcal{H}$ with exceptions

Given these parameters, together with the polymorphic $\mathcal{M}$ constants bang and alt defined in Table 6.9, inductively define the denotational semantics of $\mathcal{HX}$ according to the rules in Tables 6.6 and 6.9; denotational rule $[\![c]\!] = \mathsf{Val}|c|$ from Table 6.6 is to apply only when $Mute(c)$.

Proposition 6.36

(1) *The type assignment laws of Proposition 6.2 remain valid for $\mathcal{HX}$, except for the statements about canonical terms in Table 6.2.*

(2) *In $\mathcal{HX}$, we have the following properties of canonical terms:*

   (a) *If c::Bool then either $c \equiv \mathsf{bang}^{\mathtt{Bool}}$ or $(\exists b \in \{tt, ff\}.\, c \equiv \underline{b})$.*

   (b) *If c::Int then either $c \equiv \mathsf{bang}^{\mathtt{Int}}$ or $(\exists n \in \mathrm{N}.\, c \equiv \underline{n})$.*

   (c) *If c::$(\sigma \rightarrow \tau)$ then either $c \equiv \mathsf{bang}^{(\sigma\text{->}\tau)}$ or $(\exists e.\, c \equiv (\backslash x \text{->} e))$.*

   (d) *If c::μ then either $c \equiv \mathsf{bang}^{\mu}$ or $(\exists K, e_1, \ldots, e_m.\, c \equiv (K\, e_1 \cdots e_m))$.*

(3) *The operational semantics laws of Proposition 6.5 remain valid for $\mathcal{HX}$.*

(4) *The denotational semantics laws of Proposition 6.8 remain valid for $\mathcal{HX}$.*

Proof. Part (1) follows by easy rule inductions, similar to Proposition 6.2. Part (2) follows by inspection of the type assignment rules. Proof of part (3) is similar to that for Proposition 6.5. (4) follows by simple inductions as before. ∎

As in $\mathcal{H}$, we can prove a close correspondence between evaluation of an $\mathcal{HX}$ program and its denotation.

Proposition 6.37

(1) *For any $T\sigma$-program M, either $M\Uparrow$, or $M \Downarrow \mathsf{bang}$ or $M \Downarrow \mathsf{Val}(N)$ for some σ-program N.*

(2) *The operational behaviour of the denotational constants obeys the following rules:*

$$\frac{M\Uparrow}{(\mathsf{Let}\, v \Leftarrow M \text{ in } N)\Uparrow} \qquad \frac{M\Uparrow}{(\mathsf{alt}\, M\, N)\Uparrow}$$

$$\frac{M \Downarrow \mathsf{Val}(L)}{(\mathsf{Let}\, v \Leftarrow M \text{ in } N)\rightarrow^+ N[L\!/\!v]} \qquad \frac{M \Downarrow \mathsf{Val}(L)}{(\mathsf{alt}\, M\, N)\rightarrow^+ \mathsf{Val}\,(L)}$$

$$\frac{M \Downarrow \mathsf{bang}}{(\mathsf{Let}\, v \Leftarrow M \text{ in } N)\rightarrow^+\mathsf{bang}} \qquad \frac{M \Downarrow \mathsf{bang}}{(\mathsf{Let}\, v \Leftarrow M \text{ in } N)\rightarrow^+ N}$$

(3) *If $e \Downarrow c$ then $[\![e]\!] \Downarrow [\![c]\!]$.*

(4) *If $[\![e]\!] \Downarrow V$ then there is c such that $V \equiv [\![c]\!]$ and $e \Downarrow c$.*

(5) *$e \Downarrow c$ iff $[\![e]\!] \Downarrow [\![c]\!]$.*

Proof. Parts (1) and (2) follow by calculating from the definitions of Val, Let, bang and alt.

Part (3) follows by induction on the depth of inference of $e \Downarrow c$ as before. Part (4) follows by induction on the depth of inference of $[\![e]\!] \Downarrow V$. We show one case to illustrate the proof. Suppose that e is $(e_1 \oplus e_2)$ and that $[\![e]\!] \Downarrow V$, where $\oplus \in \{+, -, \times\}$. We have:

$$\text{Let } v_1 \Leftarrow [\![e_1]\!] \text{ in Let } v_2 \Leftarrow [\![e_2]\!] \text{ in } \mathsf{Seq}(v_1 \lfloor + \rfloor v_2, x.\ \mathsf{Val}\ (x)) \Downarrow V$$

Since each $[\![e_i]\!]$ is a program of type $T\mathsf{Num}$, by parts (1) and (3) either $[\![e_i]\!]\Uparrow$, $(\exists m_i.\ [\![e_i]\!] \Downarrow \mathsf{Val}(\lfloor m_i \rfloor))$, or $[\![e_i]\!] \Downarrow \mathsf{bang}$. Since $[\![e]\!]$ converges to V by appeal to part (2) we have only three cases to consider:

(a) $[\![e_1]\!] \Downarrow \mathsf{bang}$ and $[\![e]\!] \Downarrow \mathsf{bang} \equiv V$.

(b) $[\![e_1]\!] \Downarrow \mathsf{Val}(\lfloor m_1 \rfloor)$, $[\![e_2]\!] \Downarrow \mathsf{bang}$ and $[\![e]\!] \Downarrow \mathsf{bang} \equiv V$.

(c) $[\![e_1]\!] \Downarrow \mathsf{Val}(\lfloor m_1 \rfloor)$, $[\![e_2]\!] \Downarrow \mathsf{Val}(\lfloor m_2 \rfloor)$
    and $[\![e]\!] \to^+ \mathsf{Seq}(\lfloor m_1 \rfloor \lfloor \oplus \rfloor \lfloor m_2 \rfloor, x.\ \mathsf{Val}\ (x)) \Downarrow V$.

In each case we exhibit c such that $e \Downarrow c$ and $[\![c]\!] \equiv V$.

(a) Take c to be bang. By IH, we have $e_1 \Downarrow \mathsf{bang}$ and then $(e_1 \oplus e_2) \Downarrow \mathsf{bang}$.

(b) Take c to be bang. By IH, we have $e_1 \Downarrow m_1$ and $e_2 \Downarrow \mathsf{bang}$, so then $(e_1 \oplus e_2) \Downarrow \mathsf{bang}$.

(c) Take c to be $m_1 \oplus m_2$. By IH, we have $e_1 \Downarrow m_1$ and $e_1 \Downarrow m_2$, so $e \Downarrow m_1 \oplus m_2$. But $\mathsf{Seq}(\lfloor m_1 \rfloor \lfloor \oplus \rfloor \lfloor m_2 \rfloor, x.\ \mathsf{Val}\ (x)) \Downarrow [\![m_1 \oplus m_2]\!]$ so $V \equiv [\![m_1 \oplus m_2]\!]$ as required.

Finally, part (5) is a corollary of parts (3) and (4). ∎

We now rework the theory of operational equivalence. We conjecture that denotational equivalence could be reworked similarly, but leave this as future work.

Definition 6.38 *We adopt all the definitions to do with confined relations and applicative similarity and bisimilarity from §6.2 and §6.3 for $\mathcal{HX}$, with the following amendment. In $\mathcal{HX}$, given a confined relation $\mathcal{R}$ the confined relation $\widehat{\mathcal{R}}$ is defined by the rules in the first half of Table 6.7, together with the additional rules:*

$$\frac{}{\Gamma \vdash \mathsf{bang}\ \widehat{\mathcal{R}}\ \mathsf{bang}} \qquad \frac{\Gamma \vdash e_i \mathcal{R} e_i'}{\Gamma \vdash (e_1\ ??\ e_1')\ \widehat{\mathcal{R}}\ (e_2\ ??\ e_2')}$$

Proposition 6.39

(1) *All the properties of confined and ground relations proved in §6.2 remain true.*

(2) *Applicative bisimilarity is an operationally adequate precongruence.*

Proof. By reworking §6.2 and §6.3. We omit the details. ∎

As before we take operational equivalence to be applicative bisimilarity. We finish this section on $\mathcal{HX}$ by reworking the laws of programming introduced in §6.5:

Proposition 6.40 *The laws of $\mathcal{H}$ programming in Table 6.8 hold for $\mathcal{HX}$ given the following modifications:*

- *The beta law for call-by-value application has a new side-condition that $Mute(c)$.*

- *There are new beta laws for biased choice:*

$$\Gamma \vdash (\mathsf{bang}\ ??\ e) = e \qquad \Gamma \vdash (c\ ??\ e') = c \quad \text{if } Mute(c)$$

- Each eta law has a new side-condition that $Mute(c)$.
- There is a new eta law for biased choice:

  $$\Gamma \vdash (e \;??\; bang) = e$$

- There are additional strictness laws:

  $$\Gamma \vdash (\Omega \;??\; e) = \Omega$$
  $$\Gamma \vdash LE(bang) = bang$$
  $$\Gamma \vdash RE(bang) = bang$$

Proof. By reworking the proof of Proposition 6.29.   ■

We leave a study of denotational equivalence for $\mathcal{HX}$ as future work. The following result, stated without proof, would be useful.

Proposition 6.41 *The structure* $(T, \mathsf{Val}, \mathsf{Let})$ *introduced in Definition 6.35 is a computational monad.*

This implies for instance that the example calculation shown earlier for $\mathcal{H}$ is valid for $\mathcal{HX}$ too.

Chapter 7

Four mechanisms for teletype I/O

In this chapter we consider four widely-implemented mechanisms for I/O in functional languages: side-effecting I/O, continuation-passing I/O, synchronised-stream I/O and Landin-stream I/O. In the context of interaction with a teletype, we sketch the semantics of side-effecting I/O and give detailed semantics for the other three mechanisms. These semantics are based on the theory of $\mathcal{H}$ and $\mathcal{H}\mathcal{X}$ developed in the previous chapter. Teletype I/O is a very limited model of I/O in which the computer interacts with a keyboard and a character based printer. By concentrating on a simple I/O model the contrasts between the four I/O mechanisms can be clearly seen.

We do not describe related work on using functional languages with more complex I/O models in any detail. For the record, the interested reader is referred to papers on the following topics: asynchronous interrupts [74], polling the keyboard [87, 147], real time behaviour [29, 50], interaction with a file system [51, 64, 142], concurrency [11, 23, 57, 82, 126], controlling a window system [19, 33], writing an operating system shell in a functional language [35, 73, 84, 131] and even the whole operating system [3, 53, 69, 136, 144, 145]. Surveys by Hudak and Sundaresh [60], Jones and Sinclair [67] and Perry [108] cover much of this previous work.

In §7.1 we sketch how the denotational semantics of $\mathcal{H}$ can be extended to accommodate side-effecting I/O and discuss why side-effecting I/O is unsuitable for lazy languages.

We base the semantics of the remaining three I/O mechanisms on the language $\mathcal{H}\mathcal{X}$ defined in Chapter 6. Continuation-passing and synchronised-stream I/O can be defined in terms of $\mathcal{H}$, but for Landin-stream I/O we need the exception mechanism in $\mathcal{H}\mathcal{X}$. We use exceptions to represent demand for a value in the input stream.

We use a style of operational semantics for the remaining three mechanisms that was first used by Holmström in his semantics of PFL [57]. Holmström used a continuation-passing style to embed CCS-like operations for communication and concurrency in a functional language. Starting with an evaluation relation for the host language, he defined the meaning of the embedded operations in the style of a labelled transition system, as used in CCS [94]. A labelled transition system is a way to formalise the idea that an agent (such as a functional program engaged in I/O) can perform an action (such as input or output of a character) and then become a successor agent. This style of semantics is attractive for at least three reasons. First, it can model a wide variety of nondeterministic and concurrent computation: witness the CCS school of concurrency theory. Second, the evaluation relation for the host language is unmodified; any property of the host language without I/O will still hold after the I/O mechanism has been added. Third, the method complements an operational language definition such as that of Standard ML [98]. In §7.2 we define notions of labelled transition system and bisimilarity on programs of $\mathcal{HX}$.

We go further than Holmström by developing an equational theory of functional I/O based on labelled transitions. We adopt bisimilarity from CCS as equivalence on programs engaged in I/O. Bisimilarity is an equivalence on agents induced by their operational behaviour: two agents are bisimilar iff whenever one can perform an action, the other can too such that their two successors are bisimilar.

Bisimilarity should not be confused with applicative bisimilarity. Each is defined as the greatest fixpoint of a certain functional, but they relate different kinds of behaviour. Applicative bisimilarity (as developed for $\mathcal{M}$ in Chapter 4 and for $\mathcal{H}$ and $\mathcal{HX}$ in Chapter 6) relates the evaluation behaviour of two programs. Bisimilarity (as defined in this chapter) relates the observable communication behaviour of two programs. Bisimilarity was introduced in Milner's theory of CCS, whereas applicative bisimilarity comes from Abramsky's theory of lazy λ-calculus (which itself followed CCS in part).

Both Landin-stream and synchronised-stream I/O are based on stream transformers, functions of type [inp] -> [out], where inp and out are types of input and output values respectively. §7.3 defines some general operations on stream transformers. §7.4 gives labelled transition system semantics for Landin-stream I/O, and explains why $\mathcal{HX}$ rather than $\mathcal{H}$ is needed. §7.5 and §7.6 give labelled transition system semantics for synchronised-stream and continuation-passing I/O respectively. The main result of the chapter is proved in §7.7: that there are bisimilarity preserving translations between the three mechanisms for teletype I/O other than side-effecting I/O. In this sense we have proved that the three are of equal expressiveness. The mappings between Landin-stream and continuation-passing I/O are original, whilst those between synchronised-stream and continuation-passing I/O were discovered during the design of Haskell [59, 60], but have not hitherto been verified formally. §7.8 concludes the chapter with a discussion of the practical use of the three mechanisms suitable for lazy languages.

7.1   Side-effecting I/O

The original functional language, LISP 1.5 [83], had a **side-effecting** I/O mechanism. Side-effecting I/O, which is by far the most widely-used mechanism for functional I/O, persists in LISP and is found in other eager languages such as Scheme and Standard ML.

To accommodate side-effecting I/O in $\mathcal{H}$ we add two new non-canonical operations to the syntax of expressions,

```
e ::= read      (read a character)
    | write(e) (write a character)
```

with typing rules and informal intended meanings as follows.

$$\Gamma \vdash \text{read} :: \text{Int} \qquad \frac{\Gamma \vdash e :: \text{Int}}{\Gamma \vdash \text{write}(e) :: ()}$$

- **read** means
  "input a character n from the keyboard and return $\underline{n}$."

- **write** $\underline{n}$ means
  "output character n to the printer and return unit, ()."

For example, here is a program to read two characters and output their sum.

```
main :: ()
main = write (read + read)
```

(Pardon the cavalier identification of Int and Char from §6.1.)

The denotational semantics of $\mathcal{H}$ can be extended to accommodate side-effecting I/O. Apart from diverging, there are three things a computation can do: return an answer, ask for a number as input, or output a number. Accordingly a computation of $\mathcal{H}$ type σ can be modelled as a term of $\mathcal{M}$ type $T[\![\sigma]\!]$, with the following definition of T, and corresponding definitions of $\text{Val}(M)$, $[\![\text{read}]\!]$ and $[\![\text{write}(e)]\!]$.

$$T\sigma \stackrel{\text{def}}{=} (\mu X. \sigma + (\text{Num} \to X_\perp) + (\text{Num} \times X_\perp))_\perp \quad (X \notin \mathit{ftv}(\sigma))$$

$$\text{Val}(M) \stackrel{\text{def}}{=} \text{Lift}(\text{Intro}(\text{In}_1(M)))$$

$$[\![\text{read}]\!] \stackrel{\text{def}}{=} \text{Lift}(\text{Intro}(\text{In}_2(\lambda v{:}\text{Num}. \text{Val}(v))))$$

$$[\![\text{write}(e)]\!] \stackrel{\text{def}}{=} \text{Let}\, v \Leftarrow [\![e]\!] \text{ in } \text{Lift}(\text{Intro}(\text{In}_3\langle v, [\![()]\!]\rangle))$$

This construction is based on Moggi's notes [101, Exercise 4.1.18.1] but the basic idea goes back at least as far as Plotkin's Pisa notes [118, Example 4 in Chapter 5]. This is just a sketch of the semantics; we omit the definition of Let. An analogous object level construction is detailed in Chapter 8. (Were $\mathcal{M}$ to be used in a detailed study of side-effecting I/O it would need to be extended to include mutually recursive $\mathcal{M}$ types, such as $[\![[\sigma]]\!]$.)

We do not pursue this construction here because the primary focus of this dissertation is the study of I/O for lazy languages, and, as is well-known, side-effecting I/O does not combine well with lazy languages. There are three reasons why the use of side-effecting I/O in a lazy language is problematic. First, to use side-effecting I/O in a lazy language, a programmer must be concerned with evaluation order, which because of laziness is harder to predict than in an eager language. Side-effecting I/O compels programmers to think about something that otherwise they can usually leave to the implementation.

The other two reasons depend on the observation that Strachey's property no longer holds. Recall Strachey's property from Chapter 6: that every program either equals Ω or some canonical program. Strachey's property holds for $\mathcal{H}$ and $\mathcal{HX}$, but not for $\mathcal{H}$ extended with side-effecting operators. Programs **read** and **write**($\underline{n}$) neither diverge nor equal any canonical program.

The second reason, then, that side-effecting I/O does not combine well with lazy languages is that adding side-effects makes a functional language harder to reason about. Proofs of programs are harder to construct, because there are more cases to consider than covered by Strachey's property. This applies to eager languages as well. With side-effecting I/O, one would expect that every program either diverges or converges to a canonical program, or does some I/O to become another program. How to formulate precisely and verify this expectation is an open question.

The third reason concerns efficiency. Strachey's property is important if languages with call-by-name semantics for function application are to be implemented efficiently. Such languages are only practical if call-by-need semantics coincides with call-by-name. If so, call-by-name applications can be implemented by call-by-need as in graph reduction [109, 143] for instance. Recall the difference between the two semantics for an application $(\backslash x \to e)e'$. In both regimes the function body e is evaluated. Under call-by-name semantics, each time need arises for the value of x, argument e' is evaluated. Under call-by-need semantics, the first time need arises for the value of x, argument e' is evaluated, but its value is retained, and re-used if subsequently the value of x is needed.

We give an informal proof that if evaluation is deterministic and operational equivalence satisfies operational adequacy and Strachey's property, then call-by-name semantics coincides with call-by-need. Consider an application $(\backslash x \to e)e'$. If the value of e does not depend on x then clearly both regimes are equivalent since the argument e' is never evaluated. Otherwise suppose that the value of x is demanded one or more times. By Strachey's property, the argument e' either equals Ω or some canonical form, so by operational adequacy, e' either diverges, or converges to a unique canonical form c. If e' diverges then so does the evaluation of e under either regime. Otherwise e' deterministically converges to c so it makes no difference whether the second and subsequent uses of the argument use a retained copy of c or evaluate e' again.

If evaluation of argument e' causes side-effects, then call-by-need may not be equivalent to call-by-name, and hence an important implementation technique is invalid. Witness the examples $(\backslash x \to x + x)$read or $(\backslash x \to x + x)(\texttt{write('A')}; 205)$, where we define $(e; e')$ to mean $((\backslash y \to e')\hat{~}e)$, with $y \notin fv(e')$. Under call-by-name, execution of the two examples involves two inputs and two outputs respectively; under call-by-need, execution of the programs involves just one input and one output respectively.

In summary, side-effecting I/O and lazy languages do not combine well because of the difficulty of predicting the order of side-effects, of constructing proofs of program properties, and because call-by-need semantics ceases to be a correct implementation technique. This explains why in practice side-effecting I/O is only used with call-by-value languages such as LISP or ML.

The absence of Strachey's property by no means rules out proofs of program properties, but we leave further investigation of $\mathcal{H}$ with side-effecting I/O as future work. We conjecture that the beta, eta, strictness, precongruence and canonical freeness laws of Table 6.8 remain valid. The only work to present a theory of I/O in a call-by-value language is the algebra for FL programs developed by Williams and Wimmers [9, 151]; FL uses what is essentially side-effecting I/O. One might dispense with call-by-name semantics and develop an equational theory for call-by-need semantics, and hence accommodate side-effecting I/O. Such a theory would have to make a distinction between the first and subsequent usages of bound variables, which on the face of it is much more complicated than the theory of call-by-name and call-by-value applications developed in Chapter 6. Previous work on the semantics of call-by-need in deterministic functional languages has focused on proving that an operational semantics using call-by-need correctly implements a denotational semantics specifying call-by-name [80, 122].

In his unpublished dissertation, Redelmeier [124] sketched an I/O scheme that used side-effecting operators together with data dependencies to ensure a predictable order of side-effects. His idea was that each side-effecting operator took an additional "state" parameter, and returned a new state. He argued that if each state value has a unique successor, then there is a predictable thread of side-effects. His scheme was unsatisfactory because he did not suggest how to guarantee single-threading. Hudak and Sundaresh [60] describe a variant, known as **systems I/O**. Peyton Jones and Wadler [110] have implemented the I/O mechanism in the Glasgow Haskell compiler using side-effecting operators with an efficient translation to C. Their work is a clear advance on Redelmeier's. They have ingeniously used an abstract data type based on a monad [149, 150] to guarantee single-threading. Their scheme appears to be a promising technique for efficient implementation of I/O in lazy languages.

7.2 Labelled transition systems and bisimilarity

We adopt labelled transition systems and bisimilarity from the theory of CCS [93, 94] to give semantics for Landin-stream, continuation-passing and synchronised stream I/O.

In each mechanism for functional I/O there is a single object language type whose programs can be **executed** to interact with the teletype. We call this type the **execution type**. A program is **executable** iff it is of this type. For instance, executable programs using Landin-stream I/O are of the stream transformer type [Char] -> [Char]. We formalise the execution of programs as a labelled transition system.

Definition 7.1   *The set of **actions**, ranged over by α, is produced by the following grammar:*

$$\alpha ::= \; n \; \; (\text{input character } n \in \mathbb{N})$$
$$\mid \; \; \bar{n} \; \; (\text{output character } n \in \mathbb{N})$$

*A **labelled transition system** is a family of binary relations indexed by actions, $\{\xrightarrow{\alpha}\}$, such that if $p \xrightarrow{\alpha} q$ then p and q are $\mathcal{HX}$ programs of an execution type.*

We use $\mathcal{HX}$ rather than $\mathcal{H}$ for reasons explained in §7.4. The intuitive meaning of transition $p \xrightarrow{n} q$ is that program p can input the character n from the keyboard to become program q. Similarly, the intuitive meaning of transition $p \xrightarrow{\bar{n}} q$ is that program p can output the character n to the printer to become program q. If $p \xrightarrow{\alpha} q$ for some α and q we say that p has a transition.

We define bisimilarity and prove the standard results.

Definition 7.2 *Define function $\langle \cdot \rangle$ to be the function over binary relations on $\mathcal{HX}$ programs such that $p \langle S \rangle q$ iff*

(1) *whenever $p \xrightarrow{\alpha} p'$ there is q' with $q \xrightarrow{\alpha} q'$ and $p' S q'$;*

(2) *whenever* $q \xrightarrow{\alpha} q'$ *there is* p' *with* $p \xrightarrow{\alpha} p'$ *and* $p'Sq'$.

A **bisimulation** *is a binary relation on agents,* S, *such that* $S \subseteq \langle S \rangle$. **Bisimilarity,** $\sim$, *is the union of all bisimulations.*

Proposition 7.3

(1) *Function* $\langle \cdot \rangle$ *is monotone.*

(2) *The identity relation is a bisimulation.*

(3) *If each* S_i *is a bisimulation, then so is* $S_1 S_2$.

(4) *If* S *is a bisimulation, then so is* S^{-1}.

(5) *Bisimilarity is the greatest fixpoint of* $\langle \cdot \rangle$ *and is the greatest bisimulation.*

(6) $p \sim q$ *iff there is a bisimulation* S *such that* pSq.

(7) *Bisimilarity is an equivalence relation.*

Proof. Parts (1)–(4) follow easily from the definition. The remaining parts then follow from Proposition 1.1.   ∎

7.3   Stream transformers

Many mechanisms for functional I/O or for concurrency [72] have been based on **stream transformers**. A stream is a list type whose cons operation is lazy, such as $[\sigma]$ in $\mathcal{H}$. Stream transformers in $\mathcal{H}$ have the general type:

```
type ST inp out = [inp] -> [out]
```

The idea is simple: a stream transformer maps a stream of values of type `inp` into a stream of values of type `out`. This mapping represents an interactive computing device that consumes values of type `inp` and produces values of type `out`. Intuition: if the device has been offered the sequence of values $in_1, \ldots, in_n$ for consumption, applying the stream transformer to the stream $(in_1 : \ldots : in_n : \Omega)$ yields a stream containing the sequence of values the device can produce. The list cons operation, :, has to have lazy semantics so that the partial list $(in_1 : \ldots : in_n : \Omega)$ does not simply equal Ω, which explains why stream-based I/O is not typically used with languages like ML or Scheme where cons is eager. Implementations of stream-based I/O [3, 68] typically represent the undefined value at the end of a partial list as a memory cell that can be instantiated to hold the next input character and to point to a fresh undefined value. Such a technique is intuitively correct, but we leave open the question of how to verify formally that it correctly implements the semantics to be given here. None of the work on verification of functional language implementation has considered I/O [47, 80, 132].

Stream transformers for stream-based I/O have typically been written using explicit construction of the output list and explicit examination of the input list [53, 69]. Such a programming style can be hard to read. We can avoid explicit mention of input and output lists by using the following combinators to construct stream transformers.

```
getST :: (inp -> ST inp out) -> ST inp out
```

```
putST :: out -> ST inp out -> ST inp out
nilST :: ST inp out

getST k xs = case xs of (x:xs') -> k x xs'
putST x f xs = x : f xs
nilST xs = []
```

Thompson [141] and Cupitt [27] suggest other combinators for I/O which are related to the monadic style discussed in Chapter 8.

A programmer would use the combinators above to construct stream transformers; to give semantics to stream-based I/O we use combinators giveST, nextST and skipST. The intention is that giveST feeds an input value to a stream transformer, nextST tests whether a stream transformer can produce an output value without any further input, and skipST consumes an output value from a stream transformer.

```
data Maybe a = Nothing | Just a

giveST        :: inp -> ST inp out -> ST inp out
nextST        :: (ST inp out) -> Maybe out
skipST        :: ST inp out -> ST inp out

giveST c f xs = f (c:xs)
nextST f      = case f Ω of
                    [] ->       Nothing
                    (x:xs) -> Just x
skipST f xs   = tail(f xs)
```

The Haskell committee discovered the technique of using a mock argument Ω to test whether a stream transformer is ready to produce output. Of course, if the next output from a stream transformer f depends on the next value in its input stream, nextST f will loop.

The following proposition relates the six combinators introduced in this section.

Proposition 7.4 *For all programs* u::inp, v::out, k::inp -> ST inp out *and* f::ST inp out:

(1) giveST u (getST k) = k u

(2) nextST(putST v f) $\Downarrow$ Just v

(3) nextST(nilST) $\Downarrow$ Nothing

(4) skipST(putST v f) = f

Proof. Straightforward calculations. ∎

7.4   Landin-stream I/O

Landin [76] suggested that streams "would be used to model input/output if ALGOL 60 included such." The simplest kind of stream transformer used for I/O is one that maps a stream of input characters to a stream of output characters. We call such a mechanism **Landin-stream I/O**. Executable programs are stream transformers of type LS:

    type LS = ST Char Char

A second kind of stream-based I/O, synchronised-stream I/O, is discussed in §7.5. We use the combinators of §7.3 to specify an intended meaning for Landin-streams.

- getST k means
  "input a character n from the keyboard and then execute k n."

- putST n f means
  "output character n to the printer and then execute f."

- nilST means
  "terminate immediately."

We wish to give a semantics for each I/O mechanism in terms of the operational semantics of $\mathcal{H}$. Given a function f::LS we are to compute whether f can output a character with no further input, or whether f needs an input character before producing more output, or whether f can terminate. More precisely, we need a function **ready** of the following type

    data RWD out = R | W out | D
    ready :: ST inp out -> RWD out

and satisfying the equations:

$$\begin{aligned} \text{ready}(\text{putST } \underline{n} \text{ f}) &= \text{W } \underline{n} \\ \text{ready}(\text{getST k}) &= \text{R} \\ \text{ready}(\text{nilST}) &= \text{D} \end{aligned}$$

We show that in $\mathcal{H}$ there is no such program. Consider programs e1 and e2 of type LS:

    e1 = getST (\x -> putST 205 nilST)
    e2 = putST 205 nilST

It is not hard to see that for any xs the following equations hold:

$$\begin{aligned} \text{e1 xs} &= \begin{cases} [205] & \text{if } \exists x, xs'.\, xs \Downarrow x : xs' \\ \Omega & \text{otherwise} \end{cases} \\ \text{e2 xs} &= [205] \end{aligned}$$

and hence that e1 $\sqsubseteq$ e2 and e2 $\not\sqsubseteq$ e1 by Strachey's property. To see why there can be no function **ready** that obeys the equations shown above, we assume there is and derive a contradiction. We have **ready**(e1) = R and **ready**(e2) = (W 205), and R $\not\sqsubseteq$ W 205. But e1 $\sqsubseteq$ e2 so by precongruence for $\sqsubseteq$ (Proposition 6.23) we have **ready**(e1) $\sqsubseteq$ **ready**(e2). Contradiction.[1]

---

[1] John Hughes showed me this argument in 1988.

Intuitively, the problem is that in $\mathcal{H}$ there is no way to tell whether an expression depends on the value of one of its subexpressions, such as an element of the input stream. We can remedy this by adding an exception mechanism to $\mathcal{H}$ as we did in the previous chapter. We find that the above argument does not hold in $\mathcal{HX}$. In $\mathcal{HX}$ we have that e1 and e2 are incomparable, because e1(bang) = bang, e2(bang) = [205], and bang and [205] are incomparable.

Roughly speaking, to tell whether an expression depends on the value of one of its subexpressions, replace the subexpression with **bang** and use the handler operator ?? to see if the whole expression bangs. We can define **ready** in $\mathcal{HX}$ as follows

```
ready f =
    (case (f bang) of
        [] -> D
        (x:_) -> W x)
    ?? R
```

and from the theory of $\mathcal{HX}$ from the previous chapter it follows that the conditions above on **ready** are satisfied. Intuitively speaking, the exception **bang** in $\mathcal{HX}$ provides a computable test of whether a function needs the value of its argument.

The semantics of Landin-streams can be given for LS-programs in $\mathcal{HX}$ as the labelled transition system defined by the following two rules:

$$\frac{\text{ready } f \Downarrow R}{f \xrightarrow{n} \text{giveST } \underline{n} \ f} \qquad \frac{\text{ready } f \Downarrow W v \qquad v \Downarrow \underline{n}}{f \xrightarrow{\overline{n}} \text{skipST } f}$$

The following lemma shows that this formal semantics correctly reflects the informal intended meanings given for Landin-stream programs—apart from termination, which we have not formalised.

Lemma 7.5

(1) **ready**(getST k) $\Downarrow R$

(2) **ready**(putST v k) $\Downarrow W v$

(3) getST k $\xrightarrow{n} =$k $\underline{n}$

(4) putST v p $\xrightarrow{\overline{n}} =$p *if* v $\Downarrow \underline{n}$

Proof. Parts (1) and (2) follow from the definitions of **ready**, getST and putST. For parts (3) and (4), we can calculate the following transitions:

$$\text{getST k} \xrightarrow{n} \text{giveST } \underline{n} \ (\text{getST k})$$
$$\text{putST v p} \xrightarrow{\overline{n}} \text{skipST } (\text{putST v p})$$

These, together with Proposition 7.4 establish the required results. ∎

7.5   Synchronised-stream I/O

In the **synchronised-stream** mechanism for functional I/O, the stream transformer produces a stream of requests and consumes a stream of acknowledgements. The requests and acknowledgements are in one-to-one correspondence: the computing device specified by a stream transformer alternates between producing an output request and consuming an input acknowledgement. It is the programmer's burden to ensure that the value of each request does not depend on the corresponding acknowledgement. Synchronised streams were first reported as the underlying implementation technique for Karlsson's Nebula operating system [74]. They were independently discovered by Stoye [136], whose terminology we adopt, and O'Donnell [104]. They are the underlying mechanism of the Kent Applicative Operating System (KAOS) [27, 28, 144, 145] and of I/O in Haskell [59].

Here is the type SS of executable programs in the setting of teletype I/O, together with intended meanings of some example programs:

```
type SS = ST Ack Req
data Req = Get | Put Char
data Ack = Got Char | Did
```

- putST Get (getST k) means
  "input a character n from the keyboard and then execute k (Got n)."

- putST (Put n) (getST k) means
  "output character n to the printer and then execute k Did."

- nilST means "terminate immediately."

A wide range of imperative activity can be expressed using this mechanism, as illustrated by the Haskell I/O mechanism. We define an auxiliary function for use in examining the acknowledgement obtained from a Get request:

```
outGot :: Ack -> Char
outGot (Got x) = x
```

The semantics of synchronised-streams can be given for SS-programs in $\mathcal{H}$ or in $\mathcal{HX}$ as the labelled transition system defined by the following two rules:

$$\frac{\text{nextST f} \Downarrow \text{Just r} \qquad \text{r} \Downarrow \text{Get}}{\text{f} \xrightarrow{n} \text{giveST(Got } n)(\text{skipST f})} \qquad \frac{\text{nextST f} \Downarrow \text{Just r} \qquad \text{r} \Downarrow \text{Put v} \qquad \text{v} \Downarrow n}{\text{f} \xrightarrow{\overline{n}} \text{giveST Did (skipST f)}}$$

Unlike Landin-streams, there is no need for the problematic **ready** operation because of the synchronisation between input and output. Just as for Landin-streams, we state a lemma to show that this formal semantics correctly reflects the informal intended meanings given for synchronised-stream programs—apart from termination.

Lemma 7.6 *Suppose* k::Char -> SS *and* h::SS *are programs, define programs* f *and* g *to be:*

$$\text{f} \stackrel{\text{def}}{=} \text{putST Get (getST (\textbackslash ack -> k (outGot ack)))}$$
$$\text{g} \stackrel{\text{def}}{=} \text{putST (Put v) (getST (\textbackslash ack -> h))}$$

Then we have:

(1) `nextST f` $\Downarrow$ `Just Get`

(2) `nextST g` $\Downarrow$ `Just(Put v)`

(3) `f` $\xrightarrow{n}$ `=k` $\underline{n}$

(4) `g` $\xrightarrow{\bar{n}}$ `=h` *if* `v` $\Downarrow$ $\underline{n}$.

Proof. Parts (1) and (2) follow from the definitions of `nextST`, `putST` and `getST`. For parts (3) and (4), we can calculate the following transitions and equations using Proposition 7.4:

$$
\begin{aligned}
\text{f} \ &\xrightarrow{n}\ \text{giveST(Got } \underline{n})\text{(skipST f)} \\
&=\ \text{giveST(Got } \underline{n})\text{(getST (\textbackslash ack -> k (outGot ack)))} \\
&=\ \text{k (outGot (Got } \underline{n}\text{))} \\
&=\ \text{k } \underline{n} \\
\text{g} \ &\xrightarrow{\bar{n}}\ \text{giveST Did (skipST g)} \\
&=\ \text{giveST Did (getST (\textbackslash ack -> h))} \\
&=\ \text{h}
\end{aligned}
$$

∎

7.6 Continuation-passing I/O

In **continuation-passing I/O**, the executable type is an algebraic type with a constructor corresponding to each kind of expressible imperative activity. In the case of teletype I/O we have:

```
data CPS = INPUT (Char -> CPS)
         | OUTPUT Char CPS
         | DONE
```

Holmström's PFL [57] was the first functional language to take the continuation-passing mechanism as primitive. In earlier work, Karlsson programmed continuation-passing operations on top of a synchronised-stream mechanism [74]. A similar datatype was used by Plotkin in the Pisa notes [118] as semantics for side-effecting I/O, as discussed in §7.1. The mechanism is called continuation-passing because of the similarity between the argument to `INPUT` and continuations as used in denotational semantics [134].

The intended meaning of CPS-programs is easily given.

- `INPUT k` means
  "input a character n from the keyboard and then execute (k $\underline{n}$)."
- `OUTPUT` $\underline{n}$ `p` means
  "output character n to the printer and then execute p."
- `DONE` means
  "terminate immediately."

Landin-stream I/O

$$\frac{\text{ready f} \Downarrow \text{R}}{\text{f} \xrightarrow{n} \text{giveST } \underline{n} \text{ f}} \qquad \frac{\text{ready f} \Downarrow \text{W v} \qquad \text{v} \Downarrow \underline{n}}{\text{f} \xrightarrow{\overline{n}} \text{skipST f}}$$

Synchronised-stream I/O

$$\frac{\text{nextST f} \Downarrow \text{Just r} \qquad \text{r} \Downarrow \text{Get}}{\text{f} \xrightarrow{n} \text{giveST(Got } \underline{n})(\text{skipST f})} \qquad \frac{\text{nextST f} \Downarrow \text{Just r} \qquad \text{r} \Downarrow \text{Put v} \qquad \text{v} \Downarrow \underline{n}}{\text{f} \xrightarrow{\overline{n}} \text{giveST Did (skipST f)}}$$

Continuation-passing I/O

$$\frac{\text{p} \Downarrow \text{INPUT k}}{\text{p} \xrightarrow{n} \text{k } \underline{n}} \qquad \frac{\text{p} \Downarrow \text{OUTPUT v q} \qquad \text{v} \Downarrow \underline{n}}{\text{p} \xrightarrow{\overline{n}} \text{q}}$$

Table 7.1: Three mechanisms for functional I/O

These intended meanings are reflected in the following two rules, which define a labelled transition system for CPS-programs in either $\mathcal{H}$ or $\mathcal{HX}$.

$$\frac{\text{p} \Downarrow \text{INPUT k}}{\text{p} \xrightarrow{n} \text{k } \underline{n}} \qquad \frac{\text{p} \Downarrow \text{OUTPUT v q} \qquad \text{v} \Downarrow \underline{n}}{\text{p} \xrightarrow{\overline{n}} \text{q}}$$

7.7 Maps between three of the mechanisms

We gave detailed semantics for each of the mechanisms apart from side-effecting I/O. There are two main results in this section. First, we show that if two executable programs are operationally equivalent, then they are bisimilar. The force of this result is that the theory of operational equivalence from Chapter 6 can be used to prove properties of the execution behaviour of executable programs. Second, we show that each of the three mechanisms has equivalent expressive power in the following sense. If p is an executable program with respect to one mechanism, then for each other mechanism, there is a function f such that f(p) is an executable program with respect to the other mechanism, and p and f(p) are bisimilar.

We work in $\mathcal{HX}$ so that all three mechanisms are supported in the same language; as discussed in §7.4 the semantics of Landin-streams based on the **ready** function cannot be programming in $\mathcal{H}$.

Definition 7.7 *The **teletype transition system** is a family of binary relations on $\mathcal{HX}$ programs indexed by actions, $\{\xrightarrow{\alpha}\}$, and is defined by the rules in Table 7.1.*

Lemma 7.8 *If p::τ and p $\xrightarrow{\alpha}$ q then q::τ. Type τ is one of LS, SS or CPS, depending on whether transition p $\xrightarrow{\alpha}$ q was derived from one of the Landin-stream, synchronised-stream or continuation-passing rules, respectively, in Table 7.1.*

Proof. By inspection.   ∎

Given its simple sequential nature, one would expect the semantics of teletype I/O to be determinate. The following result makes this precise.

Proposition 7.9 *For any program* p, $p \xrightarrow{\alpha} p'$ *and* $p \xrightarrow{\alpha} p''$ *implies* $p' \equiv p''$.

Proof. By inspection of each of the inference rules.   ∎

Given this determinacy, bisimilarity can alternatively be characterised in terms of traces. If $s = \alpha_1, \ldots, \alpha_n$ is a finite sequence of actions, say that s is a **trace** of program p iff there are programs p_i with $p \xrightarrow{\alpha_1} p_1 \xrightarrow{\alpha_2} \cdots \xrightarrow{\alpha_n} p_n$. Two programs are **trace equivalent** iff they have the same set of traces.

In a nondeterministic calculus like CCS, trace equivalence does not in general imply bisimilarity. Given the determinacy result above, however, it is not hard to show that the two equivalences coincide. We omit the proof, but see Milner's book for a more general result [94, Chapter 9].

Operational equivalence (applicative bisimilarity) implies bisimilarity.

Proposition 7.10 *If* p *and* q *are programs of the same type, then* $p = q$ *implies* $p \sim q$.

Proof. Recall that we take = on terms of $\mathcal{HX}$ to be applicative bisimilarity as defined in Chapter 6. It suffices to show that ground applicative bisimilarity on $\mathcal{HX}$ is a bisimulation. Suppose that $p = q$ for τ-programs p and q. We proceed by a case analysis of τ. If τ is not one of the three types CPS, SS or LS then p and q have no transitions, so $p \sim q$ trivially. Otherwise there are three cases to consider. In each case we establish condition (1) of the definition of bisimulation, that whenever $p \xrightarrow{\alpha} p'$ there is q' such that $q \xrightarrow{\alpha} q'$ and $p' = q'$. Condition (2) follows by a symmetric argument.

Case $\tau \equiv$ CPS.

 If $p \xrightarrow{n} p'$ then $p \Downarrow$ INPUT k and $p' \equiv k\,\underline{n}$. Then $q \Downarrow$ INPUT k′ with $k = k'$ from applicative bisimilarity. So $q \xrightarrow{n} k'\,\underline{n} = p'$.

 If $p \xrightarrow{\overline{n}} p'$ then $p \Downarrow$ OUTPUT v p′ and $v \Downarrow \underline{n}$. Then $q' \Downarrow$ OUTPUT v′ q′, with $v = v'$ and $p' = q'$. So $v' \Downarrow \underline{n}$ and we have $q \xrightarrow{\overline{n}} q' = p'$.

Case $\tau \equiv$ SS.

 If $p \xrightarrow{n} p'$ then nextST $p \Downarrow$ Just r, $r \Downarrow$ Get and $p' \equiv$ giveST(Got $\underline{n}$)(skipST p). Since $p = q$ we have nextST $q \Downarrow$ Just r′ with $r = r'$, so $r' \Downarrow$ Get. We have $q \xrightarrow{n}$ giveST(Got $\underline{n}$)(skipST q), and the latter equals p′ since operational equivalence is a congruence.

 If $p \xrightarrow{\overline{n}} p'$ then nextST $p \Downarrow$ Just r, $r \Downarrow$ Put v, $v \Downarrow \underline{n}$ and $p' \equiv$ giveST Did (skipST p). Again since $p = q$ we have nextST $q \Downarrow$ Just r′, with $r = r'$, so $r' \Downarrow$ Put v′ with $v = v'$ so $v' \Downarrow \underline{n}$. Therefore $q \xrightarrow{\overline{n}}$ giveST Did (skipST q), which equals p′.

The case for $\tau \equiv$ LS follows by a similar argument and is omitted.   ∎

On the other hand, bisimilarity does not imply operational equivalence of $\mathcal{H}$ programs.

Proposition 7.11 *There are program pairs,* p *and* q, *in each of the types* CPS, LS *and* SS *such that* $p \sim q$ *but not* $p = q$.

Proof. Witness program pair OUTPUT Ω Done and Ω in type CPS, and pair putST Ω nilST and Ω in each of the types SS and LS.   ∎

Intuitively the proof depends on operational equivalence distinguishing more "junk" programs than bisimilarity. Given a richer I/O model there would be more significant distinctions. Suppose we extended the CPS algebraic type with a new constructor Par::CPS -> CPS -> CPS, with intended meaning that Par p q is to be the parallel execution of programs p and q, as in PFL. Then if $p \neq q$, programs Par p q and Par q p would be operationally inequivalent (because Par is the constructor of an algebraic type) but bisimilar (because as in CCS both lead to the parallel execution of p and q).

Before proving the second main result of this section, we import the proof technique of bisimulation-up-to-$\sim$ from CCS [94].

Definition 7.12 *A binary relation on programs S is a* **bisimulation-up-to-$\sim$** *iff* pSq *implies*

(1) *whenever* $p \xrightarrow{\alpha} p'$ *there is* q' *with* $q \xrightarrow{\alpha} q'$ *and* $p' \sim S \sim q'$;

(2) *whenever* $q \xrightarrow{\alpha} q'$ *there is* p' *with* $p \xrightarrow{\alpha} p'$ *and* $p' \sim S \sim q'$.

Proposition 7.13 *If S is a bisimulation-up-to-$\sim$ then $S \subseteq \sim$.*

Proof. We follow the proof on page 93 of Milner's book [94].

We prove that $\sim S \sim$ is a bisimulation, from which it follows by reflexivity of $\sim$ that $S \subseteq \sim$. ($\sim S \sim$ is the relational composition of $\sim$, S and $\sim$.) Suppose that $p \sim S \sim q$, that is, for some p_1 and q_1 we have $p \sim p_1 S q_1 \sim q$. Suppose that $p \xrightarrow{\alpha} p'$; we are to exhibit q' such that $q \xrightarrow{\alpha} q'$ and $p' \sim S \sim q'$. We make a sequence of deductions: there is p_1' such that $p_1 \xrightarrow{\alpha} p_1'$ with $p' \sim p_1'$; there is q_1' such that $q_1 \xrightarrow{\alpha} q_1'$ and $p_1' \sim S \sim q_1'$; and there is q' such that $q \xrightarrow{\alpha} q'$ and $q_1' \sim q'$. Altogether we have $p' \sim p_1' \sim S \sim q_1' \sim q'$, hence $p' \sim S \sim q'$ by transitivity of $\sim$. This shows that $\sim S \sim$ is a bisimulation.   ∎

Suppose there are programs p and q such that we wish to prove $p \sim q$. Proposition 7.3(6) says that one proof would be to find a bisimulation containing the pair (p, q). On the other hand, Proposition 7.13 says that another proof is to find a bisimulation-up-to-$\sim$ that contains the pair. It is often simpler to do the latter. The same idea is used extensively in the theory of CCS [94] and π-calculus [96].

We show in Table 7.2 functions ss2cps and cps2ss to map between the types SS and CPS, and functions ls2cps and cps2ls to map between the types LS and CPS. Functions ss2cps and cps2ss are similar to translations discovered by the Haskell committee.

The following is the main theorem of the chapter: that the three I/O mechanisms of Table 7.1 are isomorphic in a certain sense.

Theorem 7.14

(1) *For any SS-program f, $f \sim$ ss2cps f.*

(2) *For any CPS-program p, $p \sim$ cps2ss p.*

(3) *For any LS-program f, $f \sim$ ls2cps f.*

(4) *For any CPS-program p, $p \sim$ cps2ls p.*

```
-- ====================================================================
-- Translations between SS and CPS.
-- ====================================================================


ss2cps :: SS -> CPS
cps2ss :: CPS -> SS

ss2cps f =
  case nextST f of
    Nothing -> DONE
    Just r ->  case r of
      Get ->      INPUT (\v -> ss2cps (giveST (Got v) (skipST f)))
      Put v ->    OUTPUT v (ss2cps (giveST Did (skipST f)))

cps2ss p =
  case p of
    INPUT k ->    putST Get (getST (\ack -> cps2ss (k (outGot ack))))
    OUTPUT v q -> putST (Put v) (getST (\ack -> cps2ss q))
    DONE ->       nilST

outGot :: Ack -> Char
outGot (Got v) = v


-- ====================================================================
-- Translations between LS and CPS.
-- ====================================================================


ls2cps :: LS -> CPS
cps2ls :: CPS -> LS

ls2cps f =
  case ready f of
    R ->          INPUT (\v -> ls2cps (giveST v f))
    W v ->        OUTPUT v (ls2cps (skipST f))
    D ->          DONE

cps2ls p =
  case p of
    INPUT k ->    getST (\v -> cps2ls (k v))
    OUTPUT v q -> putST v (cps2ls q)
    DONE ->       nilST
```

Table 7.2: Translations in $\mathcal{HX}$ between three styles of I/O

Proof. (1) We prove that S, given by

$$S \stackrel{\text{def}}{=} \{(\texttt{f}, \texttt{ss2cps f}) \mid \texttt{f is an SS-program}\}$$

is a bisimulation, which is to say that $S \subseteq \langle S \rangle$. Let $\texttt{f}$ be any SS-program and we have that $\texttt{ss2cps f::CPS}$. Hence the synchronised-stream rules apply to $\texttt{f}$ and the continuation-passing rules to $\texttt{ss2cps f}$. We are to show that $(\texttt{f}, \texttt{ss2cps f}) \in \langle S \rangle$. We proceed by analysis of the evaluation behaviour of $\texttt{nextST f}$. There are five cases to consider.

(i) $\texttt{nextST f} \Uparrow$ or $\texttt{nextST f} \Downarrow \texttt{bang}$

(ii) $\texttt{nextST f} \Downarrow \texttt{Nothing}$

(iii) $\texttt{nextST f} \Downarrow \texttt{Just r}$ and either $\texttt{r} \Uparrow$ or $\texttt{r} \Downarrow \texttt{bang}$

(iv) $\texttt{nextST f} \Downarrow \texttt{Just r}$ and $\texttt{r} \Downarrow \texttt{Get}$

(v) $\texttt{nextST f} \Downarrow \texttt{Just r}$ and $\texttt{r} \Downarrow \texttt{Put v}$

Here are the possible transitions from programs $\texttt{f}$ and $\texttt{ss2cps f}$.

(i–iii) There are no transitions from either $\texttt{ss2cps f}$ or $\texttt{f}$.

(iv) The only transitions of $\texttt{f}$ are of the form
$\texttt{f} \xrightarrow{n} \texttt{giveST (Got } \underline{n}\texttt{) (skipST f)}$ for any n.
We have $\texttt{ss2cps f} \Downarrow \texttt{INPUT(\textbackslash c -> ss2cps(giveST (Got c) (skipST f)))}$.
So the only transitions of $\texttt{ss2cps f}$ are of the form
$\texttt{ss2cps f} \xrightarrow{n} \texttt{ss2cps(giveST (Got } \underline{n}\texttt{) (skipST f))}$ for any n.

(v) There is no transition from $\texttt{f}$ unless $\texttt{v} \Downarrow \underline{n}$, when $\texttt{f} \xrightarrow{\overline{n}} \texttt{giveST Did (skipST f)}$.
We have $\texttt{ss2cps f} \Downarrow \texttt{OUTPUT v (ss2cps(giveST Did (skipST f)))}$.
So there is no transition from $\texttt{ss2cps f}$ unless $\texttt{v} \Downarrow \underline{n}$,
when $\texttt{ss2cps f} \xrightarrow{\overline{n}} \texttt{ss2cps(giveST Did (skipST f))}$.

In each case the conditions for $(\texttt{f}, \texttt{ss2cps f}) \in \langle S \rangle$ are satisfied.

(2) It suffices to show that S, given by

$$S \stackrel{\text{def}}{=} \{(\texttt{p}, \texttt{cps2ss p}) \mid \texttt{p is a CPS-program}\}$$

is a bisimulation-up-to-$\sim$. Suppose that pair $(\texttt{p}, \texttt{cps2ss p})$ is in S. We have $\texttt{p::CPS}$ and $\texttt{cps2ss p::SS}$, so the continuation-passing rules apply to $\texttt{p}$ and the synchronised-stream rules to $\texttt{cps2ss p}$. We are to show that whenever $\texttt{p} \xrightarrow{\alpha} \texttt{p}'$ then $\texttt{cps2ss p} \xrightarrow{\alpha} \texttt{q}'$ and $\texttt{p}' \sim S \sim \texttt{q}'$, and vice versa. We proceed by analysis of the evaluation behaviour of $\texttt{p}$. There are five cases to consider.

(i) $\texttt{p} \Uparrow$

(ii) $\texttt{p} \Downarrow \texttt{bang}$

(iii) $\texttt{p} \Downarrow \texttt{DONE}$

(iv) $\texttt{p} \Downarrow \texttt{INPUT k}$

(v) $\texttt{p} \Downarrow \texttt{OUTPUT v q}$

Here are the possible transitions from programs $\texttt{p}$ and $(\texttt{cps2ss p})$.

(i–iii) Neither program has any transitions.

(iv) The only transitions of p are of the form p $\xrightarrow{n}$ k $\underline{n}$ for any n.

We have cps2ss p $\rightarrow^+$ putST Get (getST(\ack -> cps2ss(k (outGot ack)))). So using Lemma 7.6(1,3), the only transitions of cps2ss p are of the form cps2ss p$\xrightarrow{n}$=cps2ss(k $\underline{n}$) for any n.

(v) The only transitions of p are p $\xrightarrow{\overline{n}}$ q when v $\Downarrow\underline{n}$.

We have cps2ss p $\rightarrow^+$ putST (Put v) (getST(\ack -> cps2ss q)).

So using Lemma 7.6(2,4) the only transition from cps2ss p is cps2ss p$\xrightarrow{\overline{n}}$=cps2ss q.

In each case the conditions for bisimulation-up-to-$\sim$ are satisfied, since $= \subseteq \sim$.

(3) We prove that S, given by

$$S \stackrel{\text{def}}{=} \{(f, \text{ls2cps } f) \mid f \text{ is an LS-program}\}$$

is a bisimulation, that is, $S \subseteq \langle S \rangle$. Suppose that pair $(f, \text{ls2cps } f)$ in in S. We have f::LS and ls2cps f::CPS, so the Landin-stream rules apply to f and the continuation-passing rules to ls2cps f. We are to show that $(f, \text{ls2cps } f) \in \langle S \rangle$. We proceed by analysis of the evaluation behaviour of **ready** f. There are four cases to consider.

(i) **ready** f$\Uparrow$

(ii) **ready** f $\Downarrow$ D

(iii) **ready** f $\Downarrow$ R

(iv) **ready** f $\Downarrow$ W v

A fifth possibility, that **ready** f $\Downarrow$ bang, is impossible given the form of **ready**. Here are the possible transitions from programs f and ls2cps f.

(i,ii) No transitions are possible from either f or ls2cps f.

(iii) The only transitions of f are of the form f $\xrightarrow{n}$ giveST $\underline{n}$ f for any n.

We have ls2cps f $\Downarrow$ INPUT(\c -> ls2cps(giveST c f)).

So the only transitions of ls2cps f are of the form ls2cps f $\xrightarrow{n}$ ls2cps(giveST $\underline{n}$ f) for any n.

(iv) There is no transition from f unless v $\Downarrow\underline{n}$, when f $\xrightarrow{\overline{n}}$ skipST f.

We have ls2cps f $\Downarrow$ OUTPUT v (ls2cps(skipST f)).

So there is no transition from ls2cps f unless v $\Downarrow\underline{n}$, when ls2cps f $\xrightarrow{\overline{n}}$ ls2cps(skipST f).

In each case the conditions for $(f, \text{ls2cps } f) \in \langle S \rangle$ are satisfied.

(4) It suffices to show that S, given by

$$S \stackrel{\text{def}}{=} \{(p, \text{cps2ls } p) \mid p \text{ is a CPS-program}\}$$

is a bisimulation-up-to-$\sim$. Suppose that pair $(p, \text{cps2ls } p)$ is in S. We have p::CPS and cps2ls p::LS, so the continuation-passing rules apply to p and the Landin-stream rules to cps2ls p. We are to show that whenever p $\xrightarrow{\alpha}$ p$'$ then cps2ls p $\xrightarrow{\alpha}$ q and p$'\sim S\sim$q$'$, and vice versa. We proceed by analysis of the evaluation behaviour of p. There are five cases to consider.

(i) p$\Uparrow$

   (ii) $p \Downarrow$ bang

  (iii) $p \Downarrow$ DONE

  (iv) $p \Downarrow$ INPUT k

   (v) $p \Downarrow$ WRITE v q

Here are the possible transitions from programs p and cps2ls p.

(i–iii) Neither of the programs has any transitions.

  (iv) The only transitions of p are of the form $p \xrightarrow{n} k\,\underline{n}$ for any n.
We have cps2ls p $\to^{+}$ getST(\c -> cps2ls(k c)).
So using Lemma 7.5(1,3) the only transitions of cps2ls p are of the form
cps2ls p$\xrightarrow{n}$=cps2ls(k $\underline{n}$) for any n.

   (v) The only transition of p is If $p \xrightarrow{\bar{n}} q$ if v $\Downarrow \underline{n}$.
We have cps2ls p $\to^{+}$ putST v (cps2ls q).
So using Lemma 7.5(2,4) the only transition of cps2ls p has the form
cps2ls p$\xrightarrow{\bar{n}}$=cps2ls q if v $\Downarrow \underline{n}$.

In each case the conditions for bisimulation-up-to-$\sim$ are satisfied.   ■

7.8   Discussion

The main contribution of this chapter is to the semantics of functional I/O. We sketched
a semantics of side-effecting I/O but gave three objections to its use with lazy languages.
We considered three mechanisms suitable for lazy languages, and gave an operational
semantics for each. We showed how the notion of bisimilarity from CCS is a suitable
equivalence on programs engaged in I/O. We gave translations between the three styles,
some of which are well known, but gave the first formal proofs that the translations are
correct.

Our definition of bisimilarity is very simple, but for two reasons one might wish to develop
it further. First, although each of the three I/O mechanisms has a notion of program
termination we have not modelled termination in the labelled transition system. Hence a
program that immediately terminates is bisimilar to one that diverges. Second, we have
assumed that teletype input is observable. Consider two Landin-stream programs f and
g:

```
f xs = Ω
g xs = case xs of
          [] -> Ω
          (_:xs) -> g xs
```

Given an input stream, g unravels it forever whereas f loops immediately. We have $f =^{\mathcal{H}} g$
but $f \neq^{\mathcal{H}\mathcal{X}} g$ and $f \not\sim g$ (because g forever inputs characters whereas f diverges). One
might argue that they have indistinguishable behaviour because neither ever produces
output. On the other hand, it seems reasonable to distinguish them on the ground that
teletype input is observable to the operating system, if not always to the end user. These

points bring out the simplicity of our model, but then it is meant to be simple so as to emphasise the differences between the I/O mechanisms.

We conclude the chapter with some remarks about the practical use of the three mechanisms for I/O in lazy languages. As they stand, the three mechanisms are rather too low-level for large-scale programming. As we discussed in Chapter 1, various sets of combinators have been put forward as high-level programming models [28, 141, 154]. We will investigate a set of combinators in the monadic style in Chapter 8.

Landin-stream I/O is good for teletype I/O but does not scale to a practical I/O scheme (such as Haskell I/O). Several papers have shown how to construct elegant parsers that act on a lazy input stream of characters [36, 63, 148]. It is not clear that such parsing techniques can be based so simply on synchronised-stream or continuation-passing I/O. Landin-stream programs can be written in either Haskell [59] or Hope+C [108]. This is because the I/O mechanisms of both provide operations to obtain a lazy input stream, and hence Landin-stream I/O can be simulated.

A gulf separates the source-level semantics of the stream-based I/O mechanisms given here from their imperative implementation [3, 68]. The gulf is particularly wide between the semantics and implementation of lazy input streams. The only other semantics of stream-based I/O is Thompson's trace-based work, which is domain-theoretic and also distant from practical implementations. In contrast, the operational semantics we gave for continuation-passing I/O corresponds fairly closely to an interpretive implementation [108]. It is an open question how to relate abstract specifications of I/O to efficient implementations using side-effects [110].

The principal merit of synchronised-stream I/O over continuation-passing I/O is that the former can efficiently simulate the latter via a function such as cps2ss. Simulation of the former by the latter using a function such as ss2cps is inevitably inefficient [60]. Synchronised-stream programs suffer from problems relating to synchronisation between input and output streams that do not arise with continuation-passing [108]. High-level combinators such as for monadic I/O can be implemented on top of either mechanism [28, 43]. If all user programs are to use such combinators there seems to be no reason to choose synchronised-stream I/O as the underlying mechanism rather than continuation-passing I/O.

Chapter 8

Monadic I/O

The three I/O mechanisms of Chapter 7 suitable for lazy languages express I/O at a low level. This chapter explains how to program I/O using higher-level combinators in a style which we call here **monadic I/O**. The combinators are higher-level in two senses: the intended meaning of an executable program is a computation that performs I/O and then returns a value, rather then just performing I/O as in Chapter 7; the combinators of monadic I/O can be implemented using the lower-level operations given in Chapter 7.

This chapter discusses monadic I/O in the context of a specific application of functional programming. Over the last decade the Medical Research Council (MRC) at the Western General Hospital in Edinburgh has built a prototype machine to assist the analysis of cervical smears [62]. The prototype was implemented using dedicated hardware, C and assembly-code. A team has started work on re-implementing the machine using a commercial workstation coupled with software partly written in a lazy functional language [121]. The aim is to compare the gains of using a functional language (such as reliability, ease of programming and the potential for proofs of program properties) with the losses (such as computational speed). The system captures digitised images from a microscope that sights a movable stage holding a microscope slide. The intention is that the system will be able to locate automatically the objects on the slide that are most likely to be pre-cancerous cells, and then display these to a cytologist for diagnosis. If successful, the computerised system will allow a cytologist to process slides faster than by simply using a microscope. The MRC team have been prototyping the software for their system using a mixture of C and a lazy functional language; the prototype uses Gofer and the final implementation will use Haskell. Basic image processing will be done by a server running mature C code, while the top-level main program will be new software written in the functional language.

This chapter addresses two questions. How can the I/O requirements of the MRC computer be programmed in a lazy functional language? How can properties of programs engaged in I/O be proved? In the context of a simplified model of the MRC apparatus, we suggest how the MRC computer could be programmed in a monadic style. We consider a simple I/O transformation suggested by Ian Poole of the MRC and prove it correct. We show how the monadic style applies to teletype I/O, because the simplified I/O model for the MRC computer includes teletype I/O.

§8.1 is a tutorial on the monadic style of functional I/O. It defines a simplified model of

MRC I/O, and poses a verification problem. §8.2 and §8.3 define monadic types in $\mathcal{H}$ to model teletype I/O and the MRC I/O model respectively; the latter type is defined in terms of the former. Finally, in §8.4 we verify the motivating example.

All the programs given in this chapter are written in Haskell notation. They are to be understood as $\mathcal{H}$ (not $\mathcal{HX}$) programs as discussed in §6.1. All the programs have been type-checked and executed in Mark Jones' Gofer system. Program equivalence, written =, is operational equivalence as defined in Chapter 6.

8.1   Programming I/O in a monadic style

In the monadic style of functional I/O there is a unary type constructor IO such that a program (closed term) of type IO a is intended to mean

> "a computation, which may perform I/O, and may return an answer of type a."

Let a **computation** be a program of type IO a, for some a. To program teletype I/O (as discussed in Chapter 7) in a monadic style, one might use the following operations for constructing computations.

```
>    input  :: IO Char
>    output :: Char -> IO ()
>    return :: a -> IO a
>    (>>=)  :: IO a -> (a -> IO b) -> IO b
```

Here is the intended meaning of computations constructed from these operations.

- input means "input a character v from the keyboard and return v."
- output v means "output character v to the printer and return ()."
- return v means "immediately return v."
- p >>= f means "execute computation p, call the answer x and then execute computation f x."

An example: reading a line from the keyboard

Let us consider the problem of writing a program to read from the keyboard a string (that is, a list of characters) terminated by the newline character, '\n'. We wish to derive a function, gettingLine, with the following properties.

```
>    gettingLine :: String -> IO String
```

- gettingLine vs means "having already read the string vs, continue reading characters until a newline appears."

We can define gettingLine in terms of the basic computation constructors.

```
>    gettingLine vs =
>        input >>= \v ->
```

```
>        if v == '\n' then return vs else gettingLine (v:vs)
```

We can read off an interpretation of this definition from the intended meaning of the basic
constructors: computation `gettingLine vs` means "input a character, call it v; then if v
is a newline, return the accumulated string vs, or else add v to the accumulated string
and repeat." Here then is a solution to the problem:

```
>    getLine :: IO String
>    getLine = gettingLine [] >>= (return . reverse)
```

Function `reverse::[a] -> [a]` is the list reversal function from the Haskell prelude. The
string returned by `gettingLine []` needs to be reversed because the characters are accumulated in reverse order to avoid repeated list concatenations.

Derived operations

Sometimes two computations are to be composed in sequence, but the answer from the
first is to be discarded. This pattern can be captured by the combinator >>,

```
>    (>>)   :: IO a -> IO b -> IO b
>    p >> q  = p >>= const
```

where `const` is the Haskell version of the **K** combinator, shown in Table 6.3 Commonly
the first argument to `>>` is a **task**, a program of type `IO ()`. A task is a computation that
returns no informative answer upon termination. The simplest task is `skip`, given by:

```
>    skip = return ()
```

Sequential composition of a list of tasks is achieved by the `sequence` combinator.

```
>    sequence :: [IO ()] -> IO ()
>    sequence = foldr (>>) skip
```

The Haskell list combinator `foldr` is also shown in Table 6.3. It is not hard to verify the
following equations.

$$sequence\ [] = skip$$
$$sequence\ (p : ps) = p \gg (sequence\ ps)$$

Here is a combinator that lifts a curried function f of two arguments to one that given
two computations runs them in sequence to obtain two answers x and y, and then returns
the answer f x y.

```
>    lift2      :: (a -> b -> c) -> (IO a -> IO b -> IO c)
>    lift2 f p q = p >>= \x -> q >>= \y -> return (f x y)
```

We can use `lift2` to write a generalisation of `sequence` that runs a list of computations
in sequence and then returns the list of their answers as its own answer.

```
>    accumulate :: [IO a] -> IO [a]
>    accumulate = foldr (lift2 (:)) (return [])
```

More examples: printing a line and prompting

To illustrate how **sequence** can be used, here is a program to output a string of characters followed by newline to the printer.

```
>    putLine   :: String -> IO ()
>    putLine vs = sequence [output v | v <- vs] >> output '\n'
```

(This is an example of a Haskell list comprehension, which can be translated into $\mathcal{H}$ as discussed in §6.1.) In general we call functions such as **putLine** that have some type $a_1 \rightarrow \cdots \rightarrow a_m \rightarrow$ IO b for $m > 1$, **parametric computations**.

Finally, here is a parametric computation to print a prompt and then read a line of input.

```
>    askFor   :: String -> IO String
>    askFor xs = putLine xs >> getLine
```

Adding exceptions to the programming model

Experience of programming I/O in imperative languages suggests that an exception handling mechanism is a good way to represent and process unexpected events such as errors. For instance, the implementors of DEC SRC's Taos operating system argue that representing operating system errors by exceptions is better than returning an error code, as in AT&T's Unix for instance, because it is impossible for an exception to be ignored [85].

Exceptions can be incorporated into the monadic programming model by choosing a type **Exn** of **exceptions**, and extending the intended meaning of a program of type IO **a** to be

> "a computation, which may perform I/O actions, and may return an answer of type **a**, or may fail with an exception value of type **Exn**."

For the purpose of this chapter we take **Exn** to be **String**, but in general it can be any type. There are two new primitive ways of constructing computations.

```
>    raise :: Exn -> IO a
>    try   :: IO a -> (Exn -> IO a) -> IO a
```

- **raise exn** means "immediately raise the exception **exn**."
- **try p f** means "execute computation **p**; if an answer **v** is returned, then return **v** and ignore **f**; otherwise, if **p** raises an exception **exn**, execute **f exn**."

The intended meanings of the other primitive computation constructors are unchanged, except for sequential composition.

- **p >>= f** means "execute computation **p**; if an exception **exn** is raised, then immediately raise **exn** and ignore **f**; otherwise, if an answer **x** is returned, proceed to execute computation **f x**."

The exception mechanism in $\mathcal{HX}$ was obtained by extending the syntax and semantics of $\mathcal{H}$. Here, instead, we obtain an exception mechanism by object level programming, with no extension of $\mathcal{H}$.

Biased choice is a derived form of exception handling where the exception value is ignored:

- p ? q means "execute computation p; if an answer x is returned, then return x and ignore q; otherwise, if p raises an exception, execute q."

```
>    (?)    :: IO a -> IO a -> IO a
>    p ? q  = try p (const q)
```

An example using exceptions

Here is a parametric computation that if given a numeral—a list of digits—returns the corresponding number. Otherwise it raises the exception "parseInt".

```
>    parseInt   :: String -> IO Int
>    parseInt cs =
>      accumulate (map toDigit cs) >>=
>      (return . foldr (**) 0 . reverse)
>         where
>             (**)      :: Int -> Int -> Int
>             toDigit   :: Char -> IO Int
>             u ** t    = t * 10 + u
>             toDigit v =
>                if isDigit v then return (ord v - ord '0')
>                             else raise "parseInt"
```

This function can be used to construct a computation that returns the number found by reading a line from the keyboard and treating it as a numeral, and repeating if necessary until a legitimate numeral has been typed:

```
>    getInt :: IO Int
>    getInt  =
>        getLine >>= \vs -> parseInt vs ?
>        (putLine "Oops! That wasn't a number." >> getInt)
```

A Simplified MRC Computer

We suggest a simplified version of a programming model suitable for the Edinburgh MRC team. We wish to program a computer equipped with a teletype interface but also an external microscope assembly consisting of a microscope, an image capture device and a movable stage containing a microscope slide. Suppose there is a type **Image** whose values represent digitised images obtained from the external assembly. Define a type of two-dimensional coordinates to represent positions on the slide:

```
>    type Coord = (Int,Int)
```

We assume that the stage can be moved to a certain range of coordinates, and also to a distinguished parked position for insertion and removal of the slide.

The functional program is to run on the main computer, but we assume there is an independent I/O controller responsible for stage motion. We propose to use the teletype programming model, with exceptions, extended with the following computation constructors:

```
>    moveStage :: Coord -> IO ()
>    capture   :: IO Image
>    parkStage :: IO ()
```

- moveStage co means "instruct the I/O controller to move the stage to coordinate position co, and immediately return ()."
- capture means "wait for the I/O controller to signal that the stage is stationary, capture an image im and return answer im; but if the stage is parked, raise the exception "capture"."
- parkStage means "instruct the I/O controller to park the stage and immediately return ()."

This model motivated the development of this chapter. The MRC team use an I/O model based on this simplified model, but considerably extended.

Here is a verification problem suggested by Ian Poole of the MRC. We begin with a parametric computation called jobA. Its parameters are a list of coordinates, cos, and an image analysis function, f of type Image -> Char, where for any image im, character f im represents some human-readable result computed about im. The purpose of jobA is to capture images from each of the coordinates in cos, apply the analysis function to each of the images, and output the results.

```
>    jobA      :: (Image -> Char) -> [Coord] -> IO ()
>    analyse   :: (Image -> Char) -> IO ()
>    jobA f cos = sequence [moveStage co >> analyse f | co <- cos]
>    analyse f  = capture >>= \im -> output (f im)
```

Although the main computer together with the I/O controller permit a limited amount of concurrency, one sees that the program above does not admit any concurrent activity. In processing each coordinate, the main computer tells the I/O controller to move the stage, but then immediately tries to capture an image and so undergoes a period of idle waiting. Similarly, the I/O controller remains idle while the main computer is processing the image captured at each coordinate.

Clearly the program would run faster if immediately after capturing an image at one coordinate, the I/O controller could move the stage to the next coordinate during the same time as the main computer processes the current image. Program jobB is intended to do this.

```
>    jobB f []      = skip
>    jobB f (co:cos)= moveStage co >> jobC f cos
>    jobC f cos     = sequence [each f co | co <- cos] >> analyse f
>    each f co      = capture >>= \im -> moveStage co >> output (f im)
```

The problem is to verify that parametric computations jobA and jobB are equivalent. The remaining sections of the chapter develop a theory of the simplified MRC programming model, by modelling its semantics within $\mathcal{H}$. We conclude in §8.4 by proving that jobA and jobB give rise to equal computations.

History

The first serious use of the monadic style was in the Kent Applicative Operating System (KAOS), 14,000 lines of Miranda written by John Cupitt [27, 28]. KAOS has a type constructor interact, a type sysErr, and the following operations (in Haskell notation).

```
return :: a -> interact a
comp   :: (a -> interact b) -> interact a -> interact b
raise  :: sysErr -> interact a
catch  :: (sysErr -> interact a) -> interact a -> interact a
```

Cupitt's interact and sysErr correspond to IO and Exn respectively, and his four operations correspond to return, >>=, raise and try respectively. Cupitt based his combinators on a more complex set introduced by Thompson [141] for programming teletype I/O. Cupitt's combinators were programmed on top of a primitive synchronised-stream mechanism. He found that these combinators hid many low-level details in his implementation.

Independently of Cupitt, the author proposed an extension of Holmström's PFL [57] called PFL+ [43], which was based on a continuation-passing mechanism, and proposed the use of a type constructor and operations corresponding to IO, return and >>= (called Beh, Ret and ▷ respectively). These high-level operations were defined in terms of the low-level continuation-passing mechanism. Unlike Cupitt's scheme, PFL+ was never fully implemented. This dissertation grew out of the effort to make sense of the intuitive ideas developed in PFL+.

This style of I/O has come to be called **monadic** because the structure (IO, return, >>=) can be modelled categorically as a strong monad. As discussed in Chapter 6, Moggi [100] advocated use of such structures to parameterise denotational descriptions of programming languages. Inspired by Moggi, Wadler [149, 150] has advocated use of monads in the functional language itself (rather than the denotational metalanguage) to express imperative activity, such as teletype I/O or interaction with a mutable store. The operations return and >>= used here correspond to Wadler's operations unit and bind respectively [150]. A monadic approach to I/O is being developed in the Glasgow Haskell compiler [49, 110].

Although many lines of code in this style have been written, and it has been realised that the combinators should obey the monadic laws, there has been no previous work on reasoning about programs engaged in monadic I/O. The remainder of this chapter develops a theory of monadic I/O.

```
>    data TT a = Read (Char -> TT a)
>              | Write Char (TT a)
>              | ReturnTT a

>    thenTT :: TT a -> (a -> TT b) -> TT b

>    p 'thenTT' f =
>      case p of
>        Read g     -> Read (\v -> g v 'thenTT' f)
>        Write v q  -> Write v (q 'thenTT' f)
>        ReturnTT x -> f x
```

Table 8.1: A weak monad for teletype I/O

8.2   A weak monad for teletype I/O

Our theory of the MRC programming model is based on modelling the semantics of computations as functional programs within $\mathcal{H}$. This model admits proofs of program properties,
but it is not being proposed as the basis of an efficient implementation! Peyton Jones and
Wadler [110] discuss implementation techniques for monadic I/O.

We begin by defining what we mean by a 'monad' in the context of $\mathcal{H}$.

Definition 8.1 *For any structure* (M, returnM, thenM) *where* M *is a type constructor and
programs* returnM *and* thenM *have types*

> returnM :: σ -> M σ
>   thenM :: M σ -> (σ -> M τ) -> M τ

define three properties as follows.

> (M.beta)   returnM x 'thenM' f = f x   *(for all suitably typed* f *and* x*)*
> (M.assoc) (p 'thenM' f) 'thenM' g = p 'thenM' \x -> (f x) 'thenM' g
>   *(for all suitably typed* p, f *and* g*)*
> (M.eta)   p 'thenM' returnM = p   *(for all suitably typed* p*)*

A **weak monad** *is such a structure* M *satisfying* (M.beta) *and* (M.assoc)*; a* **monad** *is a
weak monad* M *satisfying* (M.eta).

Perhaps surprisingly, the weak monad laws suffice for the purposes of this chapter. In
fact, the full eta law fails for the two weak monads we consider. We begin with a (weak)
monad, TT, given in Table 8.1, which models teletype I/O. It is a version of the constructor
T proposed in §7.1 to model side-effecting I/O. Roughly speaking, any program of type
TT a consists of a string of Reads and Writes terminated by a ReturnTT.

Lemma 8.2 *Structure (*TT, ReturnTT, thenTT*) is a weak monad.*

Proof. (TT.beta) follows immediately by definition of 'thenTT'. For (TT.assoc) it suffices to show that relation S is a bisimulation-up-to-=, where S is defined as follows.

$$S_0 \overset{\text{def}}{=} \{((\text{p 'thenTT' f}) \text{ 'thenTT' g}, \text{p 'thenTT' } (\backslash \text{x} \rightarrow (\text{f x}) \text{ 'thenTT' g}))$$
$$\mid \text{p::TT a, f::a} \rightarrow \text{TT b, g::b} \rightarrow \text{TT c}\}$$
$$S \overset{\text{def}}{=} S_0 \cup \{(c_1, c_2) \mid c_1 \, \widehat{S_0} \, c_2\} \cup (\equiv)$$

To show that S is a bisimulation-up-to-=, it suffices to consider any pair (e_1, e_2) in S_0 and show that either $e_1 = e_2 = \Omega$, or that there are canonical programs c_1 and c_2 such that $e_i = c_i$ for each i, and that $c_1 \, \widehat{S} \, c_2$. Accordingly, let $e_1 \equiv (\text{p 'thenTT' f}) \text{ 'thenTT' g}$ and $e_2 \equiv \text{p 'thenTT' } (\backslash \text{x} \rightarrow \text{f x 'thenTT' g})$. By Strachey's property, one of the following cases holds:

(1) $\text{p} = \Omega$

(2) $\text{p} = \text{returnTT x}$

(3) $\text{p} = \text{Write v q}$ or

(4) $\text{p} = \text{Read h}$.

In each case we can establish the required conditions.

(1) $e_1 = \Omega = e_2$.

(2) $e_1 = (\text{ReturnTT x 'thenTT' f}) \text{ 'thenTT' g} = \text{f x 'thenTT' g}$.
$e_2 = \text{ReturnTT x 'thenTT' } (\backslash \text{x} \rightarrow \text{f x 'thenTT' g}) = \text{f x 'thenTT' g}$.
So $e_1 = e_2$. By Strachey's property, either $e_1 = e_2 = \Omega$ (and we are done) or there is a canonical program c with $e_1 = e_2 = c$. In the latter case we have $c \, \widehat{\equiv} \, c$ so $c \, \widehat{S} \, c$ as required.

(3) In this case, we have:

$$\begin{aligned}
e_1 &= ((\text{Write v q}) \text{ 'thenTT' f}) \text{ 'thenTT' g} \\
&= (\text{Write v } (\text{q 'thenTT' f})) \text{ 'thenTT' g} \\
&= \text{Write v } ((\text{q 'thenTT' f}) \text{ 'thenTT' g} \\
e_2 &= (\text{Write v q}) \text{ 'thenTT' } (\backslash \text{x} \rightarrow \text{f x 'thenTT' g}) \\
&= \text{Write v } (\text{q 'thenTT' } (\backslash \text{x} \rightarrow \text{f x 'thenTT' g}))
\end{aligned}$$

Define programs e_i' and c_i to be:

$$\begin{aligned}
e_1' &\equiv (\text{q 'thenTT' f}) \text{ 'thenTT' g} \\
e_2' &\equiv \text{q 'thenTT' } (\backslash \text{v} \rightarrow (\text{f v}) \text{ 'thenTT' g}) \\
c_1 &\equiv \text{Write v } e_1' \\
c_2 &\equiv \text{Write v } e_2'
\end{aligned}$$

We have $e_i = c_i$, and since $v \equiv v$ and $e_1' S_0 e_2'$ we have $c_1 \, \widehat{S} \, c_2$ as required.

(4) In this final case case, when $\text{p} = \text{Read h}$, either h equals Ω or some canonical function

$\v -> e_3$. If $h = \Omega$ we have:

$$
\begin{aligned}
e_1 &= (\text{Read } \Omega \text{ 'thenTT' } f) \text{ 'thenTT' } g \\
&= (\text{Read}(\v -> \Omega \text{ v 'thenTT' } f)) \text{ 'thenTT' } g \\
&= \text{Read}(\v -> \Omega) \text{ 'thenTT' } g \\
&= \text{Read}(\v -> \Omega \text{ 'thenTT' } g) \\
&= \text{Read}(\v -> \Omega) \\
e_2 &= (\text{Read } \Omega) \text{ 'thenTT' } (\v -> (f \text{ v}) \text{ 'thenTT' } g) \\
&= \text{Read}(\v -> \Omega \text{ v 'thenTT' } (\v -> (f \text{ v}) \text{ 'thenTT' } g)) \\
&= \text{Read}(\v -> \Omega)
\end{aligned}
$$

Since $e_1 = e_2 = \text{Read}(\v -> \Omega)$ and $\Omega \equiv \Omega$ we are done. Otherwise, $h = \v -> e_3$ and we have:

$$
\begin{aligned}
e_1 &= (\text{Read } (\v -> e_3) \text{ 'thenTT' } f) \text{ 'thenTT' } g \\
&= (\text{Read}(\v -> e_3 \text{ 'thenTT' } f)) \text{ 'thenTT' } g \\
&= \text{Read}(\v -> (e_3 \text{ 'thenTT' } f) \text{ 'thenTT' } g) \\
e_2 &= \text{Read}(\v -> e_3) \text{ 'thenTT' } (\v -> (f \text{ v}) \text{ 'thenTT' } g) \\
&= \text{Read}(\v -> e_3 \text{ 'thenTT' } (\v -> (f \text{ v}) \text{ 'thenTT' } g))
\end{aligned}
$$

Define programs c_i' and c_i to be:

$$
\begin{aligned}
c_1' &\equiv \v -> (e_3 \text{ 'thenTT' } f) \text{ 'thenTT' } g \\
c_2' &\equiv \v -> e_3 \text{ 'thenTT' } (\v -> (f \text{ v}) \text{ 'thenTT' } g) \\
c_1 &\equiv \text{Read } e_1' \\
c_2 &\equiv \text{Read } e_2'
\end{aligned}
$$

We have $c_1' \; \widehat{S_0} \; c_2'$ so $c_1' S c_2'$. But then $e_i = c_i$ for each i and $c_1 \; \widehat{S} \; c_2$ so the proof for Read is complete.   ∎

The (TT.eta) law is invalid. Here is a counterexample.

$$
\begin{aligned}
\text{Read } \Omega \text{ 'thenTT' ReturnTT} &= \text{Read}(\v -> \Omega \text{ v 'thenTT' ReturnTT}) \\
&= \text{Read}(\v -> \Omega) \\
&\neq \text{Read } \Omega
\end{aligned}
$$

If we had a theory of $\mathcal{H}$ which satisfied $\Omega = \v -> \Omega$ (the intention of the Haskell designers) we could in fact establish (TT.eta). For the purposes of this chapter the lack of (TT.eta) is unimportant; all we need are the weak monad laws, (TT.beta) and (TT.assoc).

8.3   A weak monad for the MRC computer

The MRC programming model has three components: teletype I/O, interaction with the external microscope assembly, and exception handling. We model the state of the external microscope assembly as a pair, consisting of the current position (either parked or at a particular coordinate) and a function representing the image that could be captured from any of the coordinate positions.

```
>    type State   = (Maybe Coord, Coord -> Image)
>    data Maybe a = Nothing | Just a
```

```
> either              :: (a -> c) -> (b -> c) -> (Either a b -> c)
> either f g ab       = case ab of
>                          Left a -> f a
>                          Right b -> g b

> get                 :: IO State
> put                 :: State -> IO ()
> get                 = \s0 -> ReturnTT (Left s0, s0)
> put s1              = \s0 -> ReturnTT (Left (), s1)

> return x            = \s0 -> ReturnTT (Left x, s0)
> raise x             = \s0 -> ReturnTT (Right x, s0)
> p >>= f             = \s0 -> p s0 'thenTT' uncurry (either f raise)
> try p f             = \s0 -> p s0 'thenTT' uncurry (either return f)
> output v            = \s0 -> Write v (ReturnTT (Left (), s0))
> input               = \s0 -> Read (\v -> ReturnTT (Left v, s0))

> parkStage           = get >>= \s -> put (Nothing, snd s)
> moveStage co        = get >>= \s -> put (Just co, snd s)
> capture             = get >>= \s -> case fst s of
>                          Just co  -> return ((snd s) co)
>                          Nothing  -> raise "capture"
```

Table 8.2: Deriving the MRC programming model

Modelling image capture from the loaded slide by a fixed function is extremely crude, as it ignores the effects of random camera noise, sloppy stage mechanics and the settings of the focus, lamp, objective lens and filter. It is a kind of 'idealised microscope model' whose principle virtue is simplicity. We use the type of strings to model exceptions.

```
> type Exn = String
```

Intuitively we expect a computation of type IO a to act on some initial state by performing some teletype I/O before returning an answer, either a value of type a or an exception of type Exn. We formalise this expectation in the following definition of IO.

```
> type IO a       = PrimIO (Either a Exn)
> type PrimIO a   = State -> TT (a, State)
> data Either a b = Left a | Right b
```

Recall that programs of type TT a can be thought of as a string of I/O operations ending with a result of type a. Therefore a program p::IO a is a function that given an initial state s returns p s::TT (Either a Exn, State), which consists of a string of I/O operations ending with a result of type (Either a Exn, State). Such a result consists of a final state paired with either a normal result of type a or an exception of type Exn. This definition of IO allows us to model the semantics of computations within $\mathcal{H}$, and hence use our theory of $\mathcal{H}$ to reason about programs. In practice we would almost certainly want to implement the IO type more efficiently.

We show in Table 8.2 how to program the various monadic operations, given our definition of the IO type. These programs should be understood as formal specifications of the programming model's semantics, rather than as realistic implementations. There are three auxiliary operations either, get and put. Functions uncurry, fst and snd are given in Table 6.3.

We can verify the laws (IO.beta) and (IO.assoc) as follows.

Lemma 8.3 *Structure* (IO , return, (>>=)) *is a weak monad.*

Proof. The proofs are by routine equational reasoning. (IO.beta) follows from the following calculations.

$$
\begin{aligned}
\text{(return v >>= f)s} &= \text{ return v s `thenTT` uncurry(either f raise)} \\
&= \text{ returnTT(Left v, s) `thenTT` uncurry(either f raise)} \\
&= \text{ either f raise (Left v) s} \\
&= \text{ f v s}
\end{aligned}
$$

To establish (IO.assoc) first note the following facts.

$$
\begin{aligned}
\text{either f g v >>= h} &= \text{ either (\textbackslash x -> f x >>= h) (\textbackslash x -> g x >>= h) v} \\
\text{raise v >>= f} &= \text{ raise v} \\
\text{e}_1 \text{ `thenTT` (\textbackslash x -> e}_2 \text{ x)} &= \text{ e}_1 \text{ `thenTT` e}_2
\end{aligned}
$$

The third of these, a specialised functional eta law, can be established by a simple co-induction. We can begin the proof of (IO.assoc) as follows, for any suitably typed programs p, f, g and s.

$$
\begin{aligned}
\text{((p >>= f) >>= g)s} &= \text{ (p s `thenTT` uncurry(either f raise))} \\
&\qquad \text{ `thenTT` uncurry(either g raise)} \\
&= \text{ p s `thenTT` (\textbackslash y -> uncurry(either f raise) y} \\
&\qquad \text{ `thenTT` uncurry(either g raise))}
\end{aligned}
$$

Now set e to be a subexpression of the right-hand side,

$$
\text{e} \equiv \text{uncurry(either f raise) y `thenTT` uncurry(either g raise).}
$$

From the facts noted earlier we can calculate as follows.

$$
\begin{aligned}
\text{e} &= \text{ either f raise (fst y) (snd y) `thenTT` uncurry(either g raise)} \\
&= \text{ (either f raise (fst y) >>= g)(snd y)} \\
&= \text{ either (\textbackslash x -> f x >>= g) (\textbackslash x -> raise x >>= g) (fst y) (snd y)} \\
&= \text{ either (\textbackslash x -> f x >>= g) raise (fst y) (snd y)} \\
&= \text{ uncurry(either (\textbackslash x -> f x >>= g) raise) y}
\end{aligned}
$$

Hence via the specialised functional eta law noted above we have

$$
\begin{aligned}
\text{((p >>= f) >>= g)s} &= \text{ p s `thenTT` (\textbackslash y -> e)} \\
&= \text{ p s `thenTT` uncurry(either (\textbackslash x -> f x >>= g) raise)} \\
&= \text{ (p >>= (\textbackslash x -> f x >>= g))s}
\end{aligned}
$$

as required for (IO.assoc).   ∎

```
> analyse       :: (Image -> Char) -> IO ()
> jobA f cos    = sequence [moveStage co >> analyse f | co <- cos]
> analyse f     = capture >>= \im -> output (f im)

> jobB f []         = skip
> jobB f (co:cos) = moveStage co >> jobC f cos
> jobC f cos       = sequence [each f co | co <- cos] >> analyse f
> each f co        = capture >>= \im -> moveStage co >> output (f im)
```

Table 8.3: The motivating example

Here is a counterexample to (IO.eta). Let p be const(ReturnTT Ω). We have for any state s,

$$
\begin{aligned}
(p >>= return)\ s &= ReturnTT\ \Omega\ \text{`thenTT`}\ uncurry(either\ return\ raise) \\
&= uncurry(either\ return\ raise)\ \Omega \\
&= either\ return\ raise\ \Omega\ \Omega \\
&= \Omega
\end{aligned}
$$

but p s = ReturnTT Ω which does not equal Ω in $\mathcal{H}$ (nor in Haskell) because all datatype constructors are lazy.

From (IO.beta) and (IO.assoc) we can verify the following facts about >> and skip.

Lemma 8.4

(1) $(p >> q) >> r = p >> (q >> r)$

(2) $skip >> p = p$

It would help subsequent calculations if we had the right cancellation law

$$p >> skip = p$$

(which would make (>>, skip) a monoid) but this fails because of the same counterexample as (IO.eta). Furthermore, q = return Ω is another counterexample; we have q >> skip = skip = return () $\neq$ return Ω. The problem is that () $\neq$ Ω in $\mathcal{H}$ and in Haskell. Undesirable undefined elements cause the failure of all these eta and right cancellation laws. (TT.eta) fails in $\mathcal{H}$ because \x -> Ω $\neq$ Ω, and (IO.eta) fails in both $\mathcal{H}$ and Haskell because ReturnTT Ω $\neq$ Ω. However, for the purpose of proving our motivating example all we need is a specific right cancellation law, Lemma 8.5(1).

8.4 Proof of the motivating example

We conclude this chapter by verifying the example set in §8.1 on page 124. We begin with a lemma, each part of which can easily proved by equational calculations from what we have already proved about the IO type.

Lemma 8.5

(1) output v >> skip = output v

(2) $(\text{capture} >>= \text{f})(\text{Just } \text{co}, \text{g}) = \text{f}(\text{g co})(\text{Just co}, \text{g})$

(3) $(\text{moveStage co} >> \text{p})(\text{mb}, \text{g}) = \text{p}(\text{Just co}, \text{g})$

(4) $(\text{output v} >> \text{p})(\text{mb}, \text{g}) = \text{Write v } (\text{p}(\text{mb}, \text{g}))$

(5) $(\text{analyse f} >> \text{p})(\text{Just co}, \text{g}) = \text{Write } (\text{f}(\text{g co})) \ (\text{p}(\text{Just co}, \text{g}))$

(6) $(\text{each f co}' >> \text{p})(\text{Just co}, \text{g}) = \text{Write } (\text{f}(\text{g co})) \ (\text{p}(\text{Just co}', \text{g}))$

We need a lemma to relate jobA and the auxiliary function jobC.

Lemma 8.6 *For any finite* cos::[Coord]*,* co::Coord*,* f::Image -> Char*,* g::Coord -> Image *and* mb::Maybe Coord*,*

$$\text{jobA f } (\text{co} : \text{cos}) \ (\text{mb}, \text{g}) \ = \ \text{jobC f cos } (\text{Just co}, \text{g}).$$

Proof. By appeal to the structural induction principle, Proposition 6.34, as specialised to lists in §6.6, we may prove the lemma by induction on the structure of finite list cos. We have:

$$
\begin{aligned}
\text{lhs} \ &= \ (\text{moveStage co} >> \text{analyse f} >> \text{jobA f cos})(\text{mb}, \text{g}) \\
&= \ (\text{analyse f} >> \text{jobA f cos})(\text{Just co}, \text{g}) \\
&= \ \text{Write } (\text{f}(\text{g co})) \ (\text{jobA f cos } (\text{Just co}, \text{g}))
\end{aligned}
$$

Now we consider the two possible forms of cos: (i) cos = [] and (ii) cos = co' : cos'. In case (i) it is not hard to check that both sides equal

$$\text{Write } (\text{f}(\text{g co})) \ (\text{skip } (\text{Just co}, \text{g})).$$

In case (ii) we may calculate as follows.

$$
\begin{aligned}
\text{rhs} \ &= \ (\text{each f co}' >> \text{jobC f cos}')(\text{Just co}, \text{g}) \\
&= \ \text{Write } (\text{f}(\text{g co})) \ (\text{jobC f cos}' \ (\text{Just co}', \text{g})) \\
&= \ \text{Write } (\text{f}(\text{g co})) \ (\text{jobA f } (\text{co}' : \text{cos}') \ (\text{Just co}, \text{g})) \ \ (\text{IH}) \\
&= \ \text{lhs}
\end{aligned}
$$

In both cases, then, we have the desired equivalence.   ∎

The lemma would fail if we were to remove the constraint that cos be finite. Consider cos = Ω, which is not finite (in the sense of §6.6). Program jobA f (co : Ω) (mb, g) = Write (f(g co)) Ω but jobC f Ω (Just co, g) = Ω.

Finally, we can verify our motivating example.

Proposition 8.7 *For any finite list* cos*, function* f*, and initial state* (mb, g)*,*

$$\text{jobA f cos } (\text{mb}, \text{g}) = \text{jobB f cos } (\text{mb}, \text{g}).$$

Proof. If cos is finite, then either cos = [] or cos = co : cos'. In the first case, lhs = skip (mb, g) = rhs. In the second case, we have rhs = (moveStage co >> jobC f cos')(mb, g) = jobC f cos' (Just co, g) = jobA f (co : cos')(mb, g), by the previous lemma, and hence lhs = rhs.   ∎

Chapter 9

Conclusion

9.1 Summary

We have shown how a theory of functional programming can be developed from structural operational semantics and applicative bisimulation. We might reckon this a CCS-view of λ-calculus. We developed parallel theories of a metalanguage for denotational semantics, $\mathcal{M}$, and a small functional language, $\mathcal{H}$, essentially a fragment of Haskell. Co-induction, in the form of bisimulation-up-to-equivalence, was found to be useful in circumstances where domain-theoretic Scott induction might have been needed.

We identified four basic mechanisms for teletype I/O. We gave a labelled transition semantics for three of these mechanisms and defined a notion of bisimilarity. We proved that the three mechanisms are of equivalent expressive power in the theoretical sense that there are bisimulation-preserving translations between the three. Actual implementation of these translations would not necessarily be efficient, however.

We advocated a monadic style of functional I/O in the context of an application of functional programming to medical electronics at the Edinburgh Medical Research Council (MRC). Motivated by a verification example suggested by the MRC, we developed a theory of monadic I/O as an extension of our theory of functional programming. By modelling the semantics of the MRC programming model within $\mathcal{H}$, we were able to verify the example via functional programming techniques.

Ever since McCarthy referred to the I/O operations in LISP 1.5 as "pseudo-functions" functional I/O has been viewed with suspicion. The work of this dissertation is important because it is the first to show how a theory of functional programming can be smoothly extended to admit both an operational semantics for functional I/O and verification of programs engaged in I/O.

To finish off the dissertation, for each chapter we sketch possible future work, and offer some further appraisal.

9.2   A calculus of recursive types

It is a pity that the convergence theorem for $\mathcal{M}$, Theorem 3.11, must depend ultimately on Mendler's theorem [88] which this dissertation takes on trust. It would be interesting to investigate whether the $\mathcal{M}$ convergence theorem could be based on Wraith's encoding of recursive types in the Girard-Reynolds calculus itself [153]. Another direction to pursue would be to see whether Mendler's original strong normalisation proof could be extended to cope with the new constants. The author has recently obtained a result analogous to Theorem 3.11 for a variant of $\mathcal{M}$ via a form of Tait's method (upon which Mendler's proof for $\mu\nu\lambda2$ was based).

9.3   A metalanguage for semantics

$\mathcal{M}$ is based on Plotkin's domain-theoretic metalanguage for semantics [120], in which each type represents a particular domain construction. Missing from both $\mathcal{M}$ and Plotkin's metalanguage is a type of nondeterministic computations corresponding to a powerdomain construction. Howe's original paper [58] showed that applicative bisimulation can be applied to a nondeterministic calculus. It may be worthwhile to investigate how to extend $\mathcal{M}$ with a type representing nondeterministic computations.

9.4   Operational precongruence

Chapter 4 studied how the context lemma and Howe's method can be used to prove that an operationally-defined equivalence relation is a precongruence. We expect that Howe's method will be extremely useful for constructing operational theories of programming languages. The context lemma was simple and ingenious in the setting of combinatory logic [91], but much care appears to be needed to generalise it to a more complex λ-calculus, such as $\mathcal{M}$.

9.5   Theory of the metalanguage

We developed an equational theory for $\mathcal{M}$, and proved results about certain types needed for the denotational semantics of $\mathcal{H}$. Although not itself domain-theoretic, the theory of $\mathcal{M}$ can be compared to axiomatisations of domain theory or functional programming, such as Edinburgh LCF [46], Cambridge LCF [105] and Thompson's logic for Miranda [140]. There are two major differences. First, only $\mathcal{M}$ types of the form $\sigma_\perp$ contain a divergent term Ω. Hence the presentation of the theory in Table 5.1 is simpler than in LCF or Thompson's logic. Second, there is no principle of Scott induction for $\mathcal{M}$. Smith has shown how to derive such a principle in an operational setting [133]. On the other hand, we have found in this dissertation that co-induction is sufficient to prove theorems such as Lemma 8.2 that in LCF would probably have required Scott induction.

```
infix 1 >>= >>
abstype 'a Job = JOB of unit -> 'a
with
    fun exec (JOB f)    = f ()

    fun unit x          = JOB(fn _ => x)
    fun (JOB f) >>= q   = JOB(fn _ => exec (q (f ())))
    fun getStr n        = JOB(fn _ => input(std_in,n))
    fun putStr s        = JOB(fn _ => output(std_out,s))
end;

fun p >> q = p >>= (fn u => q);
fun gettingLine s =
    getStr 1 >>= (fn c =>
    if c = "\n" then unit s else gettingLine (s^c));
val getLine = gettingLine "";
val main =
    putStr "First name:  " >> getLine >>= (fn first =>
    putStr "Second name: " >> getLine >>= (fn second =>
    putStr ("Hello "^first^" "^second^"\n")));
```

Table 9.1: A monadic style of I/O for Standard ML

9.6 An operational theory of functional programming

The most original aspect of the theory of functional programming in Chapter 6 is that it is entirely grounded in operational semantics. Note that the theory of operational equivalence in $\mathcal{H}$ does not depend in any way on Mendler's normalisation theorem [88], although the theory of denotational equivalence does.

It is interesting to compare the operational and denotational theories of $\mathcal{H}$. The denotational semantics is good for comparing different object languages (e.g., $\mathcal{H}$, $\mathcal{HX}$, and $\mathcal{H}$ with side-effecting I/O), while the operational semantics allows a simple derivation of program equivalence.

A useful future project would be to extend $\mathcal{H}$ to include eager algebraic type constructors and a more realistic exception mechanism. Such an extension would contain a non-trivial fragment of core Standard ML.

9.7 Four mechanisms for teletype I/O

The main question left open in this chapter is how to integrate an operational semantics of side-effecting I/O into a theory of functional programming. Several authors have suggested operational semantics for ML extended with side-effecting operators for concurrency [11, 126]; however, there has been little work on equational theories for functional languages extended with concurrency.

9.8   Monadic I/O

This chapter showed how to construct a crude model of the MRC computer within $\mathcal{H}$, and use functional programming techniques to verify a simple property. Before this sort of methodology is to be of any practical use, there needs to be a good deal more mechanised support for proofs of programs, and experience of specifying more realistic systems.

One can view monadic I/O as a controlled form of side-effecting I/O; the monad of side-effects has moved from the denotational semantics into the type system of the object language.

This dissertation has not discussed practical implementation, though of course the operational semantics rules give some clues. There is ongoing work at Glasgow on efficient implementation of monadic I/O [110]. Verification of an I/O mechanism is a problem not previously examined in work on verified functional implementations [47, 80, 132].

The monadic style is not confined to lazy languages. Table 9.1 shows how monadic I/O can be implemented in core Standard ML on top of side-effecting I/O. In naive experiments, this style of monadic I/O was about six times slower than side-effecting I/O. It should be possible to improve this performance if the Job type were taken as primitive (which is more or less what is proposed in the Glasgow Haskell compiler [110]). If side-effects are allowed only in the implementation of the Job type, reasoning about monadic programs in ML should not be much harder than reasoning about monadic programs in Haskell.

Bibliography

Each reference is followed by a parenthesised list of the pages on which it is cited.

[1] Harold Abelson and Gerald J. Sussman. **Structure and Interpretation of Computer Programs**. MIT Press, Cambridge, Mass., 1985.   (p 2)

[2] Samson Abramsky. The lazy lambda calculus. In Turner [146], pages 65–116.   (pp 7, 37)

[3] Samson Abramsky and Richard Sykes. SECD-M: a virtual machine for applicative programming. In Jouannaud [70], pages 81–98.   (pp 99, 104, 117)

[4] Peter Achten, John van Groningen, and Rinus Plasmeijer. High level specification of I/O in functional languages. In **Functional Programming, Glasgow 1992**, Workshops in Computing. Springer-Verlag, 1993.   (p xi)

[5] Arvind and J. Dean Brock. Resource managers in functional programming. **Journal of Parallel and Distributed Computing**, 1:5–21, 1984.   (p 3)

[6] E. A. Ashcroft and W. W. Wadge. Lucid: a nonprocedural language with iteration. **Communications of the ACM**, 20(7):519–526, July 1977.   (p 2)

[7] L. Augustsson and T. Johnsson. The Chalmers Lazy-ML compiler. **The Computer Journal**, 32(2):127–141, April 1989.   (p 6)

[8] John Backus. Can programming be liberated from the von Neumann style? a functional style and its algebra of programs. **Communications of the ACM**, 21(8):613–641, August 1978.   (p 3)

[9] John Backus, John H. Williams, and Edward L. Wimmers. An introduction to the programming language FL. In Turner [146], pages 219–248.   (pp 3, 102)

[10] H. P. Barendregt. **The Lambda Calculus: Its Syntax and Semantics**, volume 103 of **Studies in logic and the foundations of mathematics**. North-Holland, revised edition, 1984.   (pp 7, 11)

[11] Dave Berry, Robin Milner, and David N. Turner. A semantics for ML concurrency primitives. In **Proceedings of the Nineteenth ACM Symposium on Principles of Programming Languages**, pages 119–129, 1992.   (pp 6, 99, 135)

[12] Gérard Berry. Some syntactic and categorical constructions of lambda-calculus models. Technical Report 80, INRIA, 1981.   (pp 7, 46)

[13] Richard Bird and Philip Wadler. **Introduction to Functional Programming**. Prentice-Hall International, 1988.   (pp 2, 3)

[14] Bard Bloom. Can LCF be topped? Flat lattice models of typed lambda calculus. In **Proceedings of the 3rd IEEE Symposium on Logic in Computer Science**, pages 282–295. IEEE Computer Society Press, 1988.   (pp 9, 37)

[15] Manfred Broy. Nondeterministic data flow programs: how to avoid the merge anomaly. **Science of Computer Programming**, 10:65–85, 1988.   (p 6)

[16] Geoffrey Burn. **Lazy Functional Languages: Interpretation and Compilation**. MIT Press, Cambridge, Mass., 1991.   (p 8)

[17] R. M. Burstall and R. Popplestone. POP-2 reference manual. **Machine Intelligence**, 2:205–249, 1968.   (p 1)

[18] Luca Cardelli. Stream input/output. **Polymorphism—The ML/LCF/Hope Newsletter**, 1(3), December 1985.   (p 6)

[19] Luca Cardelli and Rob Pike. Squeak: a language for communicating with mice. **Computer Graphics**, 19(3):199–204, July 1985.   (pp 6, 99)

[20] Magnus Carlsson and Thomas Hallgren. FUDGETS: A graphical user interface in a lazy functional language. In **FPCA'93: Conference on Functional Programming Languages and Computer Architecture, Copenhagen**, pages 321–330. ACM Press, 1993.   (p xi)

[21] Robert Cartwright and James Donahue. The semantics of lazy (and industrious) evaluation. In **LISP and Functional Programming**, pages 253–264. ACM Press, 1982.   (p 7)

[22] P. Caspi, D. Pilaud, N. Halbwachs, and J. A. Plaice. LUSTRE: a declarative language for real-time programming. In **Fourteenth ACM Symposium on Principles of Programming Languages**, pages 178–188, Münich, West Germany, 1987. ACM Press.   (p 6)

[23] Eric Cooper and J. Gregory Morrisett. Adding threads to Standard ML. Technical Report CMU–CS–90–186, Computer Science Department, Carnegie-Mellon University, December 1990.   (p 99)

[24] R. L. Crole and A. M. Pitts. New foundations for fixpoint computations: FIX hyperdoctrines and the FIX-logic. **Information and Computation**, 98:171–210, 1992. Earlier version in LICS'90.   (p 75)

[25] Roy L. Crole. **Programming Metalogics with a Fixpoint Type**. PhD thesis, University of Cambridge Computer Laboratory, February 1992. Available as Technical Report 247.   (pp 8, 32, 75)

[26] Roy L. Crole and Andrew D. Gordon. Factoring an adequacy proof (preliminary report). In **Functional Programming, Glasgow 1993**, Workshops in Computing. Springer-Verlag, 1994.   (p xi)

[27] J. Cupitt. Another new scheme for writing functional operating systems. Technical Report 52, Computing Laboratory, University of Kent at Canterbury, March 1988.   (pp 105, 108, 125)

[28] J. Cupitt. A brief walk through KAOS. Technical Report 58, Computing Laboratory, University of Kent at Canterbury, February 1989.   (pp 5, 108, 117, 125)

[29] Roger B. Dannenberg. Arctic: A functional language for real-time control. In **LISP**

and Functional Programming, pages 96–103. ACM Press, 1984.   (p 99)

[30] J. Darlington, P. Henderson, and D. A. Turner, editors. **Functional Programming and its Applications**. Cambridge University Press, 1982.   (pp 140, 145)

[31] B. A. Davey and H. A. Priestley. **Introduction to Lattices and Order**. Cambridge University Press, 1990.   (pp 7, 12)

[32] Andrew Dwelly. Synchronizing the I/O behaviour of functional programs with feedback. **Information Processing Letters**, May 1988.   (p 5)

[33] Andrew Dwelly. Functions and dynamic user interfaces. In **Fourth International Conference on Functional Programming Languages and Computer Architecture, Imperial College, London**, pages 371–381. ACM Press, September 11–13, 1989.   (p 99)

[34] Peter Dybjer and Herbert Sander. A functional programming approach to the specification and verification of concurrent systems. **Formal Aspects of Computing**, 1(4):303–319, October–December 1989.   (p 6)

[35] John R. Ellis. A LISP shell. **ACM SIGPLAN Notices**, 15(5):24–34, May 1980. (p 99)

[36] Jon Fairbairn. Making form follow function: An exercise in functional programming style. **Software—Practice and Experience**, 17(6):379–386, 1987.   (p 117)

[37] Joe Fasel and Paul Hudak. A gentle introduction to Haskell. **ACM SIGPLAN Notices**, 27(5), March 1992. Section T.   (p 69)

[38] M. Felleisen and D. Friedman. **Control Operators, the SECD-machine, and the λ-calculus**, pages 193–217. North-Holland, 1986.   (p 30)

[39] M. Felleisen and D. P. Friedman. A syntactic theory of sequential state. **Theoretical Computer Science**, 69:243–287, 1989.   (p xi)

[40] Anthony J. Field and Peter G. Harrison. **Functional Programming**. Addison-Wesley, Wokingham, England, 1988.   (p 2)

[41] D. P. Friedman and D. S. Wise. Cons should not evaluate its arguments. In S. Michaelson and R. Milner, editors, **Third International Colloquium on Automata, Languages and Programming**. Edinburgh University Press, July 1976. (p 3)

[42] Jean-Yvres Girard, Paul Taylor, and Yves Lafont. **Proofs and Types**. Cambridge University Press, 1989.   (pp 15, 18)

[43] Andrew Gordon. PFL+ : A kernel scheme for functional I/O. Technical Report 160, University of Cambridge Computer Laboratory, February 1989.   (pp 6, 117, 125)

[44] Andrew D. Gordon. The formal definition of a synchronous hardware-description language in higher order logic. In **International Conference on Computer Design, Cambridge, Massachusetts, October 11–14, 1992**, pages 531–534. IEEE Computer Society Press, 1992.   (p 2)

[45] Andrew D. Gordon. An operational semantics for I/O in a lazy functional language. In **FPCA'93: Conference on Functional Programming Languages and Computer Architecture, Copenhagen**, pages 136–145. ACM Press, 1993.

(p xi)

[46] Michael J. C. Gordon, Robin Milner, and Christopher P. Wadsworth. **Edinburgh LCF**, volume 78 of **Lecture Notes in Computer Science**. Springer-Verlag, 1979. (pp 9, 55, 134)

[47] Brian T. Graham. **The SECD Microprocessor: A Verification Case Study**. Kluwer Academic Publishers, 1992.   (pp 104, 136)

[48] Carl A. Gunter. **Semantics of Programming Languages: Structures and Techniques**. MIT Press, Cambridge, Mass., 1992.   (p xi)

[49] Kevin Hammond, Philip Wadler, and Donald Brady. Imperate: Be imperative (summary). Department of Computing Science, University of Glasgow, 1991.   (p 125)

[50] Dave Harrison. Ruth: A functional language for real-time programming. In **Parallel Architectures and Languages Europe Proceedings**, volume 259 of **Lecture Notes in Computer Science**, pages 297–314. Springer-Verlag, 1987.   (pp 6, 99)

[51] B. C. Heck and D. S. Wise. An implementation of an applicative file system. In **International Worshop on Memory Management**, St Malo, France, September 16–18, 1992. Also available as Technical Report 354, Computer Science Department, Indiana University, June 1992.   (p 99)

[52] Peter Henderson. **Functional Programming: Application and Implementation**. Prentice-Hall, 1980.   (p 2)

[53] Peter Henderson. Purely functional operating systems. In Darlington et al. [30], pages 177–192.   (pp 3, 99, 104)

[54] Peter Henderson and James H. Morris Jr. A lazy evaluator. In **Conference Record of the Third ACM Symposium on Principles of Programming Languages**, pages 95–103. ACM Press, 1976. Atlanta, Georgia.   (pp 3, 7)

[55] Matthew Hennessy. **The Semantics of Programming Languages**. John Wiley and Sons, Chichester, 1990.   (p 7)

[56] J. Roger Hindley and Jonathan P. Seldin. **Introduction to Combinators and λ-Calculus**. Cambridge University Press, 1986.   (p 11)

[57] Sören Holmström. PFL: A functional language for parallel programming. In **Declarative Programming Workshop**, pages 114–139. University College, London, 1983. Extended version published as Report 7, Programming Methodology Group, Chalmers University. September 1983.   (pp 4, 6, 99, 109, 125)

[58] Douglas J. Howe. Equality in lazy computation systems. In **Proceedings of the 4th IEEE Symposium on Logic in Computer Science**, pages 198–203, 1989. (pp 7, 9, 37, 50, 52, 134)

[59] Paul Hudak, Simon L. Peyton Jones, Philip Wadler, et al. Report on the functional programming language Haskell: A non-strict, purely functional language version 1.2. **ACM SIGPLAN Notices**, 27(5), March 1992. Section R.   (pp 4, 69, 100, 108, 117)

[60] Paul Hudak and Raman S. Sundaresh. On the expressiveness of purely functional I/O systems. Research Report YALEU/DCS/RR–665, Yale University Department of Computer Science, March 1989.   (pp 4, 6, 99, 100, 103, 117)

[61] John Hughes. Why functional programming matters. **The Computer Journal**, 32(2):98–107, April 1989. (pp 2, 3)

[62] O. A. N. Husain, K. C. Watts, F. Lorriman, B. Butler, J. Tucker, A. Carothers, P. Eason, S. Farrow, D. Rutovitz, and M. Stark. Semi-automated cervical smear pre-screening system: an evaluation of the Cytoscan-110. **Analytical and Cellular Pathology**, 5:49–68, 1993. (p 119)

[63] Graham Hutton. Higher-order functions for parsing. **Journal of Functional Programming**, 2(3):323–343, July 1992. (p 117)

[64] Evan Peter Ireland. Writing interactive and file-processing functional programs: A method and implementation. Master's thesis, Victoria University of Wellington, March 1989. (p 99)

[65] Alan Jeffrey. A chemical abstract machine for graph reduction. In **Proceedings Mathematical Foundations of Programming Semantics IX, New Orleans 1993**, volume 802 of **Lecture Notes in Computer Science**. Springer-Verlag, 1994. (p xi)

[66] Claire Jones. **Probabilistic Non-determinism**. PhD thesis, University of Edinburgh, 1990. Available as Technical Report CST–63–90, Computer Science Department, University of Edinburgh. (p 27)

[67] S. B. Jones and A. F. Sinclair. Functional programming and operating systems. **The Computer Journal**, 32(2):162–174, April 1989. (pp 3, 6, 99)

[68] Simon B. Jones. Abstract machine support for purely functional operating systems. Technical Report PRG-34, Programming Research Group, Oxford University Computing Laboratory, August 1983. (pp 104, 117)

[69] Simon B. Jones. A range of operating systems written in a purely functional style. Technical Report PRG-42, Programming Research Group, Oxford University Computing Laboratory, September 1984. (pp 99, 104)

[70] Jean-Pierre Jouannaud, editor. **Functional Programming Languages and Computer Architecture, Nancy, France**, volume 201 of **Lecture Notes in Computer Science**. Springer-Verlag, September 1985. (pp 137, 146)

[71] Gilles Kahn. A preliminary theory for parallel programs. Rapport de Recherche 6, IRIA, January 1973. (p 3)

[72] Gilles Kahn and David B. MacQueen. Coroutines and networks of parallel processes. In B. Gilchrist, editor, **Information Processing 77**, pages 993–998. North-Holland, 1977. (pp 3, 6, 104)

[73] Y. H. Kamath and M. M. Matthews. Implementation of an FP-shell. **IEEE Transactions on Software Engineering**, SE–13(5):532–539, May 1987. (p 99)

[74] Kent Karlsson. Nebula: A functional operating system. Programming Methodology Group, Chalmers University of Technology and University of Gothenburg, 1981. (pp 4, 5, 99, 108, 109)

[75] Paul Kelly. **Functional Programming for Loosely-coupled Multiprocessors**. MIT Press, Cambridge, Mass., 1989. (p 6)

[76] P. J. Landin. A correspondence between ALGOL 60 and Church's lambda-notation:

Parts I and II. **Communications of the ACM**, 8(2,3):89–101,158–165, February and March 1965.   (pp 3, 106)

[77] P. J. Landin. The next 700 programming languages. **Communications of the ACM**, 9(3):157–166, March 1966.   (p 1)

[78] John Launchbury. A natural semantics for lazy evaluation. In **Proceedings of the Twentieth ACM Symposium on Principles of Programming Languages**, 1993.   (p xi)

[79] John Launchbury and Simon L. Peyton Jones. Lazy functional state threads. In **Proceedings of the ACM Conference on Programming Languages Design and Implementation (PLDI), Orlando**, June 1994.   (p xi)

[80] David R. Lester. **Combinator Graph Reduction: A Congruence and its Applications**. DPhil thesis, Programming Research Group, Oxford University Computing Laboratory, April 1989. Available as Technical Report PRG–73.   (pp 8, 103, 104, 136)

[81] I. A. Mason and C. L. Talcott. Equivalence in functional languages with effects. **Journal of Functional Programming**, 1(3):287–327, 1991.   (p xi)

[82] David Matthews. A distributed concurrent implementation of Standard ML. In **EurOpen Autumn 1991 Conference**, 1991. Appears as LFCS Report ECS-LFCS-91-174.   (p 99)

[83] John McCarthy, Paul W. Abrahams, Daniel J. Edwards, Timothy P. Hart, and Michael I. Levin. **LISP 1.5 Programmer's Manual**. MIT Press, Cambridge, Mass., 1962.   (pp 1, 2, 100)

[84] Chris S. McDonald. fsh—a functional unix command interpreter. **Software—Practice and Experience**, 17(10):685–700, October 1987.   (p 99)

[85] Paul R. McJones and Garret F. Swart. Evolving the UNIX system interface to support multithreaded programs. Technical Report 21, DEC Systems Research Center, Palo Alto, September 28, 1987.   (p 122)

[86] Lee M. McLoughlin and Sean Hayes. Imperative effects from a pure functional language. In Kei Davis and John Hughes, editors, **Functional Programming, Glasgow 1989**, Workshops in Computing, pages 157–169. Springer-Verlag, 1990. (p 4)

[87] Silvio Lemos Meira. Processes and functions. In **TAPSOFT/CCIPL**, volume 352 of **Lecture Notes in Computer Science**, Barcelona, 1989. Springer-Verlag. (p 99)

[88] Nax Paul Mendler. Inductive types and type constraints in the second-order lambda calculus. **Annals of Pure and Applied Logic**, 51(1–2):159–172, 1991. Earlier version in LICS'88.   (pp 15, 19, 134, 135)

[89] Paul Francis Mendler. **Inductive Definition in Type Theory**. PhD thesis, Department of Computer Science, Cornell University, September 1987. Available as Technical Report 87-870.   (p 15)

[90] Albert R. Meyer and Stavros S. Cosmadakis. Semantical paradigms: Notes for an invited lecture. In **Proceedings of the 3rd IEEE Symposium on Logic in**

Computer Science, pages 236–253, July 1988. (p 8)

[91] Robin Milner. Fully abstract models of typed lambda-calculi. **Theoretical Computer Science**, 4:1–23, 1977. (pp 7, 9, 37, 46, 134)

[92] Robin Milner. A theory of type polymorphism in programming. **Journal of Computer and System Sciences**, 17(3):348–375, December 1978. (p 11)

[93] Robin Milner. **A Calculus of Communicating Systems**, volume 92 of **Lecture Notes in Computer Science**. Springer-Verlag, 1980. (pp 7, 103)

[94] Robin Milner. **Communication and Concurrency**. Prentice-Hall International, 1989. (pp 7, 12, 99, 103, 111, 112)

[95] Robin Milner. Functions as processes. **Mathematical Structures in Computer Science**, 2:119–141, 1992. (p 7)

[96] Robin Milner, Joachim Parrow, and David Walker. A calculus of mobile processes, parts i and ii. **Information and Computation**, 100:1–40 and 41–77, 1992. (pp 7, 112)

[97] Robin Milner and Mads Tofte. Co-induction in relational semantics. **Theoretical Computer Science**, 87:209–220, 1991. (pp 7, 13)

[98] Robin Milner, Mads Tofte, and Robert Harper. **The Definition of Standard ML**. MIT Press, Cambridge, Mass., 1990. (pp 6, 100)

[99] Eugenio Moggi. **The Partial Lambda-Calculus**. PhD thesis, Department of Computer Science, University of Edinburgh, August 1988. Available as Technical report CST–53–88. (p 27)

[100] Eugenio Moggi. Notions of computations and monads. **Theoretical Computer Science**, 93:55–92, 1989. Earlier version in LICS'89. (pp 5, 65, 75, 85, 125)

[101] Eugenio Moggi. An abstract view of programming languages. Technical Report ECS–LFCS–90–113, Laboratory for Foundations of Computer Science, Department of Computer Science, University of Edinburgh, April 1990. (pp 5, 65, 75, 101)

[102] Peter D. Mosses. Denotational semantics. In Jan Van Leeuven, editor, **Handbook of Theoretical Computer Science**, chapter 11, pages 575–631. Elsevier Science Publishers B. V., 1990. Volume B. (p 7)

[103] Rob Noble and Colin Runciman. Functional languages and graphical user interfaces—a review and case study. Technical Report YCS-94-223, Department of Computer Science, University of York, February 1994. (p xi)

[104] John T. O'Donnell. Dialogues: A basis for constructing programming environments. In **ACM Symposium on Language Issues in Programming Environments**, pages 19–27, 1985. SIGPLAN Notices 20(7). (pp 4, 108)

[105] Lawrence C. Paulson. **Logic and Computation: Interactive Proof with Cambridge LCF**. Cambridge University Press, 1987. (pp 9, 55, 89, 134)

[106] Lawrence C. Paulson. **ML for the Working Programmer**. Cambridge University Press, 1991. (p 2)

[107] Nigel Perry. Hope+C: A continuation extension for Hope+. Technical Report IC/FPR/LANG/2.5.1/21, Department of Computing, Imperial College, London,

November 1987.   (p 4)

[108] Nigel Perry. **The Implementation of Practical Functional Programming Languages**. PhD thesis, Department of Computing, Imperial College, London, June 1991.   (pp 6, 99, 117)

[109] Simon L. Peyton Jones. **The implementation of functional programming languages**. Prentice-Hall International, April 1987.   (pp 2, 3, 69, 102)

[110] Simon L. Peyton Jones and Philip Wadler. Imperative functional programming. In **Proceedings 20th ACM Symposium on Principles of Programming Languages, Charleston, South Carolina, January 1993**, pages 71–84. ACM Press, 1993.   (pp xi, 103, 117, 125, 126, 136)

[111] Andrew Pitts and Ian Stark. On the observable properties of higher order functions that dynamically create local names (preliminary report). In **SIPL'93: ACM SIGPLAN Workshop on State in Programming Languages**, pages 31–45, June 1993.   (p xi)

[112] Andrew M. Pitts. Evaluation logic. In G. Birtwistle, editor, **IVth Higher Order Workshop, Banff 1990**, Workshops in Computing, pages 162–189. Springer-Verlag, 1991. Available as University of Cambridge Computer Laboratory Technical Report 198, August 1990.   (pp 65, 73, 75)

[113] Andrew M. Pitts. Relational properties of domains. Technical Report 321, University of Cambridge Computer Laboratory, December 1993.   (p xi)

[114] Andrew M. Pitts. A co-induction principle for recursively defined domains. **Theoretical Computer Science**, 124:195–219, 1994.   (pp 7, 13)

[115] Andrew M. Pitts. Computational adequacy via 'mixed' inductive definitions. In **Proceedings Mathematical Foundations of Programming Semantics IX, New Orleans 1993**, volume 802 of **Lecture Notes in Computer Science**, pages 72–82. Springer-Verlag, 1994.   (p xi)

[116] Gordon D. Plotkin. Call-by-name, call-by-value and the λ-calculus. **Theoretical Computer Science**, 1:125–159, 1975.   (pp 37, 44)

[117] Gordon D. Plotkin. LCF considered as a programming language. **Theoretical Computer Science**, 5:223–255, 1977.   (pp 7, 8, 37)

[118] Gordon D. Plotkin. The category of complete partial orders: a tool for making meanings. Unpublished lecture notes for the Summer School on Foundations of Artificial Intelligence and Computer Science, Pisa., June 1978.   (pp 7, 73, 101, 109)

[119] Gordon D. Plotkin. A structural approach to operational semantics. Technical Report FN–19, DAIMI, Aarhus University, September 1981.   (p 7)

[120] Gordon D. Plotkin. Denotational semantics with partial functions. Unpublished lecture notes, CSLI, Stanford University, July 1985.   (pp 8, 27, 65, 75, 134)

[121] Ian Poole. A functional programming environment for image analysis. In **Proceedings of the 11th International Conference on Pattern Recognition, The Hague**, volume IV, pages 124–127, August 1992.   (p 119)

[122] S. Purushothaman and J. Seaman. An adequate operational semantics of sharing in lazy evaluation. In B. Krieg-Brückner, editor, **Proceedings of 4th European**

Symposium on Programming, ESOP'92, Rennes, France, volume 582 of **Lecture Notes in Computer Science**. Springer-Verlag, 1992. Available as Report CS-91-8, Department of Computer Science, Pennsylvania State University.   (p 103)

[123] S. A. Rebelsky. I/O trees and interactive lazy functional programming. In **Fourth International Symposium on Programming Language Implementation and Logic Programming**, volume 631 of **Lecture Notes in Computer Science**, pages 458–472, Leuven, August 26–28, 1992. Springer-Verlag.   (p 4)

[124] D. Hugh Redelmeier. **Towards Practical Functional Programming**. PhD thesis, Computer Systems Research Group, University of Toronto, May 1984. Available as Technical Report CSRG–158.   (p 103)

[125] A. Reid and S. Singh. Budgets: Cheap and cheerful widget combinators. In **Functional Programming, Glasgow 1993**, Workshops in Computing. Springer-Verlag, 1994.   (p xi)

[126] John H. Reppy. An operational semantics of first-class synchronous operations. Technical Report TR 91-1232, Department of Computer Science, Cornell University, August 1991.   (pp 6, 99, 135)

[127] J. C. Reynolds. Definitional interpreters for higher-order programming languages. In **Proc. 25th ACM National Conference**, pages 717–740. ACM, New York, 1972.   (p 4)

[128] David Sands. Operational theories of improvement in functional languages (extended abstract). In **Functional Programming, Glasgow 1991**, Workshops in Computing, pages 298–311. Springer-Verlag, 1992.   (p xi)

[129] Davide Sangiorgi. The lazy lambda calculus in a concurrency scenario. **Information and Computation**, 1994. To appear.   (p 7)

[130] David A. Schmidt. **Denotational Semantics: A Methodology for Language Development**. Allyn and Bacon, Inc., 1986.   (p 7)

[131] Jon Shultis. A functional shell. In **Proc. Symp. on Programming Language Issues in Software Systems**, 1983. SIGPLAN Notices 18(6).   (p 99)

[132] Todd G. Simpson. **Design and verification of IFL: a wide-spectrum intermediate functional language**. PhD thesis, Department of Computer Science, The University of Calgary, July 1991. Available as Research Report 91/440/24.   (pp 8, 104, 136)

[133] Scott F. Smith. From operational to denotational semantics. In **MFPS VII, Pittsburgh**, volume 598 of **Lecture Notes in Computer Science**, pages 54–76. Springer-Verlag, 1991.   (pp 7, 134)

[134] Joseph E. Stoy. **Denotational semantics: the Scott-Strachey approach to programming language theory**. MIT Press, Cambridge, Mass., 1977.   (pp 2, 4, 7, 73, 109)

[135] Joseph E. Stoy. Mathematical aspects of functional programming. In Darlington et al. [30], pages 217–252.   (p 7)

[136] William Stoye. Message-based functional operating systems. **Science of Computer Programming**, 6(3):291–311, 1986. Originally appeared as: A New Scheme

for Writing Functional Operating Systems, Technical Report 56, University of Cambridge Computer Laboratory, 1984.   (pp 4, 6, 99, 108)

[137] Christopher Strachey. A general purpose macrogenerator. Technical Memorandum 65/1, University Mathematical Laboratory, Cambridge, March 1965.   (p 3)

[138] Christopher Strachey. Fundamental concepts in programming languages. Unpublished lectures given at the International Summer School in Computer Programming, Copenhagen, August 1967.   (p 88)

[139] R. D. Tennent. **Semantics of Programming Languages**. Prentice-Hall International, 1991.   (p 8)

[140] Simon Thompson. A logic for Miranda. **Formal Aspects of Computing**, 1(4):339–365, October–December 1989.   (p 134)

[141] Simon Thompson. Interactive functional programs: A method and a formal semantics. In Turner [146], pages 249–286. Originally appeared as Technical Report 48, Computing Laboratory, University of Kent at Canterbury, November 1987.   (pp 6, 105, 117, 125)

[142] Mark Tillotson. Introduction to the functional programming language "Ponder". Technical Report 65, University of Cambridge Computer Laboratory, May 1985.   (pp 3, 99)

[143] David Turner. A new implementation technique for applicative languages. **Software—Practice and Experience**, 9:31–49, 1979.   (pp 2, 102)

[144] David Turner. Functional programming and communicating processes (some design considerations for a functional operating system). In **Parallel Architectures and Languages Europe Proceedings**, volume 259 of **Lecture Notes in Computer Science**, pages 54–74. Springer-Verlag, 1987.   (pp 5, 99, 108)

[145] David Turner. An approach to functional operating systems. In Turner [146], pages 199–217.   (pp 99, 108)

[146] David Turner, editor. **Research Topics in Functional Programming**. Addison-Wesley, 1990.   (pp 137, 146)

[147] W. Wadge and E. Ashcroft. **Lucid, the dataflow programming language**. Academic Press, New York, 1985.   (pp 2, 6, 99)

[148] Philip Wadler. How to replace failure by a list of successes. In Jouannaud [70], pages 113–128.   (p 117)

[149] Philip Wadler. Comprehending monads. **Mathematical Structures in Computer Science**, 2:461–493, 1992.   (pp 5, 103, 125)

[150] Philip Wadler. The essence of functional programming. In **Proceedings of the Nineteenth ACM Symposium on Principles of Programming Languages**, 1992.   (pp 5, 103, 125)

[151] John H. Williams and Edward L. Wimmers. Sacrificing simplicity for convenience: Where do you draw the line? In **Conference Record of the Fifteenth ACM Symposium on Principles of Programming Languages**, pages 169–179, January 1988.   (pp 3, 6, 102)

[152] Glynn Winskel. **The Formal Semantics of Programming Languages**. MIT Press, Cambridge, Mass., 1993. (p xi)

[153] G.C. Wraith. A note on categorical datatypes. In D. H. Pitt, D. E. Rydheheard, P. Dybjer, A. M. Pitts, and A. Poigné, editors, **Category Theory and Computer Science**, volume 389 of **Lecture Notes in Computer Science**. Springer-Verlag, 1989. (pp 15, 134)

[154] Stuart C. Wray. **Implementation and programming techniques for functional languages**. PhD thesis, University of Cambridge Computer Laboratory, June 1986. Available as Technical Report 92. (pp 3, 5, 117)

Notation Index

Chapter One

Chapter Two

Chapter Three

Chapter Four

Chapter Five

Chapter Six

Chapter Seven

Chapter Eight

Index

actions, 103
adequacy, xi, 7, 8, 27
   operational, 37, 41, 79
advice to the reader, 10
ALGOL 60, 1, 3, 106
alpha-conversion, 11
   in $\mu\nu\lambda2$, 18

bisimilarity, 7, 12, 13, 100, 103, 133
   applicative, 9, 37, 49, 53, 82, 96
   compared with applicative bisimilarity, 100, 111
   ground applicative, 49, 82
   simplicity of, 116
bisimulation, 13
   applicative, xi, 7, 37, 49, 82
     and nondeterminism, 134
bisimulation-up-to, 56, 90, 112
Booleans in $\mathcal{M}$, 60
Budgets, xi

call-by-name, 1, 9, 67, 102
call-by-need, xi, 2, 102–103
call-by-value, 1, 9, 66, 67, 93, 102
canonical freeness, 56, 90
CCS, 7, 12, 99, 100, 103, 111, 112, 116, 133
certainly-convergent types, 27, 28, 32, 56
co-induction
   and bisimulation, 12–13
   and Scott induction, 8, 89, 134
   principle of, 56, 90
combinators for I/O
   history, 5
   monadic programming, 120–125
   stream transformers, 104–105
compatible relation, 18
computation, 120
computational monad, 86, 97

concurrency, 4, 6, 7, 99
   constructor for, 112
   in MRC model, 124
   Kahn networks, 3
Concurrent Clean, xi
confined extension, 43, 81
confined relation, 41, 79
confined term, 30, 69
congruence, 42, 79
context, 11
   canonical, 38
   instantiation, 38
context lemma, 7, 46
contextual equivalence, 53
contextual order, 44
convergence, 32, 73

denotational equivalence, 85
divergence, 32, 73

eager language, 2, 3, 100–102, 104, 135
empty type in $\mathcal{M}$, 58
environment, 28, 67
evaluation, 30, 73
evaluation contexts, 30
exceptions
   in $\mathcal{HX}$, 93–97
   in monadic I/O, 122
execution type, 103
experimental order, 44
experiments, 30
   left and right, 73

FL, 3
FP, 3
Fudgets, xi
functional extensionality, 91

Γ-closure, 43, 81
Gofer, x, 65, 119, 120